C11

C. P. SNOW AND THE STRUGGLE OF M

C. P. Snow
and the
Struggle of Modernity

John de la Mothe

UNIVERSITY OF TEXAS PRESS, AUSTIN

Requests for permission to reproduce material from this work
should be sent to Permissions, University of Texas Press, Box 7819,
Austin, Texas 78713-7819.

ⓧ The paper used in this publication meets the minimum
requirements of American National Standard for Information
Sciences—Permanence of Paper for Printed Library Materials,
ANSI Z39.48-1984.

Library of Congress Cataloging-in-Publication Data

De la Mothe, John.
    C. P. Snow and the struggle of modernity / by John de la Mothe.
      p.   cm.
    Includes bibliographical references (p.   ) and index.
    ISBN 978-0-292-72916-2
    1. Snow, C. P. (Charles Percy), 1905– .   2. Novelists, English—
  20th century—Biography.   3. Civil service—Great Britain—
  Biography.   4. Scientists—Great Britain—Biography.   I. Title.
  PR6037.N58Z62   1992
  823'.912—dc20   91-34855
                                                              CIP

Who else is going to give you a broken arrow?
Who else is going to bring you a bottle of rain?
Here we go. Moving across the water.
There you go. Turning my whole world around.
—*ROBBIE ROBERTSON, 1989*

This work is dedicated to

Donna Thompson, Fred Knelman, Horace de la Mothe,
Marion Stanton, and Bob Thompson

CONTENTS

ACKNOWLEDGMENTS

STUDIES OF this sort tend not to be the result of pure library research. Instead they seem to need sustained input from many diverse sources: knowledgeable and supportive people, the stimulation of a larger environment, and the agitation that comes with excess (such as too little sleep and too much coffee). This study is no exception. But if one activity privately signified the development of this work for me, it was tennis. This thesis was first conceived of on the tennis courts of Westmount, Quebec. Its basic parameters were first sketched out at the Players Open (Canadian Championship) in Montreal. Major theoretical difficulties were overcome in conversations that took place on the train from London to Lewes, Sussex, following Wimbledon, in the tennis bubble at the University of Sussex, and on the grass courts of Oxford. Textual refinements to the introduction were suggested and discussed at the Elmdale Tennis Club in Ottawa. To all of my partners, your patience did not go unnoticed, and I hope that my "match chatter" did not prove too distracting. Of course, many other factors also promoted the completion of this manuscript.

Many friends helped me directly to complete this work through a combination of their infliction of guilt, their warmth of affection, and their examples of professionalism and discipline. My deep thanks are due, therefore, to Debra Alcock, Charles Bertrand, Stephen Block, Grant Caverly, Jim de la Mothe, Louis Marc Ducharme, Paul Dufour, Michael Farley, Janet Halliwell, Bob Kavanagh, Andrew Molloy, Richard Nimijean, Gilles Paquet, Joy Senack, Margaret Simpson, Anita Watson, and Graham Wilson.

My access to the C. P. Snow Archives at the Harry Ransom Humanities Research Center of the University of Texas at Austin was entirely facilitated by Philip Snow. This study holds a considerable debt to him as he generously, and with care, answered all of my (sometimes delicate) queries either by correspondence, by phone, or during our many long visits.

The sustained attention of four readers made this text more interesting, rigorous, and readable. All are my friends and teachers. My debt to Fred Knelman, Harold Chorney, Michael Hogben, and Donna Thompson (who has long been my harshest and most caring critic) cannot be easily expressed. Their presence is evident in each line. Any errors are, of course, entirely my own responsibility.

Perceptive and valuable comments on this manuscript were made by three external readers. For their contribution, I would like to thank Alkis Kontos, Arthur Kroker, and Tom Staley.

Timely financial assistance and generous intellectual space were provided by the Quebec Government (FCAC), the British Council, the Science Policy Research Unit, the Natural Sciences and Engineering Research Council of Canada, and the Ministry of State for Science and Technology.

I would also like to thank all those involved in Concordia University's interdisciplinary doctoral program in arts and science (Ph.D. Humanities—Interdisciplinary Studies in Society and Culture). The research represented by this study could not have found a more congenial home. In particular, I would like to thank John Drysdale, Geoff Fidler, and Joyce Barakett. Their patience, encouragement, and belief in the value of interdisciplinarity has benefited many—myself included.

A number of individuals who either had personal recollections of Snow, or useful analytic perspectives on Snow's work, generously gave of their time for interviews or correspondence. In this regard, I would like to thank Norman Auburn, Tony Benn, Ivor Boldizar, Sir Herman Bondi, Kenneth Boulding, William F. Buckley, Jr., William Campbell, Charles Chadwick, Peter Collins, Collin Divall, Peter Dallos, Terry Eagleton, Brian Easlea, Maurice Goldsmith, Phil Gummett, Gerald Holton, Harry Hoff, Alfred Kazin, Sir Hans Kornberg, Thomas Kuhn, Sir Edmund Leach, William Manchester, John Marshal, Arthur Marwick, Leo Marx, Jonathan Miller, Erik Millstone, John Mitchell, Clarence Moll, S. G. Putt, Saguna Ramanathan, Clayton Roberts, Lord Sherfield, Anthony Storr, Albert Teich, Gary Werskey, and Roger Williams.

A number of individuals, on behalf of their institutions, also gave generously to this study. I should therefore like to thank the Master and Fellows of Christ's College, Downing College, Trinity College, and Churchill College, Cambridge, the Royal Society of London, the

International Science Policy Foundation, the General Electric Company p.l.c., the *New York Review of Books,* Cambridge University Press, and Macmillan Publishing (London). The archives of the following universities were also instrumental in completing my research: Harvard University, Leicester University, Loyola University of Chicago, Memorial University, New York University, Pace University, the Polytechnic Institute of New York, Rice University, Rutgers University, St. Andrews University, the State University of New York at Buffalo, Syracuse University, Temple University, the University of London (Birkbeck College), the University of Michigan, the University of Pittsburgh, the University of Texas at Austin, the University of Western Ontario, Warwick University, Washington University (St. Louis), and Wesleyan University.

Finally, I would like to thank Frankie Westbrook of the University of Texas Press, who—for more than three years—encouraged me to keep writing.

To all of these people and institutions, and to those at the Ritz 3, Café Toman, Café Deluxe, and the Blue Willow, my sincere thanks.

In me, past, present, future meet
To hold long chiding conference.
My lusts usurp the present tense
And strangle Reason in his seat.
My loves leap through the future's fence
To dance with dream enfranchised feet.

In me, the cave-man clasps the seer,
And garlanded Apollo goes
Chanting to Abraham's deaf ear.
In me the tiger sniffs the rose.
Look in my heart kind friends, and tremble,
Since there your elements assemble.

—SIGFRIED SASSOON

Part One

INTRODUCTION

C. P. Snow, 1963 (reproduced by kind permission of Mark Gerson).

Caricature of C. P. Snow, 1963 (reproduced by kind permission of the
Master and Fellows of Christs' College, Cambridge).

Drawing of heraldic device for Lord Snow of Leicester (reproduced
by kind permission of Philip Snow, O.B.E., J.P., M.A., F.R.S.A.).

C. P. Snow at home, with Sidney Nolan's *Kelly 1954*, on Cromwell Road, London, in 1964 (reproduced by kind permission of Mark Gerson).

Cover illustration by Sidney Nolan for *The Masters* (reproduced by kind permission of Philip Snow, O.B.E., J.P., M.A., F.R.S.A.).

Cover illustration by Sidney Nolan for *The Affair* (reproduced by kind permission of Philip Snow, O.B.E., J.P., M.A., F.R.S.A.).

Kelly 1954, by Sidney Nolan (reproduced by kind permission of the owner).

Cover illustration by Sidney Nolan for *Corridors of Power* (reproduced by kind permission of Philip Snow, O.B.E., J.P., M.A., F.R.S.A.).

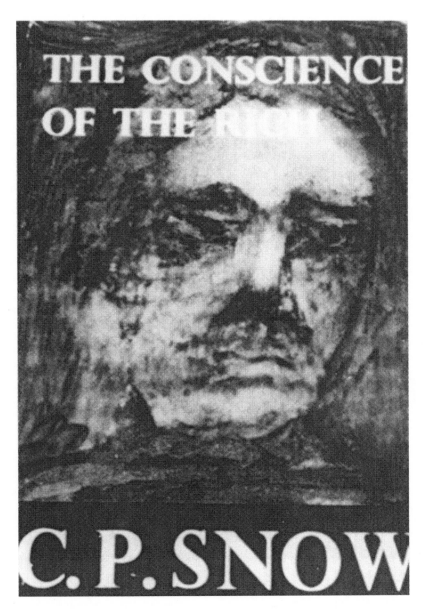

Cover illustration by Sidney Nolan for *The Conscience of the Rich* (reproduced by kind permission of Philip Snow, O.B.E., J.P., M.A., F.R.S.A.).

Avenue de Clichy, 1887, oil on paper mounted to canvas, by Louis Anquetin (reproduced by kind permission of the Wadsworth Athenaeum, Hartford, the Ella Gallup Sumner and Mary Catlin Sumner Collection).

1

LITERATURE, SCIENCE, AND THE MODERN MIND

The whole is a riddle, an enigma, an inexplicable mystery.
Doubt [and] uncertainty . . . appear the only result of our most accurate
scrutiny. . . . But such is the frailty of human reason. . . .
—DAVID HUME

We all carry within us our places of exile . . .
but our task is not to unleash them on
the world: it is to fight them in ourselves and others.
—ALBERT CAMUS

THE DISCOURSE OF MODERNITY is comprised of a cacophony of voices, the interpretation of which can only be described as a struggle. Some of these voices may seem, at the present time, to be those of academic social critics who are involved in the fashionable professional debate over the distinction between modernism, "high modernism," and postmodernism.[1] But the voices to which I refer are, more importantly, those that breeze down the streets of our modern urbanscapes and formatively (if unconsciously) reach our ears at the level of economy, fashion, and tradition. Each of these voices vies for authority and attention. Each of these voices offers us but a fragment of that mosaic that is our total identity. And in so doing, each operates within a larger cultural environment most known perhaps for its Renaissance dream of unity and for its current condition of rupture.

The struggle of modernity ultimately derives from modernity's tendency to revolt against the normalizing functions of traditions. Its "task" seems to be to keep us, as individuals, on the edge of meaning and understanding. Thus it should not be surprising that our aspiration to more precisely delineate the parameters of this struggle has become the paradigmatic idea of our age.

The signs of the struggle of modernity are well known to us. It is signified daily through the images of the crowd and by the perpetual shock of the new. Anonymity and exile are its watchwords. Its central site is the Metropolis and those institutions that are most affected by the processes of modernity, such as the government, the university, the law office, and the research lab. The science of modernity (from administration and genetics to particle physics) provides a constant recasting of our physical space and of our role in it. The politics of modernity gives up life to the perpetual dream of social rationality and individual totality but collapses in the burnout of liberal positivism. The literature of modernity describes those transformations that are taking place in the public world and in its associated consciousness. As such, it has come to be concerned with city life and, predominantly, with the experience of men.[2] The "heroes" of modernity are no longer sole romantic adventurers but are now the professional custodians of instrumental reason—the scientists, administrators, and lawyers. They are those for whom anonymity in the crowd is assured and found in the tacit norms and codified behaviors afforded to them by their profession. They move freely about the modern urbanscape, observing and being observed. But they are reluctant to develop as individuals, for as they know or sense, the modern world is one in which one can never feel entirely at home. It is a world that presses in on us daily, making demands and forcing choices. It is a world in which both history and our possible futures confront us on every street corner. It is a world that defies meaning. In such a world that is foreign yet familiar, the only "natural" persona we can seek to develop is one that—as C. P. Snow perceptively understood—is both stranger and brother.

While alienation and the disenfranchised individual are among the keywords of our period, we intuitively remind ourselves that to seek out totality or a comprehensive self-identification that is balanced between our private and public experiences may, in fact, be the only "heroism" left to us in the late twentieth century. As we will see, it is, at least in part, because of this deeply imbedded desire for totality that C. P. Snow must be considered a significant figure of modernity. This perception of cultural rupture, his appealingly aggressive "realist's" framework, as well as his personal efforts to come to terms with his own modernity all mark Snow's life as a "heroic" example of the struggle that is modernity. Social theorists have long highlighted the central role that the quest for totality plays in our modern experience. Émile Durkheim, for example, speculated that the idea of totality is reflected in the group nature of society itself. Georg Lukacs contended that it is "crucial that there should be an aspiration towards totality." And Lucien Goldman has claimed that there is a "fundamental need for coherence . . . which characterizes all human, social life."[3] Nevertheless, given modernity's destabilizing inner logic, striking such a balance has become increasingly problematic.

The time consciousness that is active in modernity is not ahistorical or antihistorical, but it uses our sense of the past in a way that both changes our preview of the future and undermines our perceived value of the present. Our perceived sense of context and totality is jeopardized. Modernity thus characterizes our present as little more than a transition period that is consumed in the awareness of speeding-up and in the expectation of the differentness of the future. Each immediate moment loses its unique meaning as it gives birth to the new. And as the present increasingly understands itself as standing at the horizon of the modern age, it recapitulates the break brought about with the past in a process of continuous renewal.[4]

The myriad dynamic concepts that emerged out of this new temporal understanding gave rise to new terms with which to handle the new meanings of experience. Words such as *progress, revolution, innovation,* and *crisis* all became key. Phrases like "the new civilization," "the new society," and "the new world" all came naturally. "New" was clearly a keyword of the emerging age of modernity. There was Art Nouveau, the New Novel of Zola, the New Drama of Ibsen and Shaw, the New Music of Wagner, the New Journalism of Newne's *Tit-bits,* the New Women of the feminist movement, and the New Men of C. P. Snow. Progress was the one quality that was demanded from novelty in art, literature, politics, and morality. While some—like Max Nordau—could sadly observe (in *Degeneration,* 1895) that "our epoch of history is unmistakenly in its decline. . . . Things are suffered to . . . fall because . . . there is no faith that is worth an effort to uphold them," others—such as H. G. Wells—could sense new hope and progress in the air. Wells's books, such as *New World for Old, A World Set Free, Men like Gods,* and *The Shape of Things to Come,* all express this. But nowhere does he declare his sense of a break with the past so baldly as when his time-traveler excitedly exclaims, "I have discovered the future" and "I flung myself into futurity." Modernity came to realize that it must create normality out of itself and that it must come to terms with its desire to escape itself. The struggle of modernity thus has become a struggle to find meaning and value within a time that is, by definition, a time of the fleeting and the contingent. It is a struggle to understand our history without being captured by it. It is a struggle to overcome our sense of alienation and exile. The pressure and interpretive difficulty that this struggle has come to imply for the individual within the context of mass society cannot be underestimated.

This failure is most serious, for as Daniel Bell has argued in his insightful book *The Cultural Contradictions of Capitalism,* once past and future became perceptually separated then modernity's "will to power" was effectively able to "flood into the void"—pervasively penetrating the values of everyday life on every level. Insofar as this is true, it should not be surprising that, as Charles-Pierre Baudelaire foresaw, those who identify and orient themselves toward interpreting the primary forces of modernity would come to be seen as our heroes—as challengers to the struggle of modernity, as strategists in our quest for totality. Given that literature, science, and politics constitute powerful primary forces of our most recent past, then C. P. Snow must be seen as one of our more prominent "strategists." Indeed, in some ways, it can be argued that nowhere can the struggle of modernity be more significantly seen than in the fiction and nonfiction work of Charles Percy Snow (1905–1980). What distinguishes C. P. Snow as a participant in the struggle of modernity is not his urge to escape culture. It is instead his wish to fully participate in culture—in the authoritative discourses of modernity—that presents him as a unique and powerful figure. As we will see, his participation comes through an aggressive realism that attempts to embrace three major dispositions of the modern mind: these being literature, science, and politics. The ultimate *raison d'être* behind Snow's work is to work out, for himself, the possible conditions for totality, and to illustrate for others the grounds upon which a mediation between public and private spheres can be realized. As such, his work amounts to a highly individual attempt to reconstitute modern culture as a cognitive and meaning-generating enterprise. His writings were consumed by an awareness of the alienation and angst that can be found in the Metropolis. But to this he brought an understanding of the influence of science and technology on our perceptions of the individual and on our notions of rationality, an understanding of the profound influence that is (often) latent in literature, as well as an appreciation of the fundamentally political quality of modern life. He refused to isolate these dispositions from each other, seeing them instead as being intimately linked. His writing was relentlessly in search of means through which to strike a balance between the necessities of social institutions and the needs of individuals. Indeed, Snow saw human fulfillment in modernity as lying not in withdrawal and despair but in participation in society. Those who choose to hide from, or ignore, social life were, in Snow's schema, anomalies who could never find a fully functional self-definition at either the aesthetic, cognitive, or political levels.

Clearly, the ambiguity and uncertainty that has followed in the wake of modernity has resulted in the widespread sense both of dehumanization in the life-world and of the demise of the integrated individual personality. The rapid shift toward this status can be easily seen by contrasting contemporary treatments of individual character with those of earlier periods. In early realist literature, for example, individual characters were presented with highly structured personality features; they developed their individuality through a life of social interaction. More recently, however, writers have felt unable to do so. "Character, for modernists like Joyce [and] Woolf," Irving Howe has written, "is regarded not as a coherent, definable and well-structured entity, but as a psychic battle-field, or an insoluble puzzle, or the occasion for a flow of perceptions and sensations. This tendency to dissolve character into a stream of atomized experiences . . . gives way . . . to an opposite tendency . . . in which character is severed from psychology and confined to a sequence of severely objective events."[5] This hegemonic aesthetic tendency (which is also discernible in music and in the visual arts) is by no means caused by the failure of the literati, or of literary techniques more generally. It is instead a stark reflection of the widespread contemporary "crisis of individuality" that is fueled by modernity. Political ambiguities also connote this tendency.

As modernity strives to perfect agencies of change, the self (the person or individual) ceases to be the privileged site of agency. Instead, to effect change, the self is forced to give itself up in hopeful mediation to the fuzzy sets of state, community, and class. (Nowhere is the locus of influence clearly discernible.) Whereas the dichotomy between the private and public spheres was once defended by classical liberalism for the simple and useful purpose of circumscribing the legitimate areas of possible government intervention in the lives of its citizens, the distinction has today been distorted to the point that the private sphere is no longer a privileged space to be associated with self-development, artistic creation, and self-expression. Instead, the private and public spheres have collapsed so that individuals in modern society are "twice alienated":[6] once insofar as the public sphere denies private meaning, twice insofar as the private sphere has been emptied of influence. Said another way, the public sphere has become an all-inclusive category that refers not only to traditional government institutions and functions (as it once did under classical liberalism) but to the workplace and all areas of everyday life where social cooperation or the cash nexus are present. In this "collapse of the spheres," the hegemonic value of individualism and of the individual's right to totality have become entirely secondary to the systemic imperatives of a homogenizing mass capitalistic society. Contrary to the elitist and neoconservative strategies of Allan Bloom, Ed Hirsch, and other ideologues of the New Right, the modern "culture of narcissism" is not necessarily a culture in which moral constraints have collapsed; instead, it is that cultural ground that mediates between our private and public worlds that is threatened with disintegration.[7] And it is on this battlefield that C. P. Snow is most present.

Although clues as to the exact character of Snow's overt interest in modernity are not readily evident, they can be found in a variety of places. For example, Snow's interests in the loneliness of the individual condition are highly visible in the cover that he chose for his 1978 book *The Realists: Portraits of Eight Novelists*. The selected painting by Louis Anquetin, *La Place Clichy* (1887), admirably displays the anonymity of the crowd, the world at dusk, the capitalist world of the shopkeeper, the Metropolis, and the world of fashion.

And Snow's interest in "man alone" is quietly evident in his use of four works by Australian artist Sidney Nolan on five dust jackets.[8] (It is no accident that a character in Snow's *Affair* collects paintings by Nolan.) Each—like the Nolan work that hung above Snow's home mantelpiece—demonstrates the hero of modernity—the New Man. The hero maintains a strange relationship with his landscape. He stands out so clearly he looks like a target. His environment neither absorbs (admits) him nor camouflages his approach. He is a man against the landscape, a man who doesn't seem to fit in at all. Yet where else could Snow's private hero exist but in the public open spaces? There is no mistaking this landscape for modernity's "country of the mind": it is too well observed, too actual. (As we will see, it is, in part, because of this that Snow eschews metaphorical literary forms for the direct form of realism.) The apparent truthfulness of the tone attests to the reality of the world Snow imprints himself upon. Snow's dramatic separation of the hero from the environment, suggested by Nolan, creates one of the most striking resonances between the figure and the landscape in the struggle of modernity. As such, a new social contract is established. The hero is anonymous, lonely and yet invincible. The figure of Kelly, for example, a prominent figure in Nolan's work, rides "in the armour of self-containment across the desolation of the wasteland." Insofar as Kelly represents Nolan's and modernity's hero, he also represents the efforts of Snow to mediate between the public and private spheres, to "invade the landscape, so the landscape . . . [can] invade him."[9] The obvious immediacy of the hero, and the way of inserting the individual into the landscape or context, is thoroughly a reflection of modernity.

Snow's concern with the mediation between the spheres, and with the potential of the individual, is symbolically reflected in his heraldic device. Designed by himself and his wife on the occasion of being made Lord Snow of Leicester in 1964, it depicts a crossed pen and telescope, which was deliberately chosen by Snow to suggest the relationship between science and literature. It also depicts a motto that Snow held as being deeply meaningful at a personal level and key to anyone's view of the struggle of modernity. That motto reads: *Aut Invenian Viam aut Faciam* (I will either find a way or make one).

Defining the terms for mediation between the private and public spheres in Snow's framework—through their sheer cognitive, "logical," and political will to power—are science, which changes our conceptions of ourselves, and technology, which changes relationships with nature and society. As Snow understood, they have become our deepest languages. They have come to pervade our politics and economy, our literature and aesthetics, and even our fashion and desire. They condition the "iron cage" that is our urbanscape, and together, they constitute our frontiers. In so doing, they contain both a moment of opportunity and danger: opportunity insofar as they perpetually encourage us to rethink the relationships between technique, society, and the individual; danger insofar as they too are driven by the inner logic of modernity. In these languages, we find further clues of Snow's interest in modernity. Throughout Snow's fiction, his heroes are rationalists, modern professionals: they are either scientists, lawyers, and administrators or politicians and industrialists. Together they represent the revolutionary New Men of modernity on whose back the promise of social change and progress is borne. They are reflective in their lives, but progressive in their rationality. Snow's fictional sites are the university and laboratory, the office or government department, and he attempts to use these settings to show us the motives and ambitions of "revolutionizing" professionals at a time when science and technology were actively redefining the modern world and the modern mind.

Luckily, despite the threatened decoupling of the public and private spheres, despite the tension between culture and society, there remains considerable covert or buried communication between such important "voices" as literature and science. The difficulty is to interpret this deeper-level discourse in a way that is useful to developing our own individual senses of totality. The success of Snow's interpretive strategy and framework lie, as we will see, precisely in his ability to decipher this discourse.

Well before Snow, and well before Hugh Kenner, Harry Levin, or Irving Howe [10] were inclined to artificially seal off the period of modernity for the purpose of study,[11] the work of critics as diverse as F. R. Leavis and Georg Lukacs was already structured by a shared presupposition that modern literature—and the modern condition generally—acts out of the loss of something primary that it wishes to regain.

Lionel Trilling's crisp designation of the "will to modernity" as a redemptive search for a realm "beyond the reach of culture" remains as clear a definition as we have of what is axiomatic in our literary assumptions about the struggle for modernity. To be sure, for Trilling and others, the exemplary high modernist James Joyce stands as such precisely because he fully represents "this intense conviction of the existence of the self apart from culture."[12] But this notwithstanding, modern literature could not resist being a part of the scientific and technological character of the new age.[13]

By 1921, when Albert Einstein visited the United States, he—and "the physicist" in general—had become the new cultural hero, and the new physics had become front-page news. The models of science presented by Werner Heisenberg, Max Planck, and Albert Einstein (to name but three prominent participants in the second scientific revolution) were dramatically different from those of the nineteenth century, and they appealed directly to modernist politics and literary aesthetics.

For example, Einstein's original formulation of the special theory of relativity in 1905 stated that whereas an event viewed from two separate moving observers may appear different to each, neither observer would be wrong, or encounter contradictions, if he or she used the same basic laws of physics. The speed of light is a constant. This could lead to apparent contradictions since one person observing a light beam might be moving faster than another person observing the same beam. What happens, according to Einstein, is that the nature of time and space is altered by motion while the laws of physics remain unchanged. Einstein's later work on a general relativity extended his ideas to cover curved time and gravity.

Max Planck's work also concerned light and motion, but he focused on subatomic phenomena. In 1900, Planck proposed that electrons absorbed or emitted light in quantum units. He also found that there was a constant by which to measure the value of such energy exchanges. These findings required the abandonment of the older notion of a continuum of energy. Einstein later showed that Planck's findings suggested that light was in fact composed of particles that behaved, or could be treated, as a wave.

Werner Heisenberg's 1927 work on the uncertainty principle built on the work of Einstein and Planck and proposed that the error in position measurement multiplied by the error in momentum measurement can never be less than one-half of Planck's constant—or, said another way, that both the position and the speed of an atomic particle cannot be simultaneously known.

This "new" physics, which Snow understood, broke down the framework of classical physics, suggesting that space and time were fluid, and that phenomena changed depending on how they were observed. As the old edifice of certainty was eroded, physicists agreed that the difficulty in defining light or measuring subatomic "wavicles" was not due to the failings of scientific instrumentation but was rather due to the actual, ambiguous nature of the physical universe. This natural ambiguity appealed to, and underscored, the ambiguities of the Metropolis and of modernity itself. Snow put it thus: "It doesn't need saying that there are some objective reasons . . . why sensible people in the cities should behave as though they were in a state of siege. The modern city, the city of the last third of this century, is not an entirely reposeful place to live in."[14]

Literature drew on the growing authority of science and technology. Foreseeing Lionel Trilling's observation that "in an age of science, prestige is to be gained by approximating the methods of science,"[15] and driven by an angst and the will to escape culture at all costs, modern literature both accepted and emulated the images of science and technology. "In an age of transparent technologies, the modernist literature evolved, for itself, a set of parallel technologies. These were both difficult and obscure. *Et ignotas animum dimittit in artes*, the epigraph to James Joyce's *Portrait of the Artist as a Young Man*, claims the sponsorship of the fabulous technologist and warns us not to expect the kind of book that we've been used to. Arcane skills, "ignotas artes," such as those that enabled the Wright brothers to triumph at Kitty Hawk, have gone into its fashioning. Their machine had nothing to hide—you could see every moving part, just like Joyce's prose—and yet it challenged comprehension. They first flew it in December 1903, and by January 7, 1904, Joyce had effectively adopted the persona of "Daedalus."[16] Like the technology of its time, literary modernism sought, as evidenced by books like *Ulysses*, to share in the authority of science and technology and to become itself deeply technological. The connection among powerful aesthetic, cognitive, and political voices was thus ensured, but only after being subjugated to modernity itself.

As Hugh Kenner has articulated, "the internal combustion engine altered our perceptions of rhythm. . . . X-rays showed us transparent planes of matter . . . [and] the wireless superimposed voices from twenty countries on top of one another (*Finnegans Wake*). . . . Words moved on wires. Distant voices sounded in our ears."[17] And under a rigorous scrutiny, both the text and ourselves began to dissolve. Science and technology began to increasingly redefine both the role of words and of ourselves in relation to the text and to nature. It simultaneously embodied and promoted modernity's aesthetic and worldview.

Despite the pervasiveness of modernity, the several superficial clues to Snow's interest in modernity, and his deep thematic and personal involvement in the struggle of modernity, the exact nature, quality, and significance of Snow's efforts have largely gone unrecognized. Certainly since his death on July 1, 1980,[18] as the noted broadcaster Robert Fulford has said, "the waters seem to have closed above Snow's head, with both the humanist and scientific communities acting as if he hadn't existed."[19] Indeed to risk only a slight overstatement, since his death, Snow's contribution to our understanding of the struggle of modernity has run the risk of being lost altogether.

In part this has been due to the sheer weight of modernity in its tendency to maintain a fragmented perception of reality and of discourses. As a result, literary assessments of Snow's work have focused almost exclusively on his literary style, plot lines, and character building—almost to the total exclusion of the importance of science and politics in his conceptual schema. Indeed literary assessments have (with the rare exceptions of Saguna Ramanathan's most sensitive introduction and Frederick Karl's articulate— if now dated—analysis) attempted to "cage" Snow either as a late-nineteenth-century realist or as a "crass Wellsian."[20] Those who have focused on the political dimensions of Snow's work have ignored the evidence of his literature and have tended to inaccurately portray Snow as an ideologue. And the central importance of science in Snow's thought has been totally ignored, with existing assessments treating Snow's scientific background and themes as if they were simply cute, unimportant, or meaningless in terms of his literature. Indeed, to date, those making assessments of Snow's work have behaved as if the barriers between what Snow called "the two cultures" of the arts and sciences were in fact real and impenetrable. As one prominent literary academic revealingly phrased it, during an interview with Snow shortly before his death, "Can you tell a dummy like me what crystallography is?"[21] Surely, if we are to understand modernity as a complex but structured totality, then we must move beyond such barriers to understanding. Fearing the unknown discourses of modernity—or refusing to confront the sources of authoritative imagery in our own individual worlds—will only freeze our actions in a continuous present and negate any prospect for future progress. Equally it will relegate us to living with an impoverished legacy of C. P. Snow.

The basic biographical details of Snow's life are, by now, well known. He was born on October 15, 1905, in the provincial city of Leicester, England. He was the second of four sons in a lower-middle-class family. He received his B.Sc. in 1927 and his M.Sc. in 1928 from what is now Leicester University. He took his Ph.D. in Physical Chemistry in 1930 from Cambridge University. He was Fellow (1930) at Christ's College, Cambridge, was made Tutor (1935–1945), and was editor of the popular science journal called *Discovery* (1937–1940). He became Commander of the British Empire (CBE) in 1943 for work carried out during the war as the technical director at the Ministry of Labour, a post in which he recruited scientific personnel during World War II. In 1943, his name appeared twice on Himmler's special search list of individuals the Gestapo thought should be "dealt with" immediately.[22] In 1944, he became director of scientific personnel for the English Electric Company (a post that he held until 1964). He was civil service commissioner from 1945 to 1964 and book reviewer for the *Financial Times* (1949–1952). In 1950 he married the novelist, friend of Augustus John, and the ex-fiancée to Dylan Thomas—Pamela Hansford Johnson. He was knighted in 1957 and made Lord Snow in 1964. He took on the post of junior minister of technology in the House of Lords under the minister of technology, Frank Cousins, in the Labour government of Harold Wilson (until 1966). He again became a regular reviewer for the *Financial Times* in 1970 and died at the age of seventy-five in 1980.

During his life C. P. Snow collected numerous awards and prizes, including thirty-one honorary doctorates from universities in the United States, the Soviet Union, Canada, and Great Britain. He was at one time generally thought to be a serious contender for the Nobel Prize in literature and for a Fellowship in the Royal Society of London—both awards that he would have cherished but that, in the end, eluded him.

Snow is most remembered, perhaps, for his controversial 1959 Cambridge lecture on *The Two Cultures and the Scientific Revolution* and for his 1960 Harvard lectures on *Science and Government*. But it is his literary output for which he is most memorable. Many of Snow's novels are still superb reads. Among these I personally include *The Search, George Passant, The Masters, The New Men,* and *The Affair.* However, others, such as *New Lives for Old,* are decidedly mediocre. Nevertheless, between the publication of his first novel in 1932 and his last book of nonfiction (published posthumously) in 1981, Snow offered the world what may rank as the most sustained and intelligent assessment of our times that has ever been attempted. Snow authored seventeen novels, twelve nonfiction books, nine plays,[23] and literally hundreds of book reviews, articles, chapters, or lectures. The largest component of Snow's fiction comprises a series of eleven large novels, written between 1940 and 1970 and known collectively as *Strangers and Brothers*.[24]

What this study offers is not a literary critique dealing with each of Snow's novels—nor is it intended to be a biographical assessment of Snow. Instead, the task of this study is both historical and constructive. Its purpose is to recover the significance, meaning, and limitations of C. P. Snow's struggle with modernity by directly focusing on the three major dispositions of modernity that comprise his framework—literature, science, and politics. I seek to demonstrate both the relationships and the tensions that made Snow, like ourselves, an intimate part of our culture. The method of this study is essentially one of critical hermeneutics in which Snow's life, fiction, and nonfiction all become texts and forms of discourse to be topographically leveled and evaluated against the contours of his specific historical context.[25] In this way, I assess what Frederic Jameson calls "the political unconscious"—that is, those links that exist between narrative and history, between form and substance. The organization of this study leads part 2 (chapters 2 and 3) to examine the historical context in which Snow developed with particular reference to those literary and scientific reactions to the modern age that were to be formative for Snow. It also attempts to provide a critical distance between ourselves and the dominant readings of Snow's most notorious text (*The Two Cultures and the Scientific Revolution*). Part 3 (chapters 4, 5, and 6) focuses expressly on literature, science, and politics in Snow's work and in so doing attempts to construct an understanding of the totality of Snow's framework. In the end, it is the purpose of this work to have evaluated the contribution that Snow has made to our understanding of ourselves and to the struggle of modernity.

Two major premises inform this study. First, I believe that the distinction between the "two cultures" has been so overquoted that it has lost all of its meaning. Our ability to view Snow in toto has suffered as a result. Second, I hold that understanding C. P. Snow's totality can teach us about our own strategies for interpreting the world around us. It can help us understand our surroundings, and it can tell us something about reading various forms of discourse that vie for our attention and combine to make up our realities.

A word of caution is in order, however, for in the "Snow" I present there is no "movement." There is only an individual—a storyteller for the atomic age—who has lived in privileged spaces and who wanted to relay something to us about our condition. In many ways, his was a voice of hope. The ultimate collapse of his hope under the sheer weight of modernity—the ultimate failure of his framework— must be seen as a decay that was not his own, but which was endemic to the rationality of his generation. He was a defender of our individuality, of our totality. He was a defender of our consciousness, of our choices, and of our ability to reason. He was the prototype of human potential—a man in touch with the dialectical frontier of the struggle of modernity. We have much to learn from Snow's struggle, for whether we like it or not, that frontier is where we all are going.

Part Two

CONTEXT AND DISTANCE

2

STRANGERS AND BROTHERS
AGAINST THE GRAIN

Science has become self-conscious.
—J. D. BERNAL

. . . a nervous and haunted imagination
—DUNCAN GRANT ON *ULYSSES*

THE PERIOD into which C. P. Snow was born was a decidedly modernist one of change, vitality, and contradiction that exerted a powerful and lasting influence on the development of Snow's individualist framework. His social migration from lower-middle-class provincial Leicester to the intelligentsia of Cambridge and the bureaucracy of London made him acutely aware of the tensions between public and private life and ensured, in the class-bound society of Britain, his permanent sense of alienation. This migration paralleled many of the transformations that were implied in the emergence of the Metropolis. His cognitive perspective powerfully reflected the convergence of responses that were carried within—and between—the radical science and literature of the period. And his unique synthesis of political insights underpinned both his social hope for totality and his ultimate collapse under the weight of modernity into a disconnected "darkening" vision reveal the extent to which Snow himself was trapped in the tensions that are modernity. However, this having been said, it would not be a profitable exercise to discuss and assess the significance of Snow's complex triptych of literature, science, and politics without first achieving an understanding of the context and debates that shaped his sensibilities, and in which he participated. Approaching such an understanding is the purpose of this chapter.

The years surrounding the birth of Charles Percy Snow in 1905 were years in which the Victorian spirit of optimism and liberal positivism continued to hold considerable sway in English thought, politics, and social practice. As Snow himself said, he was a man of his time, and nowhere else would the young Snow receive clearer signals of this than from his own lower-middle-class family and the provincial city of Leicester. He grew up in a building—purchased by his family in 1898—that was once part of the Victorian Liberal Club. His great-grandfather moved to the Midlands with the Industrial Revolution. Though illiterate, he was a self-taught engine fitter—a fact that Snow was very proud of.[1] The Snow family library included many of the typical readings of the Victorian "Self-Help" movement, including *The Discoveries and Inventions of the Nineteenth Century*, the *Penny Magazine*, the *Illustrated London News*, and *John o' London's Wide World*.

Snow's father, an organist and Fellow of the Royal College of Organists (FRCO), moved to Leicester in the late 1890s "to go where the money was"[2] and to become a clerk in a boot and shoe factory. Despite the fact that the Snow family endured the social disgrace associated with the father's involvement in bankruptcies—two with firms he was employed by and one when he was in business on his own[3]—the fact that Snow's father was "an FRCO" gave Snow an early, overt, and strong sense of social class as well as a clear idea of what some of the "markings" of successful people were.

Leicester, at the time, was growing quickly. The population between 1851 and 1905 more than tripled—rising from 60,642 to 226,547[4]—while the city became increasingly industrial and oriented toward satisfying London's expanding consumer demand. During this same period the city's employment in the footware industry, for example, rose from 1,393 to 25,978. This reflected a number of converging factors—all of which were discernible, even to a young boy like Snow—ranging from the expansion of the rail lines from London, the diffusion of mechanized technology, and the growth of London as both a hub of politics and a source of cultural ideals.

At a deeper level, the rapid transitions taking place during Snow's youth were represented by the decline of liberalism and the growing momentum of socialism. The legitimacy of the old patterns of authority was being repeatedly challenged.[5] It is not surprising, then, that Snow's definition of a "sane society" was one that embodied "liberal-socialist attitudes." The transition was manifested in myriad and unexpected ways and implicated not only long-standing political traditions but cognitive and creative patterns as well.

Underlying this shift was a clustering of moods and events that could not go unnoticed, even by the Snow family. The growing pessimism of the fin de siècle and the void caused by the collapse of la belle époque—together with the unprecedented slaughters on the battlefields of the First World War, the equally "bloody" scientific revolution that turned our physical understanding on its head, the Russian Revolution of 1917, and the economic crises of the 1920s and 1930s—gave rise within Britain to a potent mix of revulsion against the existing society and faith in the possibility of its transformation. The net effect of this broad-based renegotiation was a blurring, and at times a complete erasing, of many traditional boundaries between politics and culture that had existed in the stable premodern society.

Two of the most powerful expressions of this reaction came from the literary and scientific communities through a reconsideration of their function in this "modern world." Both sets of reactions were to be formative in the development of Snow's own outlook. In both, Snow was to be first an observer and later an active participant. His involvement in the scientific community came through several levels. For example, he was a researcher at Cambridge (1928–1935) in one of the most revolutionary fields of science.[6] He was a colleague and friend of those who forged the debate on the modern social function of science between 1914 and 1945, including J. D. Bernal and G. H. Hardy (who appear as characters in the *Strangers and Brothers* series of novels). And he was a Tutor and the editor of the Cambridge-based popular science journal *Discovery* (1937–1940). While Snow developed his scientific credentials, it became increasingly necessary and unavoidable for him—as a budding serious novelist—to observe and respond to what he perceived as being the dominant literary reactions to change that were shaping the novel form, its language, and its implied political sensitivities. Among the many who played an active part in these literary transformations during the period between 1914 and 1945 were Virginia Woolf, Evelyn Waugh, Graham Greene, James Joyce, Richard Aldington, and Wyndham Lewis. However, as we will discuss in chapter 4, Snow's literary sensibilities operated almost to the total exclusion of the Greenes and Waughs (or even Audens). Instead his aesthetics were forged more as a selective reaction against "the experimentalists" (who were broadly classified in his mind). He attempted to develop "a new school of humanistic writing" (along with William Cooper, Pamela Hansford Johnson, John Wain, and others) that would counter the experimentalists and that would combine an antiquated form of nineteenth-century realism with modern scenes and motivations. The experimentalists' voices could be heard from the Gordon Square home of the Bloomsbury Group, which was in many ways an extension of the Cambridge Society of Apostles,[7] and from such avant-garde magazines as *Blast* and *transition*. While many within the scientific and literary communities did not mix socially—either amongst themselves or with other communities[8]—both the scientists and the literalists were inexorably linked through the charged climate that they shared. Snow was to react to both, and to paraphrase Walter Benjamin and Snow, these communities were strangers and brothers who struggled against the grain.

To be sure, as a young man Snow was largely unaware of the details of debate within these communities. But there is no doubt that he was deeply affected by the contexts created by them. For some within these two broad communities, the period between 1914 and 1945 was a time of great opportunity signified by new forms of conception and action. For those caught up in the energy of the period, as were both J. D. Bernal and Richard Aldington, the many social contradictions of the age served to solidify their commitments to liberal causes while at the same time entrenching their fears of repressive governments. In their view, the tensions of the period could be effectively used to increase the political momentum of then marginal elements of society—including both science and literature. To them, political and aesthetic marginality was seen as becoming the avant-garde of effective progress and transformation.

For many others, however, it was a time between time—a period that was conceived of as being an epistemological and social no-man's-land of despair, angst, and lost meaning. From their perspective, the past was unrecoverable and the future offered no hope. Their emergent awareness of change, coupled with a growing consciousness of their marginality, was to lead not to progress and social transformation but to psychological and social collapse—as it did in 1915 for Virginia Woolf. For those who shared this view, the rise of political reactionism at this time was the result of a reversal in values that was itself grounded in the ashes of positivism.

Between these poles of reaction, no clear set of concerns is discernible. The political and cultural attitudes of the involved scientists and literati were often marked by as much contradiction, ambivalence, and electricity as the age itself. Thus, exactly where the distinction lies between a dominant modernist center, seen to be reactionary, and a more marginal political liberalism fighting for more progressive social change is not at all clear. However, what is clear of this period is that cultural innovation and revolutionary politics were powerfully drawn together. Moreover, each reaction (including Snow's) was tied firmly to the social sphere—engagé with the urban struggle for modernity and ranging across a broad frontier of tense confrontations—from the style, form, and content of literary expression to the social responsibility of science, and ultimately, to the very frontiers of liberal ideology itself.

Prior to 1914, in a time often associated with both the second phase of la belle époque[9] and the growing crisis of British capitalism,

Britain was still clinging to the polite and blithe facade of a permanent and stable society. Insofar as this is true, however, the dominant imagery of the age must be seen as being highly problematic. The arts were flourishing, as were the dance halls and galleries. Following the now-famous 1910 London exhibition sponsored by the Cambridge Apostles Roger Fry and Clive Bell, Impressionism was giving way to the achievements of Picasso and Gauguin. Debussy and Wagner were establishing musical styles. Both the formidable Sarah Bernhardt and Maurice Chevalier, with his bowler hat and cane, were entertaining the genteel classes of London and Paris. While Continental fiction was becoming more varied and distinctly bohemian, British fiction responded to the increasingly pervasive urban experience by attempting to recover a mythical past, complete with dominant values and imagery of the affluent country gentleman and home, thus forcing the novel form to become comfortably rural in its character.[10]

At the same time, deep economic and political instabilities in Britain were becoming pronounced and increasingly apparent. The antiquated paradigms of financial and industrial management that had become dominant in Britain over a century of successful overseas trading had left British firms, and the British domestic economy generally, technologically obsolete, uncompetitive, and increasingly at odds with its labor force. The Snow household experienced some of this tension in a direct fashion. The political and trade union arms of the labor movement had grown in numbers, strength, and militancy, so that between 1910 and 1914 a wave of major strikes, augmented by record high unemployment, had clearly signaled to the world that Britain was in serious political and industrial trouble.

Thus the proliferation of strikes and plant closures, the economy's decreasing productivity, and the arming of Europe all combined with a facade of social and artistic gaiety to create an environment in Britain and throughout Europe that was electric with stress and contradiction. What is clearly discernible beneath this cultural and economic veneer is a panic state in which there was an unconscious, yet widespread, yearning for the mythical stability of earlier years. Much of the fiction, poetry, drama, and music[11] was, in fact, trapped in a time warp of the prewar years in which a timid and stylized version of the past dominated. Chevalier's hat and cane were nothing more than lingering anachronisms. Art, literature, and politics were still firmly grounded in the ideas of the nineteenth century. And although life seemed affluent, stable, and peaceful, traditional society was nonetheless crumbling. The ideas that were coming to dominate the creative communities and that were to be formative for Snow regrettably represented a deep splintering of the Victorian tradition.

In response to the tensions of the period and the pressures on private life, many writers discussed the function of literature and art in the emerging society as well as the social role of the intellectual. Among the most influential expressions of this were from the Bloomsbury Group and its associated elite Society of Apostles in the 1910s and 1920s. Its membership featured many of the most prominent intellectuals at Cambridge, including Leonard Woolf, Lytton and James Strachey, E. M. Forster, Bertrand Russell, G. H. Hardy, G. E. Moore, and John Maynard Keynes.

In many ways, the Bloomsbury Group were cultural and sexual rebels—elitists whose views were to influence an elite. They had no direct mass appeal, and their preaching of personal values and disenchantment with the interwar world through their Cambridge friends was to spread only slowly to the undergraduates. And yet, the group was responsible for important changes in the dominant artistic and literary tastes. Examples abound. Two Bloomsbury-sponsored Post-Impressionist exhibitions in 1910 forced the London art world to redefine its perceptions in the images of Matisse, Van Gogh, Gauguin, and Picasso. By 1914 both Roger Fry and Clive Bell had become regular visitors to the Saturday evening salons hosted by Gertrude Stein in her Paris apartment where their influence on discussions on the merger between art and literature was rivaled only by Stein herself, who was then trying to become a "cubist of letters" in response to her own discussions with Picasso, Fry, and Bell.[12] Other attendees who were part of this circle and who helped to diffuse these new ideas were Augustus John and Wyndham Lewis. In addition, many of the leading literary and political papers of the day were controlled by friends of the Bloomsbury Group and by relatives. Desmond MacCarthy was at the *New Statesman* and Leonard Woolf was at the *Nation;* therefore, reviews and wide circulation of the work, ideas, and opinions of the group were assured. As a result, a formidable younger group of soon-to-be influential writers and critics fell under the spell of Bloomsbury. They included Harold Nicolson and his wife Vita Sackville-West, Roger Stenhouse, and George Brenan. To many, Bloomsbury seemed to be unforgivably successful—particularly as they possessed their own means of (re)production, the Hogarth Press, which published T. S. Eliot's unsettling *Waste Land*. Thus, in idea and in fact, the group seemed to dominate literary tastes and styles of the times.

Under the dominant moral philosophy of G. E. Moore and as a re-action to the distasteful developments of the period, the Bloomsbury Group drew on classical Greek ideals, focusing attention on conceptions of beauty and "pure aesthetics." In so doing, they developed and restated the ideal of "art for art's sake," which had been heard in France and in the work and rhetoric of Oscar Wilde at various times since the 1870s.

The argument implied in this line of reasoning involved an attempt to justify art and literature purely in terms of their own aesthetic values.[13] As such, they must be seen as being separate from society in moral or political terms, and their aesthetic value was discerned only with reference directly to the work in question.

Proponents of this view did not ignore the world around them but developed the central image of a vehicle for social transformation consisting of a class of people who would act as custodians for the arts. They would promote and encourage the arts, even in the face of a hostile society. This class would be committed to the pursuit of artistic standards of excellence and the provision of the necessary atmosphere in which the artist could flourish. Clearly, Bloomsbury and the related Apostles saw themselves as being a living laboratory for this new class, even though after the war some members would reject the isolation of art from society as an ideal while maintaining their commitment to the aesthetic and political power of the arts. However, during this period their ideas were often carried to such extremes that accusations of dandyism could justifiably and regularly be made. These criticisms—many of which were published in Bloomsbury-controlled periodicals—came from such writers as D. H. Lawrence and Wyndham Lewis, who accused the Bloomsbury Group of launching an irreverent and indiscriminate assault on all values. In *The Apes of God*, for example, Lewis portrayed the *l'art pour l'art* Bloomsbury Group as being a diabolical lab for the inauthentic self in which there could be no art.

In a symbolic rebuttal of these attacks, some members of the group attempted to further isolate themselves from society—intending to demonstrate their commitment to their principles. But this was hardly a difficult strategy for any of them to follow, as all of them came from either aristocratic or acceptably middle-class backgrounds that afforded them both the education and the financial means to support such isolation—if only barely. But even this could not deflect the more deeply problematic aspects of Bloomsbury. In many ways, the efforts of the group represented an attempt to transfer the intellectual vitality of Cambridge to a noninstitutional home in London. But in the process there was a strong element of over-cultivation that ultimately gave their artistic and critical acclaims a shrill shallowness.[14]

Whether as immoralists (to use Keynes's own self-description) or as hyperaestheticists, the Bloomsbury Group—which formed a self-conscious "high culture" movement—were, ultimately, unable to sustain their convictions in the face of an active avant-garde. For Bloomsbury, the problematic relationship of the intellectual to society was never to be resolved or successfully renegotiated. As Michael Holroyd has written:

> For all of their elegant and ingenious tinkerings, most of the Bloomsbury writers and artists were unable finally to sever the umbilical cord joining them to the inherited traditions of the past. Theirs was a tenuous transitory mood, largely barren and inbred, a suspension bridge that now forms our authentic link back to the solid cultural traditions of the nineteenth century. They modified, romanticized, avoided those traditions with varying degrees of success. But rather than being the real founders of a new and originally conceived civilization as Virginia Woolf supposed, they were, in the words of Roger Fry himself, "the last of the Victorians."[15]

This realization of the Bloomsbury Group's own historicity came to be one that was seized upon and bitterly reacted against by the more aggressive avant-garde movements of the period. In October 1913, Wyndham Lewis and others complained that Bloomsbury was "nothing but a kind of backwater" that clung to "a typically Cambridge sort of atmosphere" and featured "a sort of aesthetic playing around" in which "the Idol [was] still Prettiness with its mid-Victorian languish of the neck."[16] The break that was to result from this clash of sensibilities was fundamental to the development of a modern literary response and was to be felt throughout the literary community.

In 1914, Wyndham Lewis had published nothing more than a few stories, but he had become known as a revolutionary visual artist. His work, which showed the strong influence of cubism, was praised by fellow critics and artists including Augustus John and Roger Fry. However, in the closing months of 1913, Lewis and Fry quarreled bitterly, ostensibly over a commission that Lewis felt had been dishonestly diverted from him to Fry's Omega Group. More importantly, however, the quarrel was over Bloomsbury's version of Post-Impressionism and cubism that often confused art with decoration.

In March 1914 Lewis founded the Rebel Art Center in direct opposition to both Bloomsbury and the Omega Group, and all the work and ideas that they represented.

Immediately there was support from a small number of writers and artists. Ford Madox Ford argued that "what contemporary literature [needed most was] intolerance, and not the mawkish flap doodle of culture."[17] A flurry of activity swelled around the more radical ideas between January and July of 1914. The journals *Blast* and *Egoist* were launched, while the anthology *Des Imagistes* appeared. All of these carried contributions by Richard Aldington and his wife, H.D., as well as by Joyce, Pound, Ford, and T. S. Eliot. In these pages, the various positions of "the new art" were articulated, including the work of the vorticists, the Imagistes, and the Futurists.[18] Lewis published (in the January 1914 *Egoist*) a passionate defense of the new directions being taken in vorticism and imagism in an essay called "The Cubist Room." These were vigorously expanded upon by Lewis, Pound, and T. E. Hulme in lectures delivered on January 22 at the London Quest Society on "Modern Art and Its Philosophy." Each speaker bitterly harangued the aestheticist's polite involvement in social reform and asserted that the artist had been fed out of the hand of bourgeois society too long. As a result, said one,

> "the arts have grown dull and complacent. . . . We are sick to death of the general acquiescence of artists, of their agreement to [exhibit] perfect manners, and to mention absolutely nothing unpleasant. If 'real' social and artistic progress is to be made, then what is needed is a manifest hostility to the social order, and now the artist has at least been aroused to the fact that the war between him and the world is a war without truce. . . . The artist has been at peace with his oppressors for long enough. He has dabbled in democracy and he is now done with that folly."[19]

Thus, in a sense, Pound and others struck out with Lewis to forge what was effectively a position as antidemocratic as that of Stirner and Nietzsche.

The strongest—even belligerent—expression of this attitude came in *Blast*. Vorticism appealed "TO THE INDIVIDUAL"; it was a popular art, but it had nothing to do with "The People" or the homogenized and fashionable tastes of the masses. As such, art could allow no involvement with popular progress or social reform, nor could it depend on a fidelity to nature. "We want to leave Nature and Men alone; We believe in no perfectibility except our own." Moral constraints dropped away as there could only be "one truth, ourselves."[20] The fundamental and recurring principle throughout this avant-garde philosophy and art was of the self-sufficiency of the artist. In the extreme, this led to antagonism not only between art and society but between art and tradition as well.

This latter point was the preoccupation of Futurism, which at the time was the dominant avant-garde sect. Under the leadership of Filippo Marinetti, Futurism dedicated itself to the pursuit of a "new beauty" derived strictly from contemporaneity: "power under control, speed, intense light, happy precision . . . the conciseness of effort, the molecular cohesion of metals . . . the simultaneous concurrence of diverse rhythms . . ."[21] all of which implied a complete break with previous art.

Futurism was highly visible on the London scene from 1912 to 1914, with lectures and performances attracting crowds as well as the attention of the press. In the June 7, 1914, edition of the *Observer*, F. T. Marinetti announced his desire "to cure English art of that most grave of all maladies—passéism." With characteristic sweep he attacked "sentimentality," "sham revolutionaries," "the conservatism of English artists," and the "worship of tradition." He then gave the Futurist cheer: "HURRAH for motors! HURRAH for speed! HURRAH for lightning!" and called upon the English public to "support, defend and glorify" futurist tendencies in culture and the "advance-forces of vital English art."[22]

Ford Madox Ford, T. E. Hulme, Wyndham Lewis, and Ezra Pound all utterly rejected the cult of technology, speed, and machinery that was advocated by the Futurists, but they all shared—with Marinetti—a strong sense of renaissance and a hostility toward certain forms of art and literature that have a legitimacy sanctioned simply by tradition and long use. To the extent that they shared an awareness of the new, they were, in the words of Pound, "all Futurists."[23]

The traumatic event that punctured the past, and all perceptions of the future, was the outbreak of the Great War. As Gertrude Stein put it, "The world collapsed on August 1, 1914"—with the mobilization of troops in France—"It was then that the twentieth century began." D. H. Lawrence agreed and observed that, to him, "the old world [had] ended . . . [and was replaced by] a vortex of broken passions, lusts, hopes, fears and horrors. . . ."[24] Henry James echoed aggressively that his was "the imagination of disaster" in which life became "ferocious and sinister." James finally conceded that he stopped writing novels because "the social aspect of the world changed so much. I had been accustomed to write about the old-fashioned world with its homes and its family life and its comparable peace. All that went, and though I think about the new world I cannot put it into fiction."[25] Virginia Woolf, as well, chronicled the fundamental meaning of a world in turmoil. She noted, along with everyone else, that "human character changed. . . . All human relations [had] shifted. . . . And when human relations change there [would be] at the same time a change in . . . politics, and literature." To many of the literati, the new or emerging (as yet unclear) conditions of life were confounding. Old styles of writing now seemed inadequate. Old subjects of writing were dusty or no longer extant. And old relationships, ranging from friendships and family units to the once-felt "security of knowing one's place" in a rigid social class system, were suddenly inverted or collapsed; once-private lives were thrown into the streets of the Metropolis. In response to this condition, Henry James advised other would-be writers that "there is one word—let me impress upon you—that you must inscribe upon your banner, and that word is Loneliness."[26] It is little wonder then that literature developed the dominant themes of exile and isolation, especially given that the social mood of the time embodied—as Ruth Benedict phrased it—a doctrine of despair.[27]

This acute perception of social and cultural instability was in many ways fueled by the profound sense of loss that the war delivered through the powerful legacy of the "lost generation." At the same time, conflict arose between the generation too old to fight (but still able to "manage" the carnage), those who supported the war effort or who fought in the trenches, and those who conscientiously objected to the war. These complex tensions gave rise to a profound questioning and reorientation of postwar politics—which were poignantly felt at Cambridge.

The support for the war effort of those attending Cambridge was clear. This was a matter of national loyalty that extended even to the scientists. Indeed many accounts of the war years reveal a veritable stampede of dons and undergraduates who were eager to sign on for active duty. And yet to fight as an officer (as many Cambridge enlistees would) meant probable death, mutilation, or injury. Of those who graduated in the five years between 1909 and 1914, more than a quarter were killed and more than half were wounded. Indeed, in many ways, what the war amounted to was nothing less than a massacre of a class that expected to rule. At one time during the fighting, the survival time for a lieutenant at the front was estimated at six weeks. A privileged birth and an education seemed to have somehow become a privilege to death and extinction. The impact that this had on revising a once hopeful sense of the future was deeply felt. As Duff Cooper, first viscount of Norwich, wrote to Lady Diana

Manners in 1918, "Our generation becomes history instead of growing up."[28]

Never before had there been such a total decimation of the country's future leaders and genius, and the impact of this realization on those who remained was profound. As J. B. Priestley, who himself was a lieutenant in the war and later an undergraduate at Trinity Hall, Cambridge, wrote: "Those of us who are left know that we are the runts." Although the "lost generation" was *numerically* only a legend, the impact on English political and intellectual life was staggering. Nevertheless, the numbers and quality of the dead were somewhat exaggerated, partly because those who had survived carried with them a deep sense of disorientation and guilt. Of the 700,000 British combatants who died, 375,000 were officers. There had been 5 million males between the ages of twenty and forty before the war, but there were the same number three years after. The weapons of death that had included machine guns, artillery, mines, aerial bombs, and chemical gas were random in their devastating effects and were not targeted against the elites of Cambridge. Thus, an entire generation had not, in fact, been killed, though many of its promising members had been.[29]

The lasting emotional impact of the slaughter and horror of the war was profound, even on the young Snow. Even though he was only a boy of 9 when the war began, and despite the fact that Snow's father was too old to join the armed forces, while his brother Harold was underage when he joined and thus was never sent abroad to see action, the signs of war were all around Snow. Regularly, he would see troop and hospital trains filled with heavily bandaged soldiers on the viaducts of Leicester. And in 1926, while still in uniform and when Snow was 21, Snow's oldest brother, Harold, died suddenly of complications from pneumonia, which he had contracted during the war and which had been aggravated during damp, late-night guard duty. This event suddenly made Snow the eldest of the three remaining sons and thus bestowed on him a mantle of responsibility and courage that he took very seriously. In many ways, it is significant that he responded in this way, for a generation of writers against whom Snow would later react recognized that the war had taught "us courage, extravagance, and fatalism; [it] made us fear boredom more than death [and] it instilled into us what might be called a *spectatorial* attitude."[30] The works of such emerging writers as Wyndham Lewis, which stood language on its ear, became imbued with this attitude. To others, including Noel Annan, these works of energy and imagination only proved that the old political and cultural values had been wrong and had probably been responsible for the catastrophe.

However, the growing disenchantment was not simply a result of the horrors of war, nor indeed was it associated solely with the guilt of coming to terms with the lost generation. Instead it was the direct result of the final social collapse of the old order signaled by the disillusionment with the political and economic terms of peace. John Maynard Keynes, whose brilliance Snow recognized at Cambridge and who was a leading member of the Bloomsbury Group and the Cambridge Society of Apostles, was the chief representative of the Treasury at the postwar negotiations in Versailles. He shared many of the antiwar views of his friends and wrote in a polemic called *The Economic Consequences of the Peace* that the punitive reparations that had been exacted from Germany, coupled with the self-interested land exchanges of the victorious powers, would only lead to the financial ruin of Europe and to yet another world war. "Vengeance," he predicted (echoing the views of many), "will not limp." In this ultimate conflict, "the progress of our generation" would be destroyed.

This was to become something of the governing attitude for many of the leading scientists and literati. The feeling of utter betrayal that many felt toward the old generation governing them was acute. In exchange for unquestioning support of the war effort, the country had been repaid with slaughter, unemployment, and political revolutions in Europe. Oswald Moseley later phrased it directly: in his view, the "old men" had "muddled my generation in the crisis of 1914, . . . [and had] laid to waste the power and the glory of the land."[31] Arthur Koestler echoed this sentiment and noted that "no longer was democracy the only form of government conceivable. Socialism (in a vague and undefined way) [had become] the hope of the 20th century."[32] The myth of the lost generation had helped to produce a bitter dissatisfaction with the society to which the survivors of the carnage returned. They were determined never to allow the repeat of the slaughter of war and the attendant unemployment. With this conviction, the mood of postwar Britain had a wedge driven into it. Gone was the neat and stable prewar Britain divided simply into the governing and governed classes.

The sentiment of interwar Britain was distinctly antiauthoritarian. The period became an era of revolt against all manifestations of the assertive will. Lord Acton's dictum that "absolute power corrupts absolutely" became a popular symbol for an entire generation. The temper of the age, as it would be with the novel, was distinctly anti-heroic. The hero of this period was a person to whom things happened rather than someone who exercised his or her will on life. The whimper had replaced the bang. The future had been dissolved in the mud and blood of the trenches and in the political turmoil of social reconstruction. Even at Cambridge, where entry had once been the sole preserve of the powerful bourgeoisie, scholarships were now beginning to bring middle- and lower-middle-class students who would traditionally never have had the opportunity to gain either a Cambridge education or any higher education. Snow was to be one such student.

Neither writers nor the general public could ignore the manic energy of the period. "The war," wrote Wyndham Lewis, "was like a great new fashion: everything had become historical; the past had returned."[33] To W. H. Auden, the period was one of the "lowest and [most] dishonest" during which time the greatest enemy of all was politics. And for Cyril Connolly, the ultimate "political problem [was] how not to get killed."

Politics and social awareness were unavoidable for anyone in this milieu. The depression of the 1920s–1930s, the collapse of Labour in the election of 1931, the rise of fascism and communism in the late 1930s, the Munich crisis of September 1938—all of these salient events signaled just how much the public sphere had come to matter for the private self. Connolly knew exactly what the writer must do: "He has to be political to integrate himself and he must be political to protect himself. Today, the forces of life and progress are raging on [the] one side, those of reaction and death on the other."[34]

But at the same time, the consumer of the writer's work—the reading public—also reacted, but not in a way that helped the literati. "The reading public panicked with the fall of France and their literary curiosity, dependent on a background of security and order, vanished over night."[35] People returned their books to lending libraries en masse. Publishers had no idea what was going to happen. Just when the need was greatest for a literary "counter voice," all fell silent. There was a great slaughter of journals and magazines. In the wartime frenzy, many literary journals of new writing, such as *Criterion, New Stories, New Verse, Seven, Twentieth Century Verse,* and *The Writer's Own Magazine*, were all closed.

Writers began to voice their complaints about the general stagnation of cultural life, as it become increasingly difficult to support oneself, let alone to create art. As George Orwell wrote in his diary: "The money situation is becoming completely unbearable. . . . Wrote a long letter to the Income Tax people pointing out that the war had practically put an end to my livelihood while at the same time the government refused to give me any kind of job."[36] Snow later registered his own recognition of both this situation and the character of the age by noting (in *George Passant*) that "money is desperately short again. The trickle from the agency is lessening. I shall have to borrow. What does it matter in this *fin de siècle* time?"[37] The gravity of this widespread situation was suggested by Cyril Connolly who, playing on the symbol of high literary culture, no longer wrote in an ivory tower but in an "Ivory Shelter,"[38] lamenting that "as human beings artists are less free now than they have ever been; it is difficult for them to make money and impossible for them to leave the country."[39] Mrs. Robert Henley reiterated these themes in an article on "The Liquidation of the Free-Lances (by One of Them)." "No young writer or artist, after this war is over, will ever dare to be without a safe job. . . . When the free-lance is finally liquidated, our art and literature will all be produced by little men in striped trousers, Anthony Eden hats and rolled umbrellas, who are punctual at their offices and incapable of dangerous thoughts."[40]

These practical and cultural shifts were carefully monitored by a sociological organization called Mass Observation, which was set up by anthropologist Tom Harrison and poet Charles Madge. Mass Observation used hundreds of volunteers to register the variety of activities and opinions of the wartime population. In their study, *War Begins at Home*, they concluded what everyone already knew, that the Blackout was having the greatest impact on people's, including writer's, lives. All regular outings and activities, from walking the dog to attending political meetings, declined, while staying in and going to bed early increased. The word *blackout* itself became a synonym and a symbol of a shutdown on all intellectual life. The air war, as Snow himself noted in a *Discovery* editorial entitled "A New Means of Destruction,"[41] had blacked out civilization.

Indeed there was an inhibiting and self-isolating awareness that this was a period that was cut off from both the past and the future. Prewar experience was no longer valid material for the writer, while the present was too close to communicate. And yet, it was tremendously difficult to conceive what postwar life would be like. As Mass Observation noted: "One very vital effect of the air raids is the blurring of the future. There is a tendency for people's whole outlook to be foreshortened, so that life exists from day to day."[42] Self-alienation reached a symbolic extreme in R. D. Marshall's "A Wrist Watch and Some Ants," in which a soldier cuts off his own arm after being wounded and then lies looking at it abstractedly, a part of his own body no longer part of him.

Expressing this same sense of alienation within the darkening noon of politics and culture, George Orwell—in his essay *Inside the Whale*—expressed his deep fear that "the autonomous individual is going to be stamped out of existence. . . . The literature of liberalism is coming to an end. As for the writer, he is . . . merely an anachronism, a hangover from the bourgeois age, . . . from now onwards the all important fact for the creative writer is going to be that this is not a writer's world."[43]

Virginia Woolf's novel *Between the Acts* conveys this strain and menace in imaginative terms. In the oppressive atmosphere of a hot day close to rain in June 1939, the owners of a small country house play host to the village pageant. Everywhere there is the feeling of suppressed violence: a snake chokes trying to swallow a toad; animal blood splashes a man's shoes; the newspapers talk of a rape, the falling franc, and the uncertain news from Europe. The pageant is interrupted by low-flying planes. Its climax, "The Present Time," is a jangled collage of the past, becoming vicious as the players turn mirrors on the audience, who see nothing. The imagery clearly implies the tensions felt by many aware of the struggle of modernity— a loss of connection with the past, a loss of individual control over our lives, a loss of interpretative meaning as to our place in the world.

In *Between the Acts* the disintegration of modernity is symbolic, while in Leonard Woolf's *Barbarians at the Gate* the disintegration is at a political level. While German and Russian totalitarianism posed an external threat, equally dangerous are the internal weaknesses of liberal civilization and culture. The barbarians are at the gate, but the more insidious peril is the collapse of values within.

Thus, the collapses of the interwar years were to have a decisive effect on literature. Bloomsbury itself, in both figurative and literal terms, had ended. The literary avant-garde as a vehicle of progressive social reform had been defused and denied a public. The *Daily Mail* could write that "there is no such thing as culture in wartime."[44] The political and cultural prospects that had been hoped for all seemed to be only collapsed into a new disorder. As E. M. Forster put it (perfectly understating the enigmatic character of the age) this was not the best time to start a literary career. But it was an exciting time to start a scientific career.

Prior to 1914, the relationship between science and politics was remote. Not only did government *not* have a strong interest or involvement in scientific education or research but the leadership of science worked hard to maintain their long-standing social and political apathy.

Several factors contributed to this fusty conservatism among scientists. Class background was among the most significant. Most had come from the economically privileged strata as the sons of upper- and middle-class families. This conservative tendency was only to be reinforced by such institutions as Cambridge where the meeting of a preindustrial town, a precapitalist university, and an aristocratic conception of science together forged a powerful cultural bond.

Augmenting this "natural" conservatism was the fact that the training ground of "High Science"—research that scientists held in the greatest esteem—was Cambridge. As Gary Werskey has pointed out, High Science in twentieth-century Britain was undertaken for purely intellectual—not utilitarian—reasons. It was both "hard" and "experimental," implying a bias toward the techniques, theorizing, and problems of the physical sciences. To a degree, High Science was also research of outstanding promise or continuing excitement. And it was, above all else, the work of first-rate practitioners.[45]

Without question, the locus for High Science between 1914 and 1945 was Cambridge, site of the research teams at the famous Cavendish Laboratory under Sir Ernest Rutherford and at the Dunn Institute of Biochemistry with Sir Frederick Gowland Hopkins. During this period, an affiliation with Cambridge was practically mandatory for anyone with thoughts of a bright career in scientific research. Nowhere else in Britain was there such an abundance of human and physical resources to devote to disinterested research. Its researchers were, quite naturally, the "big men" in their chosen fields, and by sitting on important government and research committees both inside and outside of Cambridge, they were effectively able to determine the style, ethos, and direction of pure science in Britain.[46] Thus it is not coincidental that the leaders of the scientific community and their brightest students were involved with such organizations as the Royal Society and that a high proportion of Fellows of the Royal Society (FRSs) of this period were involved in two of the most revolutionary and exciting subjects—physics and biochemistry—at Cambridge. As Snow learned from his father, the designation of FRS was a social distinction reserved for "great men." It was to be highly prized and sought after.

But there was far more to becoming "a Cambridge man" than simply studying a branch of physics or biology. One had also to acquire the culture of Cambridge High Science. As Gary Werskey put it: "Once admitted into this ancient university, your research interests were woven into a way of life and a set of attitudes which you were expected to uphold. The values generated from this culture were surprisingly elitist. . . . Among the most prized virtues were loyalty to your lab and dedication to your work. Political commitments were your own affair, as long as they did not impede your full participation in the activities of your chosen research community. . . . [However,] any overt preoccupation with them was bound to cast some doubt on your 'soundness.'"[47]

Cambridge science clearly transmitted to its students a deeply hierarchial view of what science was, how it worked, and how it related to society. Thus, once inside the labs, researchers at Cambridge were exposed, in unrelenting ways, to the norms and values of High Science. The overwhelming majority of scientists at Cambridge were socially and financially well-off males, with women representing less than 5 percent of the students. Few at this time entered, as Snow did in 1928, through scholarships from the lower-middle class. Interest in politics or in carrying out industrial research was seen as being clearly at odds with the interests of High Science. As a result, they were both intellectually and morally suspect endeavors. This view was exemplified by all of Cambridge's scientific leaders. The mathematician G. H. Hardy wrote that industrial work was dull and "only fit for second rate minds."[48] This was emphasized by Hopkins, Rutherford, and Lowry (the director of the Physical Chemistry laboratories at which Snow worked), who had no interest whatsoever in technical problems or in technology. Indeed, they seemed to nurse prejudices against them.

That Cambridge scientists had what could be described as a powerful and coherent culture at this time is clear. As Snow himself wrote, the cultural cohesion of Cambridge was, in part, based upon the scientists' knowledge that "this was the golden age of science"[49] and that Cambridge was its center. But in the years ahead, there was much that came to test this cohesion.

Although scientists were, collectively, far from being politically astute, the social pressures for political reform were such that the scientific community could no longer avoid responding in some way. The war brought with it a dramatic increase in government support for science,[50] and many scientists at Cambridge, revealing their support for the war effort generally, reciprocated by clamoring to take part in weapons, operations, and tactical systems research. This included work on poison gas and the development of both the tank and fighter aircraft. Moreover, the Battle of Jutland is said to have been acted out on the banks of the Cam by groups of Cambridge scientists. The once avowedly apolitical character of scientific research was beginning to change rapidly.

The net effect of these shifts was far-reaching and included a rapid increase in demand from industrial and government labs for individuals with scientific training; the acceleration of the professionalization process among scientists; the initiation of a much closer and formal relationship among science, government, and industry;[51] and the first attempts by scientists at forming their own trade union.

Among the responses that came from within Cambridge was the establishment in 1918 of the National Union of Scientific Workers (NUScW). This organization represented a variety of interests and groups, principal among which were the pro-Soviet socialist cells that were becoming increasingly vocal at Cambridge. Active in the formation of the NUScW were Maurice Dobb and Roy Pascal (both Marxist scholars from Pembroke College), C. P. Dutt (a member of the Communist party), the crystallographer J. D. Bernal, and the eclectic mathematician from Trinity College G. H. Hardy.

In some ways, Hardy's involvement in the NUScW may seem out of character. He was, after all, a staunch and vocal supporter of the intellectual rigor of High Science. But within the British context of postwar science and society, Hardy had been deeply impressed by a statement made in April 1920 by Oxford professor Frederick Soddy, who declared that if "the world is to be made safe for democracy, scientific men must at all costs make themselves masters in their own house without delay."[52] For Hardy, this sentiment was intensified by the many criticisms leveled at government's exploitation of scientists during the war. Sir Frederick Gowland Hopkins, a colleague of Hardy's, arranged for some preliminary meetings to discuss both the criticisms and the idea of founding a professional organization of some kind.

The NUScW was the first scientists' trade union anywhere in the world and was in many ways an unusual sort of organization for scientists to join. But many did join, and if some scientists kept aloof from it, it was largely because of its radically left-wing, pro-Soviet views. The union made many rhetorically savage attacks on government and the war office for its immoral use of science in the war effort. It was concerned about support for the Bolsheviks and the revolution in Russia. Indeed, Hardy, with the support of at least one other Apostle, urged that the union seek cooperation with the Soviet Union—if not politically, then at least to exchange information. On this theme, the union's official publication, the *Scientific Worker,* stated that "the attention of members is directed to the letter from the British Committee for Aiding Men of Letters and Science in Russia" and suggested that members might wish to send gifts.[53] This gift exchange campaign did not go very well, but as a result of its pro-Soviet activities, the NUScW formed the first "think tank." It was strongly supported by Bernal and Hardy, as well as by other pro-Soviet scientists including Joseph Needham, J. G. Crowther, J. B. S. Haldane, and P. M. S. Blackett—many of whom were to visit the Soviet Union in the interwar years and all of whom were to become (between 1928 and 1935) close friends or acquaintances of Snow's. One of the first problems considered by the group was how to aid the Soviet Union in its problems of industrialization and mechanization.

However, before the union could make any real contribution on this front, internal imbalances began to take hold. Many more moderate members began to show signs of dissatisfaction with the union's socialist leanings. At the same time, the scientific membership of the union had effectively become outnumbered by economists, sociologists, and other sympathetic onlookers. Dame Helen Gwynne Vaughan resigned from the office of union president. Finances dwindled, and in 1924 Hardy took on the presidency in an attempt to revitalize the union's membership and finances. However, in his two years in office he was effectively able only to mount a rearguard action to maintain trade union status. A lack of funds finally settled the issue, and the NUScW was deregistered. Hardy resigned as president in 1926 and was soon replaced by Julian Huxley.

Within this brief period, one of the accomplishments of the NUScW was to clearly show scientists at Cambridge that they could no longer ignore either the social impact of their work or the close relationship that science now had with both society and government. The growing persecution of Jewish scholars, and their systematic expulsion from universities, powerfully underscored this point, while appealing to the scientists' sense of internationalism that underpinned their definition of the "Republic of Science."[54] J. B. S. Haldane put it most succinctly. By this time "we knew that science had a lot to do with politics."[55] But quite beyond these pressures on science were the public pressures.

The government's military use of scientific expertise served to link science in the public mind with destruction. At the same time, rising unemployment that was caused, at least in part, by technological change helped further align science in the popular mind with government interests and with the causes of the general social and cultural collapse.

Well into the early 1920s, scientists were often attacked in public as being defenders of an old and distorted social order. What is perhaps the most incisive and unforgiving indictment of the scientist's apathy came in the 1933 article "Scientist as Citizen" by sociologist Read Bain. He wrote: "Scientists, with few notable exceptions, are the worst citizens . . . ; they, more than any other single factor, threaten the persistence of Western culture. They are wholesale, if unconscious, traitors to the civilization they have created. . . . They do not vote, they sneer at politics and politicians. . . . In short, the scientist . . . lacks moral courage, . . . has tremendous . . . egotistical smugness, feels no social obligation . . . and [is] so highly specialized that he is almost psychopathic."[56] Of course, very few adopted Bain's polemical flourishes, but many of his complaints could nevertheless be heard in the writings of those less acerbic commentators. These critics generally attacked scientists for ignoring the effects that their science was having on society, and thereby for unquestioningly supporting the status quo. Clearly, the scientists' social and political aloofness could no longer remain unquestioned. As B. E. Schaar, chair of the Chicago section of the American Chemical Society, wrote in 1932 following a visit to England: "The scientific man . . . apparently forgets his training, accepts without question prevailing opinions and becomes a tool in the hands of others for maintaining the status quo."[57] The *New Republic* echoed this view and identified scientists' conservatism with the "unfortunate progeny" of the ideological mix between science and industrial interests. The scientist has, "by force of his alliance with Philistine business men, . . . become something of a Philistine himself, frequently unsympathetic to . . . [the] struggle against a reluctant and conservative society [by intellectuals, artists, and writers]."[58]

However, whereas scientists may have been conservative as a group, their conservatism was not rooted in a blind loyalty to a tradition, nor was it rooted in a worldview that paid homage to the values of business. On the contrary, they viewed themselves as being the prime agents of both cognitive and social progress. They saw themselves as being proponents—due to their inherent internationalism—of social amelioration. Hence, the practical achievements of science, which at the time included increases in agrarian production, radio communication, flight, and improved health care and conditions made the objectives of political and cultural reform seem transitory and superficial in comparison.[59] The optimism that infused their scientific work and the social organization of the scientific culture carried over into a broader social optimism in which scientists thought of themselves as being the modern engines of change, political reform, and social improvement. As noted philosopher of science Gerald Holton has written, the one thing scientists had in common was an unreasonable amount of optimism concerning the ultimately successful outcome of their research. Whereas the stereotype of the humanists is that of a rearguard group, gallantly holding up the flag of a civilization that is now being destroyed by barbarians, the scientists tend to feel that the most glorious period of intellectual history is about to dawn—and they will be there to make it happen. As C. P. Snow has said, they have the "future in their bones."

It was this sense of science as the embodiment of progress, as a source of unemployment, and as an alleviator of such human distresses as malnutrition and ill health—at a time when social change was on everyone's mind—that made science highly discussed. The output of books, articles, and public lectures on science and its social applications grew steadily. Among the most widely received were the books by J. B. S. Haldane and Bertrand Russell and the series of articles that appeared in the *Daily Herald* and on the BBC. The *Daily Herald* pieces on "How Science Can Help Us" were organized by Ritchie Calder, while the BBC radio talks were given by Julian Huxley.

As Peter Collins has detailed, the 1920s and 1930s were the principal decades of the "science and society movement" in England.[60] A number of prominent scientists, all of whom were to become either close friends or acquaintances of Snow's, espoused to varying degrees the Wellsian scientific utopia. For them, the experience of the war, economic collapse, and mass unemployment, far from constituting some sort of case against science, actually confirmed the need for science and scientists to take a more active role in the activities of society. The rulers and politicians, trained in obsolete disciplines and shaped by class experiences that would have made them more at home in the eighteenth century than in the twentieth, were the carriers of an antiquated technique and philosophy that was bringing the modern world to the brink of catastrophe. Not less, but more, science was the necessary antidote.

Among the leaders in the science and society movement in England was the biologist J. B. S. Haldane and the physicist J. D. Bernal. In 1924, Haldane published *Daedalus, or Science and the Future*, in which he posed the questions that were the fundamental underlying motif of the whole antiscience critique: "Has mankind released from the womb of matter a Demogorgon which is already beginning to turn against him, and may at any moment hurl him into the bottomless void? Or is Samuel Butler's even more horrible vision correct, in which man becomes a mere parasite of machinery, an appendage to the reproductive system of huge and complicated engines which will successively usurp his activities, and end by ousting him from the mastery of the planet? Is the machine minder engaged in repetitious work with the goal and ideal to which humanity is tending?"[61]

Haldane's answer was an exuberant vindication of science, its claims and possibilities. H. G. Wells, he thought, had been too modest in his scientific prophecies to demonstrate sufficiently the truly emancipatory promise of modern science. Haldane was correspondingly bolder in his speculations. He foresaw the energy problem posed by the exhaustion of coal and oil fields and proposed to solve it by the exploitation of wind and solar energy. Developments in transport and communications "are only limited by the velocity of light," and "we are working towards a condition when any two persons on earth will be able to be completely present to one another in not more than one-fifteen-hundredth of a second." Novel drugs, such as acid sodium phosphate, which do not have the harmful effects of nicotine and alcohol, were proposed as beneficent stimulants to physical and mental activity. Chemistry would be applied to the production of food, so that within a century all necessary food could be artificially produced. This would eliminate agriculture and the agrarian way of life, a prospect Haldane cheerfully looked forward to. "Human progress in historical time has been the progress of cities dragging a reluctant countryside in their wake."

Haldane's little book caused quite a stir and was quickly answered in an admonitory tract by Bertrand Russell, entitled *Icarus, or the Future of Science* (1924). Science, Russell countered, was more likely to promote the power of dominant groups than to make them happy. Science had become the driving force of industrialism and, to an extent, had been responsible for some improvement in the general welfare of the population; however, industrialism had remained bound to the interests of the dominant social groups and had served to largely increase the destructive power of the nationalist wars. Russell concluded: "Science has not given men more self-control, more kindliness, or more power of discounting their passions in deciding upon a course of action . . . man's collective passions are mainly evil . . . therefore at present all that gives men power to indulge their collective passions is bad. That is why science threatens to cause the destruction of our civilization."[62]

While Russell's arguments stimulated considerable debate within the literary and scientific communities, they did not dissuade Bernal from putting forward an even more extravagant vision of science than Haldane's. In 1929, with the publication of *The World, the Flesh, and the Devil*, Bernal confronted "the three enemies of the Rational Soul" and sought to rout them once and for all with science. Physics would tame "the massive, unintelligent forces of nature"; biology would cure the problems of the human body; and psychology would control man's "desires and fears, his imagination and stupidities."

As far as the material world went, Bernal quickly went through a conventional recitation of expected developments (which could be predicted with "mathematical exactness"): the age of metals would give way to new synthetic materials, food would be synthetically and abundantly produced, and the world would banish want and achieve a high degree of luxury. The only limit that Bernal saw to material expansion was the second law of thermodynamics—the entropy law—and even here, he suggested, by "intelligent organization" we can defy it for a long time.

The flesh, in Bernal's view, was not so easy to subjugate, but his inventiveness was wonderfully fertile. Surgery and "physiological chemistry" would take over and speed up the process of natural bodily evolution. Undaunted by the shades of Dr. Moreau, or by the ridicule that was heaped upon Wells for a similar vision, Bernal proposed dispossessing the "man of the future" of his inefficient limbs and organs and substituting them with artificial parts that could be linked to the brain. Any new powers and functions required could be met by incorporating new artificial organs as part of the new cerebromotor system. "We badly need a small sense organ for detecting wireless frequencies, eyes for infra-red, ultra-violet, and X-rays, ears for supersonics, detectors for high and low temperatures, or electrical potential and current, and chemical organs of many kinds." Through such artificial additions and modifications, "a mechanical stage, utilizing some or all of these alterations to the bodily frame, might . . . become the regular culmination to ordinary life."

A much more moderate tone was heard in the BBC talks that were the result of a decision to dispatch "three modern pilgrims" to conduct nationwide surveys of agriculture, industry, and science. Julian Huxley was given science, and as Peter Collins points out, the experience served to sharpen his thinking. The process of having to conduct a personal investigation into the relation of science to war, food, building, clothing, industry, communication, and health and of visiting most of the relevant institutions in the country all opened his eyes to the great extent that science was involved in society. It made him acutely aware of the extent to which its development, through technology, was bound up with political and economic questions. What also impressed him was "the fact that both our existing structure of civilization, our hope of progress are based on science, and that the lack of appreciation and understanding of science among business men, financiers, educational authorities, politicians and administrators was a serious feature in our present situation."[63]

In his first talk, Huxley expressed his faith in the crudest scientific rationalism: "Why, certainly, any subject is capable of being examined by the scientific method."[64] As the series progressed, he expanded upon this view and asserted, "In the long run human reason, employing the scientific method, will enable us to control our destiny."[65] And by the series's end he retained his confidence that "science, if it were allowed a free hand, could control the evolution of the human species."[66] To this bland optimism, however, Hyman Levy and Blackett were bitterly opposed. Blackett warned Huxley that "if society thinks the scientist is going to be its savior, it will find him a broken reed."[67] Levy explained why: "Science is used, when it is used practically, to develop and further the ends of present-day society, and is restricted and circumscribed by the possibilities inherent in that social order. We have to study our desires in this matter—our prejudices, our bias if you will—and deliberately set about acquiring power in order to create with help of science such a biased society."[68] Science might serve as the tool of social reform, but it could never dictate its direction. Huxley, on the other hand, looked to the application of the scientific method to social problems for both the means and the ends of social progress. But, Levy argued, "We have to get rid of the myth of impartiality, for we have to recognize that whatever we set about doing is simply a method for fulfilling the desires of some person or group, and the only *scientific* question we can ask is whose bias has it been in the past, and whose is it to be in the future?"[69] Furthermore, according to Levy, "we must give up the claptrap about science *always* being the benefactor of humanity."[70] Huxley, wilting, finally conceded that "the form and direction [science] takes is largely determined by the social and economic needs of the place and the period,"[71] but he nevertheless maintained that in the long run scientific advance could help prepare the way for a world state.[72]

Although Julian Huxley's radio series served to identify the more prominent controversial issues in the debate over the social function of science, it was not able to resolve them.

Other important vehicles for the discussion of the social function of science did emerge, however, that usefully served to augment Huxley's and Bernal's contributions. Among these were the prestigious scientific journal *Nature*. One reason for the longevity of this debate in these pages was Sir Richard Gregory, who was *Nature*'s editor for all but five years of the 1914–1939 period. Gregory was an enormously influential figure in science during the interwar years through his active involvement with the British Association for the Advancement of Science, the British Science Guild, the National Union of Scientific Workers, as editor of *School World* and the *Journal of Education,* and as a director of Macmillan's science department, which was responsible for publishing *Discovery* while Snow was editor. Apart from these positions, Gregory forged a number of links between himself and key academic, industrial, and government leaders, many of whom he met with (as he did with Snow) at the London Athenaeum Club.

Gregory's opinions about the role of science in the economic recovery of Britain were well known. To him, the preeminence of the scientific elite rested on the commonplace belief in Britain that "there is one Science and the University [is] its teacher." This was a perspective that Gregory's *Nature* promoted and regularly elaborated on. To Gregory, science was essentially a pursuit of truth for its own sake, an enterprise whose object was to understand nature better. Engineering and industrial research were clearly necessary and valuable, but it was the realm of the inventor whose goal was the control of nature for a material end. Although these were at times dependent on scientific advance, they were not suitable for the man of science.[73] On the basis of this somewhat soft distinction, he concluded that "as the font of all science, High Scientists had to serve as the state's leading makers of science policy. Only they sufficiently understood the 'inner logic' of their disciplines to know where the next scientific breakthrough might be made." Without their guidance science would cease to advance and so eventually, argued Gregory, would technology and industry. Therefore High Scientists had to exercise their hegemony over all forms of research. . . . Gregory would not, however, offer industrial or governmental researchers anything like that measure of autonomy. As one of *Nature*'s leading articles asserted, "though they may regret the gradual encroachment of bureaucracy on the freedom of scientific investigations [applied scientists] have to recognize that they are primarily public servants whose first duty is to perform their allocated tasks in the social machine."[74]

But if scientists were to advance from being politically removed to being policy leaders, then not only was there much ground to be covered in terms of gaining social and political legitimacy, but they also had to address many contradictions that were internal to High Science itself.

The set of ideas that are subsumed beneath this title was far from homogeneous. There were essentially two distinct philosophies involved. These have been authoritatively analyzed by both Gary Werskey and Peter Collins, who have correctly distinguished between the debate's "radical" and "reformist" elements. Briefly put, it can be said that the radicals believed that "only a society transformed along socialist lines would be prepared to make the fullest and most humane use of scientists and their discoveries. They presented their plea for an improvement in the cultural and political status of the scientist as an essential but subsidiary clause in their demand for a broad revolution."[75]

The principal architects of the radical movement were mainly "the young charismatic figures of the 1920s" whose radicalism predated the depression.[76] Its center was undoubtedly Cambridge. Among its principal members were Bernal, P. M. S. Blackett, Haldane, Joseph Needham, Lancelot Hogben, C. H. Waddington, Hyman Levy, and W. A. Wooster. As Snow noted, "They tended to be either physicists or biochemists whose sciences were being revolutionized at this time."[77] Bernal, Haldane, and Levy were at various times paid-up members of the Communist party of Great Britain, and Blackett, Needham, Waddington, and Wooster all expressed sympathy with its ideology.[78] Needham and Hogben, however, preferred to remain on the left wing of the Labour party. While there were considerable differences in outlook, they can all be called members of what Werskey has called a "Visible College."

In addition to their long-standing interest in the relationship between science and left-wing politics, those associated with the radical elements of science were deeply stimulated by the visit of the Soviet delegation at the Second International Congress of the History of Science and Technology, which was held in London from June 29 to July 4, 1931. The delegation, led by Nikolay Bukharin, who was director of the Industrial Research Department of the Supreme Economic Department, included leading physicist A. F. Joffe, biologist Nikolay Vavilov, and the director of the Soviet Institute of Physics, Boris Hessen. Despite the delay of their formal presentation of papers until a special session could be arranged for July 4, copies of the Soviet papers were made available in a bound edition entitled *Science at the Crossroads*. The thrust of these papers was that science was a dependent variable in society, grounded within—and largely determined by—a historically specific configuration of social classes and productive forces. The members of the Soviet delegation employed Marxist analysis to challenge the prevailing view of the history and practice of science that saw science as being socially removed. They contrasted the constraints that bore on science within a capitalist world in decline to the unlimited potential that, to their perspective, was just beginning to be realized under socialism. Somewhat unexpectedly, it was Hessen, one of the lesser lights of the delegation and a Stalin purge victim shortly thereafter,[79] whose paper had the most impact. In his paper, "The Social and Economic Roots of Newton's *Principia*," Hessen entirely rejected the internalist approach to the history of science, demonstrating that Newton was not an isolated genius, but instead a product of a seventeenth-century bourgeois society.

J. D. Bernal, one of those most intensely moved by the Soviet contributions, later noted that "Hessen's article on Newton . . . was for England the starting point of a new evaluation of the history of science." Bernal credited this major contribution with sparking an English interest in dialectical materialism and for showing what "a wealth of new ideas and points of view for understanding the history, the social function and the working of science could be and were being produced by the application to science of Marxist theory."[80] Bernal was not alone in his estimation. Hyman Levy noted that the 1931 Congress was "epoch-making." What became clear, he said, "was not only the social conditioning of science and the vital need for . . . anticipating the social effects of discovery, but the impossibility of carrying this through within the framework of a chaotic capitalism."[81]

Unlike the radicals who tended to emphasize the interaction *between* science and society, the reformers tended to stress the impact of science *on* society. For the most part, reformers were prepared to accept the social order as given, provided that they and their kind could have a greater voice in public affairs. As Peter Collins has usefully argued, the reformers were also known for their emphasis on the supremacy of scientific rationality in questions of social or political concern. Since the First World War, reformers attempted to publicly promote their ideas of the importance of science to society and to impress upon the government the potential of science in improving national prosperity. Much of their work was carried out through such ginger groups as the British Science Guild,[82] which was absorbed into the British Association for the Advancement of Science in 1936. Unlike the radicals, the reformers emphasized the international character of science and grew deeply concerned over the issue of freedom as the threat of war grew nearer in 1938. They tended to be more established scientists who wished to promote social change from *within* social institutions, and their political affiliations were either to the Labour party or to the more progressive elements of the Conservative party. Their spokespersons included Richard Gregory, Sir Frederick Gowland Hopkins, and Julian Huxley.

The motivations underlying the various perspectives on the emerging "social relations of science movement" can be briefly summarized as follows. The radicals felt that science was grossly undervalued in British society and in capitalist society generally; socialism, on the other hand, seemed to be geared to the fullest possible use and development of science. The fullest advancement of science was therefore seen to depend on the advent of socialism. Moreover, the Marxist interpretation of science taught that scientific activity was in fact determined by the social and economic needs of society. For each of these reasons the scientist was professionally bound to be closely concerned with social and political affairs. Within the radical camp, there seemed to have been some confusion as to whether the involvement of the scientist in social affairs was the cause or effect of a socialist society. Both Blackett and Levy, for example, insisted that the salvation and progress of society depended on the advent of socialism and that the scientist could help only insofar as he worked toward socialism. Bernal, on the other hand, felt strongly that "Marxism and Communism are not ends in themselves. [They are rather] the best available means of achieving the transfer of power to the scientist."[83]

The reformers, on the other hand, were also sensitive to the "social frustration of science," but no matter how much this might have been bound up in the inefficiencies of parliamentary democracy, they were not prepared to work for socialism. In *Nature,* at least, the exaltation of rationalism was generally tempered by reference to the "spirit and service of science,"[84] temperance conspicuously absent from Bernal's harsh rhetoric.

While socialism was unacceptable, the rationalists were prepared by the mid-1930s to concede the radical view that the "form and direction of science . . . are largely determined by the social and economic needs of the place and period."[85] At the same time, they insisted that science could (and indeed must), in turn, influence those needs. It was a duty of almost moral proportions. *Nature* was continually advocating an expansion of rational or scientific thinking "in place of prejudice, if mankind is to avert disintegration and regain control over events."[86] Social problems were a result of unthinking prejudice and needed the "ministrations of that professional practitioner of cool, unbiased thought—i.e., the scientist—for a cure."[87] The reformers were inspired by the "vision of the new and greater social possibilities if knowledge is sincerely and courageously applied, and the faith that human reason—by using wisely the scientific method—can give us the control of our destiny."[88] The reformers' involvement in social relations was therefore a matter of bringing scientists to this missionary view of their social responsibilities, and of educating the public in the virtues of scientific rationalism. "Once science had been placed at the centre of social consciousness, statecraft would mainly become a question of making humanity fit for science or, at least, of modifying the political and economic systems of the world to enable its inhabitants to enjoy the fruits of scientific endeavour."[89] In such a happy world, of course, the scientist would be duly esteemed.

These tensions within the political, literary, and scientific realms, which Snow was to sense—first at the general level as a growing adolescent caught up in a modernist world of change and later at a more focused ideological level as science and literature responded in radical and reformist tones to the new world—left a profound mark on his intellectual development. Snow's strong reaction to the literary positions of the experimentalists reflected his deep sense of loss of the "stable" Victorian tradition. His real excitement over the second scientific revolution, and its relationship to politics, reflected his deep sense of possible futures. The complex tensions implied between these two forces situated C. P. Snow squarely within modernity. His most repeated and readily discernible response to this dialectical culture was to come in the form of his "two cultures" hypothesis.

3

BLINDNESS, INSIGHT, AND
THE TWO CULTURES

Every picture has its shadows—
as it has some source of light.
Blindness. Blindness and sight.
—JONI MITCHELL

GIVEN THE DIALECTICAL CONTEXT of modernity, it is in many ways
not surprising that C. P. Snow's *The Two Cultures and the Scientific
Revolution* has become one of the significant signs of our age and
the dominant image associated with Snow himself. A statement on
the social, cognitive, and communicative dichotomy between the
arts and sciences, Snow's May 7, 1959, Rede Lecture at Cambridge
University[1] spoke directly to an essential tension in the struggle of
modernity between science and literature that acts as a veil through
which change and totality is viewed and which powerfully influ-
ences the modern mind.[2] Snow's seemingly simple thesis gained an
authoritative appeal at many levels. The lecture gained resonance
through Snow's own personal appeal as something of a Renaissance
Man or New Man (being a scientist, civil servant, literary critic, and
novelist). It gained a timely appeal as a result of the growing strategic importance throughout the West of science, technology, and education as was reflected by the atom-bombings of Japan, the launching of *Sputnik,* and the commencement of the space race between
the superpowers. And finally, the lecture carried a deep substantive
appeal to a series of long-standing dichotomies in the Western philosophical memory, such as those cryptically referred to in terms of
science/religion, facts/values, facts/fiction, objectivity/subjectivity,
numeracy/literacy, rich/poor, ends/means, quantitative/qualitative,
and masculine/feminine. However, to the extent this is true, Snow's
lecture has also become deeply problematic as far as an interpretation meaningful to a larger, more precise understanding of Snow is
concerned.

More specifically, in the thirty years since Snow's statement on
science, literature, and the modern condition, so many interpreta-

tions that were "reader specific" have emerged that a distancing has taken place between Snow's original idea, which was deeply grounded in his own personal experience and which stands as a core element throughout his work, and the multiple meanings that have since been attributed to Snow's words. These have varied widely and have included interpretations arguing for a "return" (if this is indeed the correct term) to a liberal education at one extreme and a surrender of the education system to programs of computer literacy at the other.[3] Few of these interpretions at any time use Snow's lecture for anything more than a springboard for their own agendas; consequently, numerous dense, interpretive layers now lie between us and Snow.

Thus beyond his seven original statements,[4] his numerous clarifications,[5] the initial response, and the subsequent debate that emerged between 1959 and 1964,[6] there also coexists the multiple disconnected references to Snow's image that appear regularly today and that shape our dominant impressions of Snow.[7] All drew on Snow's original image of two cultures, or cultural dichotomy, but few share more than a cursory grounding in his concerns. The net effect of this vast heap of multilayered meaning is that a new sense has been constructed that is distant or foreign to Snow. His own discourse on the fragmentation of society has itself been fragmented. A decontextualized reading of Snow's thesis has, in typically modernist fashion, created meaning above the text. Consequently, the original voice of the 1959 Rede Lecture, along with its considerable prejudices and its place within Snow's conceptual framework, has effectively been buried beneath an ontological scaffolding of considerable proportions.

However, this is not to suggest that these distant readings are in any way invalid. While they make our task more difficult and interesting, they are not only clear expressions of the interpretive difficulties represented by modernity itself and to which the authors themselves are responding, but they are also partly responsible for the creative rereadings of Snow that have demonstrated the continued vitality (and potential validity) of his notion. Indeed, engaging in the sort of energetic and critical discourse, the sort of which surrounds and engages Snow's thesis, can make possible the full recovery both of the statement's meaning and of the author's blindness and insights.[8]

With this engaging possibility in mind, it is the purpose of this chapter to recover Snow's original meaning in the "two cultures" hypothesis by closely reexamining the relevant texts, to assess its strengths and limitations as well as its biases, and to prepare the ground through which its relationships to his larger corpus can be demonstrated, thus revealing its significance for modernist politics and culture.

Clearly Snow's two cultures hypothesis has been received as being a compelling image of our age. Regular citations in learned and popular journals reveal its contemporaneity.[9] Citations in books suggest the substantive appeal of the lecture.[10] The almost annual organization of international symposia to discuss the thesis suggests the deep *problématique* contained in Snow's formulation.[11] That the Rede Lecture remains in print in more than a dozen languages and is required reading at more than five hundred universities further attests to the continued allure of the hypothesis.[12]

Yet at the same time, ungrounded interpretations of the lecture and their judgments on its validity have led to anything but a unanimous view. For example, Robert Gorham Davis has offered the influential view that "if we, by act of will, forget temporarily about 'The Two Cultures' and read carefully through Snow's fiction to see what actually occurs there, we find it almost totally inconsistent with what we had been led to expect."[13] At the same time, Nora Graves was confident enough in her reading of the Rede Lecture to argue precisely the opposite view: that is, that the hypothesis is the *only* idea in Snow's fiction. In less oppositional fashion, Aldous Huxley has referred to Snow's thesis as "a bland scientism"; Gertrude Himmelfarb, the noted New York scholar, has relegated Snow and his lecture to being little more than bald expressions of late-Victorian values and morality; George Levine and Lance Schacterle, cofounders of the Society for Science and Literature, have claimed that Snow's contribution to twentieth-century thought has been little more than his phrase "the two cultures," and that even this is "not a very helpful cliché"; Lord Sherfield, chairman of the House of Lords Select Committee on Science and Technology, and who was recently before the Royal Society of London, dismissed the idea as being "largely bunk"; the late Raymond Williams saw Snow's lecture as one that was "generous and passionate" but "hopelessly confused"; physicist and noted philosopher of science Gerald Holton edited a collection of essays by prominent scholars, the sum purpose of which was to "dismiss the . . . 'Two Cultures' thesis once and for all"; and meanwhile, in what has been seen as one of the most vitriolic and rabid attacks in modern intellectual history, the literary critic of Downing College, Cambridge—F. R. Leavis—argued, in his 1962 Richmond Lecture at Cambridge University, that Snow assumed an undue authority and knowledge, passing himself off as a genius. Leavis went on to say that Snow was "blind, uncon-

scious and automatic; . . . a portent, a poseur, a vulgar stylist, a dis-
penser of clichés and an expounder of 'Sunday paper culture.'" And
yet, as recently as 1986 the president of Rutgers University, Edward
Bloustein, recalled the thesis to our attention as one of the most
"critical issues that affects us all." [14]

From these random but representative statements, it can be
clearly seen that Snow's thesis has been received as being both important and contentious. But without a close inspection the basis for
this impression can only remain obscured.

To begin to gain an understanding of Snow's concern, it is important to appreciate that the Rede Lecture was one of a series of public
elaborations upon the theme. A forecast of these concerns can be
seen as early as 1936 in Snow's *Spectator* article called "What We
Need from Applied Science"; [15] however, the first true expression of
these appeared in the *New Statesman and Nation* on October 6,
1956. Many others were to follow in the form of university lectures,
articles in popular and scientific periodicals, and radio shows with
such dignitaries as Eleanor Roosevelt. These essentially came to an
end by 1970 following the advice of such close friends as Sir J. H.
Plumb and Maurice Goldsmith who agreed with Snow that the
ongoing debates, though on an important theme, were no longer
leading to fruitful discussions and were consequently interfering
with his writing and his reputation as a writer. Indeed, Snow later
felt that all the attention surrounding the Rede Lecture had in effect
removed any possibility of him being considered for a Nobel Prize in
literature. [16]

It is equally important to understand that the theme did not arise
because of Snow's "objective observations" of the postwar tone of
Britain. Instead it is a theme that became definitive and personally
meaningful for Snow between 1914 [17] and his early years at Cambridge. It is an expression of the blindness and the insights of his
being a perennial outsider. The formulation of this theme in terms
of "two cultures" was tacitly suggested to Snow at least as early as
1934 via a review of his own novel *The Search*, which appeared in
the prominent scientific journal *Nature* and which was written by
noted historians of Chinese science Joseph and Dorothy Needham.
In part that early review read: "It is curious that in spite of the overwhelming influence exercised by science on our civilization, there
has been so few attempts to express its ethos in literature. . . . Many
causes have probably contributed to this not least of which has been
the fact that most writers are not in any sense within the boundaries
of science, and must take those essential . . . details on which the
whole complex of human relations . . . depend at second or third

hand."[18] This clearly demarked the social realm of science and
literature that Snow experienced and attempted to bridge. The
Needhams went on to remind Snow that in order to more adequately
bridge this gap, he would need "a more definite socio-political outlook." If he could develop such a perspective for the "political education of mankind," they suggested, then "we are not willing to suggest a bounds for his possible achievement."[19]

With this kind of encouragement from within the radical arms of
the scientific community, coupled with his own personal motivations, Snow went on to focus persistently on the relationship between science and literature as well as on their role in world affairs.
In so doing, however, he at times showed a degree of intolerance
with traditional culture. As Snow said, for example, "the clashing of
two disciplines . . . ought to produce creative chances. In the history of mental activity, that is where some of the breakthroughs
came. . . . [But although] the chances are there now . . . it is bizarre
how very little of twentieth-century science has been assimilated
into twentieth-century art. Now and then one finds poets conscientiously using scientific expressions, and getting them wrong."[20]

And finally, it is important to bear in mind that Snow's prominent
(but neglected) second half of his Rede Lecture's title dealt with "the
Scientific Revolution."

Beyond these, though, one important but rarely examined element of Snow's focus on world affairs was cogently presented in his
1960 lectures at Harvard University in which he suggested that not
only is it dangerous to have a scientist with bad judgment in a position of isolated power, but it is equally dangerous to have any scientist in such a position.[21] This theme—of emerging relationships
between science and government—gave Snow's lecture immediate
credibility in the pages of the Harvard *Crimson Tide*, at the meetings of the American Association for the Advancement of Science,
and at the United Nations General Assembly, which Snow visited in
conjunction with his role at the Ministry of Technology. But these
Godkin Lectures generated little reaction with either the less specialist public or the professional literary and social science communities. This widespread and more vehement reaction was to come
only with the two cultures theory.

Although versions of Snow's two cultures thesis appear in many
places, its quintessential elements were presented in the October 6,
1956, issue of the *New Statesman and Nation*. Even in this page-
and-a-half-long piece, his casual yet aggressively realist tone solic-
ited the reader's acquiescence. In this article, which I will quote at
length and comment upon briefly before moving to a more substan-

tive discussion, Snow wrote: " 'It's rather odd,' said G. H. Hardy, one afternoon in the early Thirties, 'but when we hear about "intellectuals" nowadays, it doesn't include people like me and J. J. Thompson and Rutherford.' Hardy was the first mathematician of his generation; J. J. Thompson was the first physicist of his; and Rutherford, he was one of the greatest scientists who have ever lived."[22] Thus from the earliest expression of his concern, the personal importance that the 1930s held for Snow is clear. This importance was both social and cognitive—through his friendships with Hardy and others as well as through his training in the twentieth century's most revolutionary sciences in the shadows of men like Rutherford. His friendships and training both reinforced Snow's sense of cultural divide. He continued: "Some bright young literary person (I forget the exact context) putting them outside the enclosure reserved for intellectuals seemed to Hardy the best joke for some time. It does not seem quite such a good joke now. The separation between the two cultures has been getting deeper under our eyes; there is now precious little communication between them, . . . different kinds of incomprehension and dislike. "The traditional culture, which is, *of course* [emphasis added] mainly literary, is behaving like a state whose power is rapidly declining. . . ."

In these passages, Snow not only aligned the whole of traditional culture with the literary communities but also implicitly associated the political decline of the West with a presumed loss of character or leadership within the literary community and literature itself. In so doing, Snow suggested his sympathetic recognition and concern with the emergence of a postliterary society. He did not see the inner logics of technology and capitalist economies as being implicated or problematic. He went on ". . . standing on [literature's] precarious dignity . . . occasionally letting fly in fits of aggressive pique quite beyond its means, too much on the defensive to show *any generous imagination to the forces which must inevitably reshape [traditional culture]*" [emphasis added]. At this point, Snow revealed one of his major prejudicial beliefs regarding the nature of scientific and social progress, as well as the innate power of science as opposed to the influence of literature. "The scientific culture is expansive, not restrictive, confident at its roots, . . . certain that history is on its side, impatient, intolerant, creative rather than critical . . . and brash." This was a feature Snow referred to frequently. He described science, and the scientific culture, as being "diachronic"; that is, it is cumulative and progresses forward through time. Science, he said, builds on its past and incorporates it but also moves steadily away from it. As an example, "any decent eighteen year old student of physics in [the year 2070] will know more physics than Newton."[23] But, striking the balanced tone that was to win him favor with a wide readership, Snow added:

> *Neither culture knows the virtues of the other* [emphasis added]; often it seems they deliberately do not want to know. The resentment which the traditional culture feels for the scientific is shaded with fear; from the other side, the resentment is not so much as brimming with irritation. When scientists are faced with an expression of the traditional culture, it tends (to borrow Mr. William Cooper's eloquent phrase) to make their feet itch.
> . . . Scientists are losing a great deal. Some of that loss is inevitable; *it must* [emphasis added] and would happen in any society at our technical level. . . . But . . . we make it unnecessarily worse by our educational patterns. On the other side, how much does the traditional culture lose.
> I am inclined to think even more. Not only practically—we are familiar with those arguments by now—but *also intellectually and morally* [emphasis added]. The intellectual loss is a little difficult to appraise. Most scientists would claim that you cannot comprehend the world unless you know the structure of science, in particular of physical science. In a sense, *and a perfectly genuine sense, this is true* [emphasis added]. Not to have read *War and Peace* and *La Cousine Bette* and *La Chartreuse de Parme* is not to be educated; but so is not to have a glimmer of the Second Law of Thermodynamics. *Yet this case is not to be pressed too far. It is much more justifiable to say that those without any scientific understanding miss a whole body of experience.* . . .

This kind of genuine temperance was further augmented: "It does not need saying that generalizations of this kind are bound to look silly at the edges. There are a good many scientists indistinguishable from literary persons, and vice versa. . . ." ". . . Nevertheless, as a first approximation, the scientific culture is real enough, and so is its difference from the traditional. . . ."

But Snow quickly returned to an uncritical stance with regards to science. "For anyone like myself, by education a scientist, by calling a writer, at one time moving between groups of scientists and writers in the same evening, the difference seemed dramatic. The first thing, impossible to miss, is that *scientists are on the up and up; they have the strength of a social force behind them*" [emphasis added]. And then, strangely succumbing to a cognitive-cultural belief of the Cambridge scientific elite in a way that is contrary to what he himself excelled at illustrating in his fiction, Snow wrote: *"In a sense oddly divorced from politics, they are the new men* [emphasis added]. "There is a touch of the frontier qualities, in fact, about the whole scientific culture."

As we shall see, this view is one that is utterly out of character for Snow. If his writings reveal anything clearly, it is the firm belief in the fundamentally political nature of human relations. Nevertheless, at this point in our discussion, the above noted passage illustrates implicitly the extent and power of the scientific culture's influence on Snow. And yet, at the same time, Snow was able to express the basic affinity he saw between scientific culture and the frontier world of the modern condition. He continued this strain loosely by saying: "The climate of personal relations [in science] is singularly bracing, not to say harsh: it strikes bleakly on those unused to it. . . .

"No body of people [the scientists] ever believed more in dialectic as the primary method of attaining sense. . . ." He then returned to his rather uncritical rhetorical overview of science. "The intellectual invasions of science are, however, penetrating deeper . . . [into the] problems of will and cause and motive. [Those] *who do not understand the method will not understand the depths of their own culture"* [emphasis added].

This categorial position, which Snow retained throughout his career, was refined into his concluding remarks on the two cultures in which he linked private and public experience:

> [The] greatest enrichment scientific culture could give us is . . .
> a moral one. Among scientists, deep-natured men know, as
> starkly as any men have known, that the individual human con-
> dition is tragic, *therefore the social condition must be tragic, too*
> [emphasis added]. Because a man must die, that is no excuse for
> his dying before his time and after a servile life. The impulse
> behind the scientists drives them to limit the area of tragedy, *to
> take nothing as tragedy that can conceivably lie within man's
> will* [emphasis added]. They have nothing but contempt for those
> representatives of the traditional culture who use a deep insight
> into man's fate to obscure the social truth . . . [for example] the
> political decadence of the *avant-garde* of 1914. . . . [This is a
> symptom] of the deepest temptation of the clerks—which is to
> say: "Because man's condition is tragic, everyone ought to stay
> in their place, with mine as it happens somewhere near the

top." *From that particular temptation, made up of defeat, self-indulgence, and moral vanity, the scientific culture is almost totally immune* [emphasis added]. It is that kind of moral health of the scientists which . . . the rest of us have needed most; and of which, because two cultures scarcely touched, we have been most deprived.[24]

The impact of this article was not great; however, it did attract some attention around Cambridge. This was not only due to the article's topic, but also to the public attention that had recently been coming to Snow. As the winner of the James Tait Black Memorial Prize for Fiction in 1954, because of critical acclaim levied on *The Masters* and *The New Men*, and as a Fellow of Christ's College in physical chemistry, Snow had a reputation that made certain circles at Cambridge take note. The result was an invitation in September 1958 from the vice-chancellor of Cambridge University, Lord Adrian (Master of Trinity College), to give the 1959 Rede Lecture. As had become the custom, it was agreed that the lecture would be published by Cambridge University Press;[25] it appeared in September 1959.

In important respects, the Rede Lecture did not differ from the 1956 article. However, Snow did take the opportunity to clarify and expand certain themes. Principal among these was his central notion of a fundamental split in Western society into two cultures. "I intend something serious. I believe the intellectual life of the whole of Western society is increasingly being split into two polar groups. When I say intellectual life, I mean to include also a large part of our practical life, because I should be the last person to suggest the two can at the deepest level be distinguished." This split existed in Snow's view between the two spheres of life that together exerted a powerful formative and reflective influence on the totality of our experience. "At one pole we have the literary intellectuals . . . at the other scientists, and as the most representative, physical scientists. Between the two a gulf of mutual incomprehension. . . ."[26]

This division operated at the level of attitude.

They have a curious distorted image of each other. Their attitudes are so different that, even on the level of emotion, they can't find much common ground. Non-scientists tend to think of scientists as brash and boastful. They hear Mr. T. S. Eliot, who just for these illustrations we can take as an archetypal figure, saying . . . that we can hope for very little, but he would feel content if he and his co-workers could prepare the ground for . . .

a new Greene. That is the tone, restricted and constrained, with which literary intellectuals are at home: it is the subdued voice of their culture. Then they hear a much louder voice, that of another archetypal figure, Rutherford, trumpeting: "This is the heroic age of science! This is the Elizabethan age!" Many of us heard that . . . and we weren't left with any doubt whom Rutherford was casting for the role of Shakespeare. What is hard for the literary intellectuals to understand, imaginatively or intellectually, is that he was absolutely right. . . . [In contrast], compare [the literati sentiment] "this is the way the world ends, not with a bang but a whimper." . . .[27]

Snow further focused on this division at the level of social interaction.

[They have] so little in common that instead of going from Burlington House or South Chelsea, one might have crossed an ocean. . . . In fact, one had travelled much further than across an ocean—because after a few thousand Atlantic miles, one found Greenwich Village talking precisely the same language as Chelsea, and both having about as much communication with M.I.T. as though the scientists spoke nothing but Tibetan.[28]

The non-scientists have a rooted impression that the scientists are shallowly optimistic, unaware of man's condition. On the other hand, the scientists believe the literary intellectuals are totally lacking in foresight, peculiarly unconcerned with their brother men, in a deep sense anti-intellectual, anxious to restrict both art and thought to the existential moment.[29]

Thus, moving beyond these elements of his assessment, Snow defined his conception of culture

not only in an intellectual [sense] but also in an anthropological sense. That is, its members need not, and of course do not, always completely understand each other. . . . [In science, for example,] biologists more often than not will have a pretty hazy idea of contemporary physics; but there are common attitudes, common standards and patterns of behaviour, common approaches and assumptions.[30]

In [the scientists'] working, and in much of their emotional life, their attitudes are closer to other scientists than to non-scientists. . . . Without thinking about it, they respond alike. That is what culture means.[31]

In this more extended definition the last two sentences are often extracted and condemned by antagonistic critics. F. R. Leavis in particular has emphasized the "without thinking."[32] But Snow again was careful to qualify his assertion. Between what Snow described as a scientific and literary culture, "as one moves through the intellectual society from the physicist to the literary intellectuals, there [are] all kinds of tones of feeling on the way."

This type of mediation has led many reviewers of the lecture to conclude that Snow's analysis is balanced, and that what he is advocating is (reasonably, it appears to many) the striking of an equilibrium in intellectual and (consequently) social terms; what in essence is a praxis that is suitable to the fundamentally dialectical nature of the age. Such readings, however, flow out of the angst that developed in living at the end of liberal ideology or the fin de millenium. For Snow, writing in this context while denying the apparent fatality of the anxious moment, such a balance was neither tenable nor attractive. He introduced his own preferred approach very subtly by noting, "I believe the pole of total incomprehension of science radiates its influence on all the rest." This, he argued, was the most serious consequence of the cultural divide, because "that total incomprehension gives, much more pervasively than we realize, . . . an unscientific flavour to the whole 'traditional' culture, and that unscientific flavour is often, much more than we admit, on the point of turning anti-scientific."[33]

The importance of this key observation, made early on in the lecture, is often overlooked. However, its pivotal significance in terms of its connection to a major division in the text—absent from the 1956 article—is undeniable. Indeed, so important is the section that Snow affixed it clearly to the lecture's title: "The Two Cultures *and the Scientific Revolution*"[34] (emphasis added). But far more than simply demarking a section of text, Snow's interest in the scientific revolution stemmed from the belief that the events that demarcate it, more than any other, determine and express the character of modern society. This conviction permeates all of Snow's analysis and mediates—in successful and unsuccessful directions—all of his perspectives.

Snow distinguished between the scientific revolution and its industrial precursor.

> The distinction is not clear-edged, but it is a useful one. . . . By
> the industrial revolution, I mean the gradual use of machines,
> the employment of men and women in factories, the change . . .
> from a population . . . of agricultural labourers to a population

mainly engaged in making things in factories and distributing them. . . . That change . . . crept on us unawares. . . . One can date it roughly from the middle of the eighteenth century to the early twentieth. . . .

Out of it grew another change, closely related to the first, but far more deeply scientific, far quicker and probably more prodigious in its results. This change comes from the application of real science to industry, no longer hit and miss, no longer the ideas of odd "inventors." . . . Dating this second change is very much a matter of taste. . . . For myself, I should put it . . . not earlier than thirty to forty years ago. . . .[35]

And in so doing, he defined what to him makes modern society unique: "I believe the industrial society of electronics, atomic energy, automation is in cardinal respects different in kind from any that has gone before, and will change the world much more. It is this transformation that, in my view, is entitled to the name of 'scientific revolution.'

"This is the material basis of our lives: or more exactly, the social plasma of which we are a part. And we know almost nothing of it."[36] In this connection, Snow did casually note that "it is only fair to say that most pure scientists have themselves been devastatingly ignorant of productive industry. . . . [They] have by and large been dim-witted about engineers and applied science. . . ."[37]

But it was against the literati that Snow leveled the most ardent blame. This he said quite clearly, "If we forget the scientific culture, then the rest of western intellectuals have never tried, wanted, or been able to understand the industrial revolution, much less accept it. Intellectuals, in particular literary intellectuals, are natural Luddites.[38]

"If the scientists have the future in their bones, then the traditional culture responds by wishing the future did not exist."[39] To back up this claim, Snow asserted that

the agricultural and industrial-scientific [revolutions] are the only qualitative changes in social living that men have ever known. But the traditional culture didn't notice; and when it did notice, didn't like what it saw. Not that the traditional culture wasn't doing extremely well out of the revolution . . . [but] almost none of the imaginative energy went back into the revolution that was producing the wealth. . . . Far-sighted men were beginning to see, before the middle of the nineteenth century, that in order to go on producing wealth, the country needed to train some of its bright minds in science, particularly in applied science. No one listened. The traditional culture didn't listen at all.[40]

The academics had nothing to do with the industrial revolution. [Indeed] intellectual persons didn't comprehend what was happening. Certainly the writers didn't. Plenty of them shuddered away . . . some, like . . . Ruskin, . . . Thoreau and Emerson and Lawrence, tried various kinds of fancies which were not in effect more than screams of horror.[41]

Moreover, Snow commented, "Most writers take on social opinions which would have been thought distinctly uncivilized and demode at the time of the Plantagenets. . . . Wasn't that true of most of the famous twentieth century writers? Yeats, Pound, Wyndham Lewis . . . [all] those who have dominated literary sensibilities in our time—weren't they not only politically silly, but politically wicked?"[42]

Snow did "forgive" these supposed traits of the modern literati, arguing that since literature, contrary to science, is slow in changing and lacking in automatic correctives, "it is ill-considered of scientists to judge writers on the evidence of the period 1914 to 1950."[43] However, against these persistently harsh and overstated themes, Snow went on to counterpoint—in a strident Bernalian voice—with the strengths of an expanding scientific revolution: medical care, an adequate food supply, literacy—"everyone able to read and write because an industrial society can't work without. . . . [h]ealth, food and education; nothing but the industrial revolution could have spread them right down to the very poor. Those are the primary gains—there are losses too. . . . But the gains remain. They are the base of our social hope."[44] And the basis for this hope emanates squarely for Snow from within the "scientist's optimism."[45] This final thread is perhaps the most resilient throughout all of Snow's work. It can be found thinly disguised within the motto of his heraldic device ("I will either find a way or make one"), in the titles of his fiction (*The Search, A Time of Hope, The Physicists: A Generation That Changed the World*), and in the core ideas and tensions behind *Strangers and Brothers*; moreover, it is briefly and simply described by Snow as he recalled Blaise Pascal's dictum *on mourra seul* (we die alone), which appeared in the 1956 article. This optimism, Snow claimed, is based

on a confusion between the individual experience and the social experience, between the individual condition of man and his social condition. . . . The individual condition of each of

us is tragic. Each of us is alone: sometimes we escape from
solitariness, through love or affection or perhaps creative moments, but those triumphs of life are pools of light we make for
ourselves while the edge of the road is black; each of us dies
alone. . . . [Nearly all scientists]—and this is where the colour of
hope genuinely comes in—would see no reason why, just because the individual condition is tragic, so must the social condition be. Each of us is solitary; each of us dies alone: alright,
that's a fate against which we can't struggle—but there is plenty
in our condition which is not fate, and against which we are less
than human unless we do struggle.[46]

The two truths that emerged from the totality of Snow's thesis were
"straightforward": that "industrialization is the only hope for the
poor,"[47] and that a rethinking of our education is "the only way
out."[48] The price of this polarization, and of inaction, was "sheer
loss to us all. To us as people, and to our society. It is at the same
time practical and intellectual and creative loss, and I repeat that
it is false to imagine that those three considerations are clearly
separable."[49]

The response to Snow's statement was immediate. By commencement of term in October 1959, *The Two Cultures and the Scientific
Revolution* was being read aloud throughout Sixth Form classrooms
across Great Britain. Similarly, by 1961 it was being discussed
within the nation's newspapers and periodicals, in which form it
quickly spread to North America. The wide variety of periodicals attested to the lecture's timely appeal and did no harm for Snow's
growing fame. These ranged from *Cambridge Review: A Journal of
University Life and Thought*, *First Person*, and *Bulletin of the
Atomic Scientists*, to *Spectator*, *Encounter*, and the *New York
Times*;[50] however, commentary did not come from any one "cultural
camp."

Many of the criticisms of this initial exposure were of a superficial
textual character. Many—including Norman Cousins and Allan
Bullock—objected to the term "two," claiming that there were
"N-cultures." And despite the pervasive political themes of Snow's
fiction, these critics also questioned Snow for his "neglect of the political" in social circles.[51]

Others attacked Snow for his use of the term "culture," claiming
that the social sciences clearly made up a culture neglected by the
Rede Lecture.[52]

Others rightfully complained of Snow's choice of examples to
stereotype each side of the cultural divide. Most distracting of these

was the suggestion that everyone should have more than a passing knowledge of the concept of acceleration, the second law of thermodynamics (which, according to Snow, was roughly the equivalent of asking, can you read?), or the nonconservation of parity. However, on the other side, plenty of scientists, Snow pointed out, when asked about literature responded by saying that "well I've tried a bit of Dickens rather as though Dickens were an extraordinary esoteric, tangled, and dubiously rewarding writer, something like Rainer Maria Rilke."[53] And finally, still other critics took Snow to task for the general lack of a philosophical framework for the lecture.[54]

However, it was only with the February 28, 1962, Cambridge Richmond Lecture, given by F. R. Leavis, that what is widely referred to as the "two cultures debate" gained truly widespread attention.[55] Leavis was a gifted literary critic, whose influence paralleled that of his predecessors, I. A. Richards and E. W. W. Tillyard. He clearly possessed the necessary talents to tidily deal with Snow's Rede Lecture and its growing popularity. This is particularly so given his passionate concern for cultural decay and the popular press. For some inexplicable reason, however, rather than trying to counteract the damage he felt Snow was infringing on the schools through his popularity and cultural views, he chose instead to adopt the role of the obsessed crusader—of the "fearless vampire killer." The main points of Leavis's lecture dealt with Snow's loose use of the English language and with his view that though Snow is thought of as a "public relations man for science," he "is often far from being regarded with favour by all scientists."[56] However, the majority of Leavis's polemic amounted to no more than a direct and personal attack on Snow. It is not my purpose here to examine the motives of Leavis's actions, but it is instructive to present one or two examples of his tone on this occasion. In Leavis's opinion, "Snow [was] in fact portentously ignorant."[57] "The judgement I have come out with is that not only is [Snow] not a genius; he is intellectually as undistinguished as it is possible to be."[58] He continued that Snow's Rede Lecture exhibits a total "vulgarity of style"[59] and that this should not be surprising since "as a novelist [Snow] doesn't begin to exist."[60]

The reaction to Leavis was strong and immediate; however, the net effect of the discussion was not to shed light on the thesis under debate but instead to defend either Leavis or Snow.[61] The author William Gerhardi, who had been a complete recluse for a dozen or more years, broke his silence and wrote to say that the fact that Snow had written eleven novels while Leavis had written none was a fact not lost on detached observers. J. D. Bernal commented that "if I find Snow's novels interesting and worth reading, it is because he, almost alone among writers today, seems to know the kind of world of organization and machines in which we are now living,"[62] while J. D. Scott sarcastically "congratulated" Leavis on successfully replacing Boris Pasternak as the most controversial writer in the world. It is largely this intense exchange that has left a lasting impression on our contemporary image of Snow's lecture, but clearly it is one that is distorted. Nevertheless, the worldwide discussion of Snow's lecture was sufficient to bring Snow to write *A Second Look* in 1964.

Snow's reasons for doing so are made clear. On the one hand, the plethora of criticism, censure, and commendation demonstrated to him that his two cultures theory was unoriginal. As Snow had recognized, original ideas could not travel as fast as discussion of his lecture had. And yet, on the other hand, there was something in his idea that must be true.[63] These I will discuss shortly. But Snow also took this occasion to revisit the Rede Lecture and clarify points that had been misinterpreted or misquoted in the debate. In regards to his use of the term "culture," he cites a dictionary meaning—"intellectual development, . . . development of the mind"—and an anthropological meaning—"a group of persons living in the same environment [who are] linked by common habits, common assumptions, a common way of life."[64] Both of these meanings, he reasserted, are necessary to his thesis. In addition, he still maintained that the use of the number two is adequate for his discussion. However, reiterating the caution expressed in his original lecture, he noted that any "attempts to divide anything into two ought to be regarded with much suspicion. I have thought for a long time about going in for further refinement: but in the end I decided against."[65] In *A Second Look* he stated, "So the phrase 'the two cultures' still seems appropriate for the purpose I had in mind."[66]

Snow's other rejoinders focused on what had become a popular misquotation by Leavis—"we die alone"[67]—in place of his "each of us dies alone," to which Snow objects because of the attempt to pluralize what he intended to be an essentially singular condition: the solitariness of the human being.

And finally, Snow emphasized that while his statements had been attacked for privileging science over literature, neither culture was "adequate for our potentialities for the work which is in front of us, for the world in which we ought to begin to live."[68]

At the outset I argued that Snow's two cultures hypothesis highlights important elements within his conceptual framework. However, not only have the popular interpretations of his thesis distorted this continuity but the severe limitations and biases of the Rede Lecture itself have contributed to its current disconnected status.[69]

One of the least important of these is the lack of originality of the thesis. As I have already pointed out, this was something that Snow himself recognized. Indeed, Snow pointed specifically to such similar statements as can be found in Jacob Bronowski's *Educated Man in 1984*. Others, which Snow did not mention, include the bland contributions of J. Robert Oppenheimer entitled *The Open Mind* (1948) and *Prospects in the Arts and Sciences* (1954) and the more enlightened work of Alfred North Whitehead, who tried to alert society to "the quiet growth of science" and to its effect upon the modern world, the production of "minds in a groove and the lack of intellectual balance."[70] Even before Snow arrived at Cambridge, the arts-and-science dichotomy was noted and discussed, as it was when the young poet Julian Bell, son of Vanessa Bell (painter and sister of Virginia Woolf), maintained in the 1928 debate at the Cambridge Union—on the notion "The Sciences Are Destroying the Arts"— that "the scientist, the inquirer, the interrogator, was innately incapable either of creating, or appreciating art. The business man, the waste product of Science, was the immediate murderer."[71] Indeed, many observers have pointed to the rough similarity of the argument put forward by Snow and that by T. H. Huxley in response to Matthew Arnold's 1882 Rede Lecture. Huxley, the champion and popularizer of Darwin's evolutionary theory (and whom many have designated as being the person most responsible for driving a wedge between science and the rest of society by arguing on behalf of "value-free" research), suggested that the state should guarantee the happiness of Everyman through wealth, security, science, technology, and knowledge. In Huxley's eyes, science was both intellectually and materially rewarding for civilization.[72] But as to any real claims of originality, Snow makes none. While others deride him for his apparent lack of awareness of the 1882 debate, Snow merely states that the two cultures is an important problem of modern societies.

A related flaw in the lecture stems from Snow's distorted historical portrayal of the conflict, by which I mean to suggest something more serious than simply an error in chronology. More specifically, Snow saw the cultural split as being quite a recent phenomenon, being coincidental largely with the emergence of the industrial revolution during the late eighteenth century. However as both the noted cultural historian Leo Marx and the historian of science Lynn White, Jr., have each convincingly argued, the roots of the contemporary debate can easily be traced to much earlier periods in the history of Western culture. They both focus as an example on twelfth-century Europe when there developed a distinct awareness of the gulf between the two cultures. They note that up to this point the seven traditional liberal arts were divided into the trivium (grammar, rhetoric, and logic) and the quadrivium (arithmetic, geometry, astronomy, and music—with music conceived as the study of mathematical proportions). However, this was a time at which mathematical sophistication accelerated rapidly. According to Marx, "as late as 1100 there were few scraps of Euclid's *Elements* known in Europe. But within one hundred years there were six complete versions of the *Elements* widely available, and as confidence in the results increased quadrivially, conviction of the cogency of trivial arguments declined." By the year 1200, in other words, the "scientists of the day" were already beginning to narrow their research and methods to subjects that were tangible, physical, and quantifiable. By the fourteenth century, White tells us, the two cultures divide could be illustrated by the strenuous efforts of Bishop Nicole Oresme, who invented the graph and who futilely attempted for many years to graph beauty. Comments White concisely: "It didn't work." He elaborates, noting that "natural reason had become too identified with its most precious expression, mathematics, to cope with a vivid but diffuse experience like that of beauty. The inherent limitations of reason were now recognized so clearly that the whole realm of qualitative value—beauty, goodness, even truth—when the nature of that truth were not precisely calculable found refuge in theology with its epistemology of revelation." As Leo Marx put it, "All that was holy, all that was intangible, [all that was] immeasurable had been purged from Nature."[73] Thus the essence of Snow's two cultures can be found in Europe six hundred years ago.

Snow's historical weaknesses are even more apparent in his likening of the literati to being "natural" Luddites. Quite apart from Snow's erroneous representation of all those associated with the new literary community as a homogeneous group that responded alike to all modern situations, he nevertheless was able to successfully draw on a popular misconception that he himself appears to have held.[74] The very name of "Luddite" still evokes a powerful image of half-crazed men and women blindly striking out against the forces of progress—a handful of isolated, desperate people, irrationally smashing machines because they were "afraid of new things."[75] Indeed, this is the image that Snow wished to solicit. But as Albury and Schwartz, E. P. Thompson, and others have demonstrated, this was far from being an accurate reflection of reality. As

Thompson has noted: "The men who organised, sheltered or condoned Luddism were far from primitive. They were shrewd and humourous; [they] were amongst the most articulate of the 'industrious classes'. A few had read Adam Smith, more had made some study of trade union law. Croppers, stockingers, and weavers were capable of managing a complex organization; undertaking its finances and correspondence. . . . All of them had dealings through their representatives with Parliament. . . ."[76] Indeed, the Luddites—far from being on the whole wild machine wreckers—were in fact responsible agents of technical change who were extremely concerned with managing the introduction of a new technology in a way that mitigated against de-skilling and unemployment. They were not ignorant of technology but were, rather, intensely aware of it. Thus Snow's suggestion of a rough equivalency between writers and Luddites simply does not work. Nor does his claim that "traditional culture" was profoundly unaware of the changes that were taking place within society. Mechanics and apprentices throughout Britain were flocking to newly established Mechanics Institutes for courses in science and engineering between 1800 and 1850; the majority of people were beginning to work in automated factories or move from rural settings to industrial cities during the same period; and Britain—at that time—was leading the world in reaping the productive and wealth-creating benefits of the world's first industrial revolution—all facts that seem to have missed Snow's uncritical notice.

A somewhat more serious difficulty with Snow's Rede Lecture is its casual manner. Taking Snow's realist prose to an extreme, the lecture adopts a style far too anecdotal and autobiographical. The effective result is a caricature of a serious concern that only really works because, as with any effective caricature, it contains a grain of truth. Nevertheless, the style is distracting and has trapped critics into a consideration of terms ("two," "culture," "without thinking," "reacting as if they wished the future didn't exist") instead of ideas.

A more serious flaw of the lecture arises from conflation of language and ideas. An example is illustrative. Throughout the text, Snow appears repeatedly to equate literary, "traditional," and managerial culture. He refers to novelists, critics, managers, and politicians almost interchangeably. As he said in *The Two Cultures*, "Literary intellectuals represent, vocalize, and to some extent shape and predict the mood of the non-scientific culture: they do not make the decisions, but their words seep into the minds of those who do."[77] But clearly to suggest that the literary community shapes the sensibilities of government and industry, that they reflect those sensibilities, or that they are so coherent as to represent a focused community is clearly mistaken. Surely Snow knew this, and yet the inconsistency goes maddeningly unresolved.

Another distracting element of Snow's lecture stems from the superficial treatment that he gives his own central recommendation vis-à-vis rethinking our educational systems. At no point does he elaborate on this. Some have tried to take Snow's basic diagnosis in designing and implementing a "two cultures curriculum": two notable examples being the now discontinued core curricula of the University of Sussex and C. P. Snow College at the State University of New York at Buffalo. But Snow himself never specified what a two cultures curriculum would look like. He observed approvingly the Soviet and American ability to expand their science and engineering education in response to perceived national needs, as well as the central role that public policy can play in this process, but beyond this Snow only mentioned education or students twice in his fiction—both times in a fashion that decries boring science teaching. Perhaps the answer to this problem lies in the observations of the distinguished historian of science A. R. Hall who recalled that Snow, while a demonstrator of physical chemistry during the 1930s at Cambridge, had a reputation for being something of a boring lecturer himself who was only interested in college politics—and not in education, teaching, or the subject. But elsewhere in his nonfiction, Snow argued in a polite but uncommitted way that "the history of science, if properly taught, might redress the gap."[78] And yet Snow went no further. For someone so apparently (arguably) interested in higher education as Snow was—and keeping in mind that it was only scheduling problems that made it impossible for him to accept an invitation from Prime Minister Harold Macmillan to sit on the Robbins Committee on Higher Education in 1963[79]—the two cultures and Snow's other work only leave the reader with something that is inconsistent with what one had been led to expect. The recommendations, though compelling in the policy and educational language of the day, remain unanimated and strangely superficial. Furthermore, Snow's major implicit assumption that science and literature should have parity—both educationally and in the terms of society at large—seems remarkably naive. Science has become an exceptionally powerful, mathematically specialized discourse, and as such it establishes the "instrumental horizon" behind which the intent of the epistemological project is suppressed. To a large degree, its use (except on purely ideological grounds) is inadequate for anything except the understanding and control of the natural world. At the same time, literature—which is written in the "language" of

Dickens, Kundera, and Shakespeare—is exactly that discourse used in every aspect of our lives to describe and communicate the political, social, emotional, and cultural realms. As such, the attempt to achieve equal status between each form of discourse is to deny the practical roles, flexibility, and constraints of each.

But perhaps the most serious flaw of the Rede Lecture is its philosophical shallowness. As we have already seen, part 2 of Snow's lecture, called "Intellectuals as Natural Luddites," seems to miss entirely the scope and cogency of the critical reaction to the industrial and scientific revolutions. Snow argues that intellectuals other than those who are within the scientific culture "have never tried, wanted, or been able to understand the industrial revolution much less accept it. Intellectuals—literary intellectuals in particular—are natural Luddites." Snow's point here seems to be that intellectuals other than scientists and engineers were allied with wealth and power—the governing elites—and that they simply disdained the practical, equalizing power of science-based technology. Much of what Snow said argues that science is morally and practically on the side of Everyman while traditional culture has been corrupted by its long-standing affiliation with aristocratic power.

Clearly there is some truth in this view. But in his eagerness to align the advance of science and technology with the interests of the poor, Snow overlooked not only the increasing co-optation, and direction of modern science (since the First World War) by government and industry—science's alliance with the state and capitalism. He has also dismissed the critiques of the modern writers and their role in leading the emergence of a new and widespread paradigm concerning the nature of progress. All Snow hears in the critics of modern material progress—and in this connection he names Ruskin, Thoreau, D. H. Lawrence, Yeats, Pound, Emerson, and those writers who shaped literary culture—is what he calls "screams of horror." As Leo Marx has said, clearly it is ridiculous to paint all of these writers with such a broad brush. Indeed, as elements of their writing clearly show, some were deeply cognizant of a fundamental change in modern mass culture to which Snow appears to have remained partially blind. Indeed, many influential writers were not at all oblivious to the power of the new technology. Many embraced the new technology for their own productive and creative purposes. Many others grasped the subtle changes that were taking place in thinking about progress long before the general public had made sense of the changes. Not unlike Snow himself, many began to see science and technology as a possible tool for social good through an epistemological, moral, political, and economic liberation from the dominant aristocratic, class-bound forms of social life. Through the 1950s, such writers as J. B. Priestley and Malcolm Muggeridge ascribed to this view. However, many of the writers whom Snow specifically identified and criticized saw a transformation of the belief in "scientific progress which was in the service of Man" into an increasingly complacent belief in the sufficiency of the advancement of science, technology, and industrial innovation as an end in itself. If it can be said that modernist writers have been typically critical of science, it has not been because they didn't understand science (it is surely an overstatement to suggest that everyone should understand the principles underlying the workings of the internal combustion engine or the microwave oven), but rather it has been because they saw a danger, at a time of deep-seated political and cultural turmoil, of a new blind faith or ideology emerging.

Thus when Snow sarcastically mocked Thoreau by saying that it is all right "to *do* a modern Walden if one doesn't give a damn about the welfare of the poor," it is clear he has missed the point of Thoreau's critique of industrial society. Indeed, a careful reading of *Walden* reveals that it is in fact a sustained criticism of the disintegration of progress into a materialistically oriented, science-bound, technocratic culture. As Thoreau noted, technological innovation was on the road to becoming merely an "improved means to an unimproved end." While Snow is correct in noting that by the year 2070 undergraduates will know far more physics than Newton did, the point he seems to miss is that it is unlikely that they will de facto be better individuals. This is precisely the point that he ignores in his Rede Lecture, however, and to which he pays attention in his fiction. How can we learn to manage the power of science, technology, and knowledge from a private and public perspective? In his identification of the literary community as Luddites, as opponents to the new power—and even taken as caricature—Snow is quite wrong: he has revealed in himself the same tone deafness to sensibility that he has accused modernist writers of having. Many of the writers he singled out not only recognized the new potentials of science but also understood that these potentials could only ever be fully realized if their proponents could also bring their power to bear under morally and politically defensible purposes. Hence Snow's analysis of the two cultures is weakened by his failure to recognize the cogency and authenticity of the modern literary and cultural reactions to the mechanistic and technocratic revolutions.

And yet having said all this, it is still clear that despite the considerable flaws, weaknesses, and biases that exist in Snow's lecture, there is a deep appeal or resonance in Snow's concern that goes to the heart of modernity's ruptured condition. Forget that his use of the word *culture* is vague and misleading, and that his analytical division into *two* cultures is arbitrary—given that he identifies these almost solely with literary intellectuals, on the one hand, and with physicists, on the other. Although Snow's lecture at many points echoed the Heroic Age of the morally upright, "gentleman's," amateur tradition of science, this is a caricature that is now passé. Science, even by the 1950s, had become a highly complex social and political activity that was fundamentally aligned with corporate and government structures. Thus the problem is not just an isolated one of knowledge in a modern democratic society. Nor is it simply a problem of intellectual or educational dimensions. And yet, as a close examination of Snow's other materials shows, he was well aware of the depths and meaning of this.

If we restrict our reading of Snow solely to those writings that deal with the two cultures hypothesis, we are met by a variety of hermeneutic difficulties that give us few points of access into his larger conceptual framework. And yet it is only within this framework that we can gain a clear view of how Snow saw the enigmatic modern self and its potential for meaningful reintegration. It is only at this level that we can see how he treated literature, science, and politics as intimate and coextensive elements of his own quest of totalizing self-definition. Only once we appreciate the parameters of Snow's larger response to his own modern condition can we assess his strategy vis-à-vis both the struggle of modernity and our own personal quests. This is the purpose of the next three chapters.

Part Three

SNOW'S TRIPTYCH
OF LITERATURE,
SCIENCE, AND POLITICS

4

LITERATURE AND THE
STATE OF SIEGE

Making use . . . of what
he has beneath his eyes
—CLAUDINE CHONEZ

The system that works—this, and
nothing but this is reality
for the realist.
—J. P. STERN

NOVELS OF EVERY AGE have concerned themselves with the enigma of the self, and neither Snow's novels nor the novels of modernity are exceptions. Indeed, as soon as a literary character, such as Snow's "Lewis Eliot," is created, questions regarding the author's definition of "the self" inevitably arise. Within the struggle of modernity, what can "the self" mean? How can it be grasped in its aesthetic, cognitive, and political totality, and how can it be communicated to readers? These are among those fundamental questions on which the novel form is based and which it must address. However, the answers authors choose to give to these questions not only reveal a variety of literary responses to the demands of the novel form but also expose differing conceptual and political responses—both to the individual self and to the individual self's place in the historical context of the period. In Snow's case, he was aesthetically something of an outsider striving for the center. Cognitively, he deeply understood some of the scientific forces that continue to define the Metropolis. And politically, he was undeniably a part of the broad reconstitution of liberalism.[1] As a result, Snow's responses to these questions place him squarely within the embrace of the struggle of modernity.

Given the modern public sphere's will to dominate and submerge individual life in what Martin Heidegger called an active "forgetting of being," it should not be surprising that much talk today has come to be concerned with the abandonment of the self, the novel's *raison d'être*, and hence of the "death" of the novel. This is indeed a theme that is considerably developed by Georg Lukacs in his treatment of the tension between realism and modernism.[2] Through Heidegger's perceptive phrase, we are reminded of the crisis situation of our time on at least two fronts. First, through this forgetfulness, we have participated in an active undermining of the social function of the novel form itself. This has led us to talk of "the postliterate" society in which the novel is seen as providing little more than a vehicle of escape, entertainment, or commodity fetishism. No longer is it seen as a potential instrument for the probing of meaningful themes. Second, we can sense in Heidegger that—following his teacher Edmund Husserl—our roots of "forgetfulness" are to be found in the method and authority of our sciences.[3] Insofar as this is true, we include the historical view that as the world came to be comprehended as a whole, so too it became apprehended as a question to be answered.

Stimulated by the conviction that there is nothing without its reason, science energetically explored—as it continues to today—the *why* of everything, to the point that whatever exists is seen as being explainable, calculable, and (to a large degree) predictable. Thus, in effect, science reduced the natural and life worlds to the status of objects for investigation. The more men and women advanced their themes of knowledge through specialized disciplines, the less could be seen either of the world or of the self in clear and comprehensive terms.

As I suggested at the outset, science and technology have been effectively used and emulated by literature in the modern era. Thus to suggest that the novel form has lost its potential for totality— that the novel's social and aesthetic function have been surpassed— is to miss the unique strength of the novel form. Throughout the history of the novel, its sole *raison d'être* has been to identify those sites of contemporary existence that had become problematically hidden. A most successful preoccupation of the novel, in fact, has dealt with gaining knowledge of the self no matter how distant or imperiled the self may have seemed. Even within our own period in which both the self and the novel appear forgotten and in a state of siege, it can be asserted that the novel has not forgotten the self.

To move beyond the resigned acceptance of our tendency to forget our own being, we must recognize that we are also beings of the world (or, what Heidegger characterized as *in-der-Welt-sein* [being in the world]). As such, we can redress our passive tendencies and recognize that the human self does not relate to the world as an object to subject—or as an eye to a painting. Instead the state of humanity and the world are inexorably bound together. The world is a part of humanity. It is the human dimension—the human *milieu*— and as the world changes, so changes the self and its recognition of existence. Formulating modernity's central problematic in this way can be reassuring, for it says, in effect, that our task is not to *find* a bridge between our private and public selves but only to *see* the bridge(s) that already exist. But how is this to be done? The answer, as Snow asserted, is to be found in the self, in the characteristics that the self has come to embody in its period, and in literature's ability to communicate elements of our condition. Snow believed that the study of the individual condition could only be effected through the study of the individual in society, because he found that most, if not all, modern individuals could only be meaningfully understood if both the private and public sides of their lives could be examined. He found, moreover, that the fundamental interactions between the individual and society are most alive in their rationality and politics, and aesthetically in their literature.

Seen in these terms it should not be surprising that within our context of a public sphere dominated by both science and administration, it is the *thinking self*—that is, one who is aware of his or her modern environment, asks questions of it, and acts—that has come to be the measure of all things. Thus, it can be said that the thinking self is not only capable of clearing the air that obscures the bridge(s) between our public and private selves but is also capable of bringing us directly into contact with that vital literary device of "the hero," and of helping to define a central element of modern liberal individualism.

Of course, conceptions of the hero and the heroic vary. But whether one adopts a benign definition of hero, such as "the chief personage in a poem, play or story around whom the interest in story or plot is centered,"[4] or a more Hegelian conception of the modern hero—as one who faces the world alone—it is clear that the thinking self must be one who "acts." It is through action that one steps out from the repetitive everyday and distinguishes oneself from others to fully become an individual. Indeed this, in effect, is the modern quest. Dante said as much: "In any act, the primary intention of he who acts is to reveal his own image."[5] But this quest can clearly take on many forms. Action can be seen as being a self-portrait of the actor, regardless of whether our own heroic self-image is that of Robert Musil's "man without qualities" or of Snow's New Man.

But clearly, action—in and of itself—is not a sufficient precondition for the definition of a meaningful literature, be it modern or otherwise. In Kafka, Joyce, and Proust, for example, the actor cannot recognize himself or herself in action. Although he hopes to reveal himself through his acts, the image bears no resemblance to him. In one sense, at least, it can be argued that this is one of the great discoveries of modern literature. But in another sense it suggests that, in order for it to realize its historical mission in the quest of the self, modern literature needs—in addition to action—to turn away from the visible world in order to examine the interior life. Thus it could be argued that only by doing so will the author, or the novel form itself, be able to examine those motives and ambitions that are an integral part of the modern self—those that are meaningful within our own historical setting.

However, it must be remembered that, at their best, novelists are neither prophets nor historians. Novelists are explorers of existence; a novel is a prose form through which the author explores, by means of "experimental selves" or characters, some great themes of contemporary existence. The great novelist can make no issue of his ideas. As Milan Kundera has said, the novelist "is fascinated not by his voice but by a form he is seeking, and only those forms that meet the demands of his dream become part of his work."[6] It is against these considerations that we will begin to find the significance of C. P. Snow. On a beach in Marseilles in 1935, Snow articulated the full scale of his *Strangers and Brothers* series of novels. He was to spend the next thirty-five years seeking to fill the form that would satisfy the demands of his dream.[7]

It is in some ways ironic that the principal point of entry into Snow's aesthetics should come through his flawed critique of modernist literature that is found in his Rede Lecture, but this is indeed the case. Snow's sweeping depiction of the modern "writer as Luddite" does embody the untenable argument that modern literary genres and criticisms have been developing in a way that in some sense is antiscientific. It also suggests a view that—when given sufficient room to breathe outside the service of a narrow thesis—can lead to a more accurate perception of Snow's aesthetics that sees the responses of so-called modernist literature to the modern condition as being stylistically inflexible and substantively distant from any understanding of the modern self. These differences between the dogmatic Snow of the Rede Lecture and his more subtle literary sensibilities are meaningful, for in remaining open to his subtleties, we can more usefully see Snow as forwarding a lively critique of literature and the struggle of modernity. This element of Snow's work is too often missed when readings of Snow are closely based on the two cultures. As we will see, Snow's "literary Luddite" thesis is a poorly articulated aspect of his own realist aesthetic, which underpins his cognitive and political realism and upon which he bases his reconciliation between modernity's public and private self.

This is not to suggest, however, that what Snow offers is a fully articulated critique of literature. Rather, anything Snow presents by way of direct criticism is decidedly partial—ranging from a prolegomenon to an intuitive reaction. Rarely, if ever, does his literary assessment achieve the status of a full-blown analysis. Rather, he critiques literature by using a broad brush—employing the sweeping voice of experience and common sense, instead of precise and comprehensive analysis, to suggest his aesthetic preferences. It is these partially exposed, and partially developed, views that he amplifies through fiction.

Gaining access to Snow's critical thought on literature is difficult, not only on the level of ideas but on the level of sheer evidence as well. Snow was impressive in his output as a writer, but any search of his nonfiction will only reveal sketchy allusions to his problems with modern fiction. While it is possible to gain some insight into Snow's aesthetics either by reference to early and lucid assessments made by Snow's friend the author William Cooper[8] or by supposition, noting, for example, that Snow's wife was herself an influential Proustian scholar would result in little more than patchwork conjecture.

A more meaningful assessment of Snow's literary criticism can only come directly through his writings on writing. The principal sources of this are to be found in Snow's book reviews for the London *Sunday Times* (1949–1952) and the *Financial Times* (1970–1980), in such rare articles as his 1961 essay "Science, Politics, and the Novelist,"[9] and through brief introductions to his own *Trollope* (1975) and *The Realists* (1978). What these writings reveal, even in their own unique and fragmentary fashion, is quite interesting.

Snow's attacks on modernist writings are almost as well known as Leavis's assault on Snow.[10] James Joyce and Virginia Woolf were the novelists most often criticized by Snow. Indeed, Snow admitted that his own literature was "quite [a] deliberate reaction . . . against the kind of purely aesthetic novel represented by, say, Joyce and Virginia Woolf."[11] But they were by no means his only targets. At times, his list of grievances expanded to include several imagist poets, many experimental novelists, as well as their descendants, such as Dorothy Richardson, Yeats, Eliot, and Pound. However, Snow's list was not all-inclusive. The modernist Wyndham Lewis, for example, escaped Snow's commentary (owing, perhaps, to Lewis's own rejection of Futurists and hyperaesthetics, which would have pleased Snow),[12] as did Richard Aldington. Despite Aldington's unique modernist credentials as a writer, husband of Hilda Doolittle (H.D.), and friend of D. H. Lawrence, he became one of Snow's favorite authors following the publication of *Death of a Hero* in 1929, which starkly described the rough war experiences of World War I. Indeed, following Aldington's 1934 visits to Cambridge, Snow recorded his view that "anyone in touch with twentieth century literature knows . . . you can scarcely read [Aldington's] work and remain indifferent."[13] Soon after Snow's publication of *Richard Aldington: An Appreciation* in September 1938, Aldington reciprocated with a letter to *Discovery,* of which Snow was then editor. The letter, which undoubtedly appealed to Snow's developing interest in both the social aspects of modern science and the desirability of encouraging a dialogue between the two cultures, discussed the responsibility of persons with scientific training and was published on the eve of World War II as "Science and Conscience."[14]

Nevertheless, despite a few apparent inconsistencies in whom he included among the "problematic" modernists, Snow had no trouble in temporally situating what was for him the problematic modernist novel. This he identified firmly with the period between 1914 and 1945,[15] a period arduous for literature itself, Snow, and society. Yet underscoring the shock of the war, Snow claimed that these restrictions on the novel's range "happened almost overnight."[16]

Furthermore, Snow had no difficulty in categorizing these modern novel forms that he found to be especially problematic. These he referred to variously as "the stream of consciousness novel," the "moment to moment" novel, fiction that was concerned principally with "the continuum of sensation," novels of sensibility, and the "novel of total recall." However, Snow refused to accept the popular phrase "experimental novel," as the word *experiment* has real meaning in inductive thought. Snow found the misappropriation of this term (which, he tried to suggest, was fostered by the literary community) to be even more bizarre than that expressed in his favorite story of a cantankerous physicist howling of modern writers, "Why do these idiots think that *polarized light* is a *specially superior* form of light?!"[17] In Snow's view, the application of the term *experimental* to a fictional style of writing that has not budged for four decades is ludicrous. Snow included Dorothy Richardson's *Pointed Roofs,* Virginia Woolf's *To the Lighthouse,* Harry Green's *Party Going,* Carson McCuller's *Heart Is a Lonely Hunter,* and Joyce's *Finnegans Wake* in his list of unprogressive—even retrograde—novels.

To Snow, these various writers and forms (whatever they are called) were producing work that was "arid and mindless." The new modern novel was "meaningless in semantic terms and certainly in human terms."[18] In so saying, Snow repeated his harsh literary criticism that was revealed in the Rede Lecture. But he also suggested that the forms of writing then becoming dominant in the interwar period were in part themselves a reaction against the success of science. Science, in effect, was driving serious literature "underground."

> [The] science which has made novel writing diminish and hide is the science which is the dominant expression of our entire industrial society, the science which is both the cause and effect of the technological revolution in which we stand. And the devitalizing effect which science has had on novel writing . . . is not because it is evil or antihuman, but simply because it has been so overwhelmingly successful.
>
> In the same year that T. S. Eliot wrote about the world ending not with a bang but a whimper, Ernest Rutherford, the British physicist, was saying, loudly and with his usual unselfconscious abundant delight in his own genius, that this was the Golden Age of Science. . . . [It was] hard for art to live in his shadow or the shadow of all he symbolized.
>
> For science had lived up to all its boasts. It has seemed to know all the answers (even though the real point about science is not that it knows the right answers but the right questions). Anyways, it works. Against the supreme achievements of twentieth century science . . . what is there for a writer to do? No one ever said so consciously to himself, of course, but it is that feeling which has made the frontiers of novel-writing . . . shrink. . . .
>
> The reflective mind has been sacrificed. All that is left is an attempt to reproduce the moments of sensation, to convey just what it is like to experience this instant of the here-and-now.[19]

This was a view that Snow held throughout his life but it was not one that was static, despite popular perceptions to the contrary. This hypothesis led Snow to overtly recognize that in order for a work of fiction to be truly meaningful, or even "viable" in the modern world, it must lead a difficult double life. Snow understood that, through its own internal integrity, every work of fiction must maintain contact both with other literary works and with the world. Overemphasize the "lived world," and a novel risks falling into propaganda or the merely documentary (even though this can have its uses). Overemphasize language, and a novel will collapse into meaninglessness and endless self-reflection. Following these simple rules brought Snow to hold that in the truly great novels "there must clearly be a presiding, unconcealed, interpreting intelligence. They are all of them concerned with the actual social setting in which their personages exist. The concrete world of physical fact, the shapes of society, are essential to the [realist's] art. . . ."[20] As such, the many routine misrepresentations and doubts of the self in life have a chance to be tested, to be uncovered and replaced by a more comprehensive and functional sense of self. This literary view had important implications for Snow's view of social change and politics. But for literature in itself to fully embrace its possibility of social change, it must reflect on its own duality through its language and structure.

It is not surprising then that Snow felt the new novel forms to be incapable of either progress or duality. Snow noted that these new novel forms had revealed "a remarkable suicidal tendency to narrow literature's range."[21] The principal literary techniques that effected this narrowing were the "stream of consciousness" and the "interior monologue." At a time when the images, definitions, and functions of the self were under siege, "the new literature" and "the new criticism" had begun to retreat from literature's traditional activity of engagement, becoming responsive only to the demands and fetishes of the text. As a result, Snow accused not only the new forms of shedding the duality vital to the success of literature but also of being party to the abandonment of the self in a world now seemingly devoid of meaning. Technically this development in literature can be documented in several ways: through the "disappearance" of the author, through the development of the anti-hero, or through the privileging of language and text over representation of the social-life world. The significance of these developments for the self in a late-capitalistic, bureaucratic Metropolis has been well documented. But in Snow's view, these developments resulted in an aesthetic *cul de sac* for which there could be no corrective and no progress.[22] The new fiction had "stayed remarkably constant for 30 years. . . . Between [Richardson's] *Pointed Roofs* in 1915 and its successors there was no significant development. In fact, there could not be; because [the interior monologue and stream of consciousness] effectively [cuts] out precisely those aspects of the novel [from which] a living tradition can be handed on."[23] Indeed, Snow and many of his literary colleagues, such as John Wain and William Cooper, were suspicious of the fact that "the Modern movement [or] 'the Men of 1914' were still known as 'Modern' forty-six years later [thus showing] that we are not dealing with any historical situation in a serious sense."[24] In Snow's mind these writers were dishonestly and uncritically presenting themselves as a future wave when in fact they themselves were trapped—frozen—within an *avant-garde* that had become *passé*.

What the novel was losing as a result of the modernists' textual preoccupations and social withdrawal was far more than a stylistic convention. In the new forms, "reflection had to be sacrificed, [as was] moral awareness [and] investigatory intelligence. . . ."[25] As far as such intelligence was concerned, Snow distinguished between the modernist's insight "which tells us what it is like to be in a certain mood and his preferred insight which asks, why should I be driven by these motives [or] capable of this action?"[26] This distinction is important, for Snow found that the new novel's preference for interior monologue plus its almost compulsive emphasis on images and patterns served only to distance the subject of fiction from the fiction itself. A piece of evidence that Snow liked to cite was that the new and popular literary techniques of the modernists were no longer seen as *a* way of writing but "as the *only* way of writing." They served to work only as they could—as proxies for the direct complexities inherent in the struggle that is modernity. Snow "streamlined" the cognitive sensualities of reality by referring simply to "flux." Any written attempt to express the flux of "our sensations and mental experience must, of course, rest upon a convention. [In reality], the flux is very largely non-verbal. . . . [The technique of the] stream of consciousness, at its highest point, as in Joyce, is an attempt to find a verbal equivalent for [this] non-verbal flux. [Its] strategy is straightforward: adopt what looks like a naturalistic approach, write the verbal equivalent as though it were the flux itself, discard the reflective intelligence, and try to make the words suggest what scientists call a one-to-one correlation with the elements of the verbal flux."[27]

Snow saw such literary techniques as being limiting not only in terms of the range of experience that the novel could address but also in terms of their access to a necessary insight through which the persona of the self is located and explored. "The essence of introspective insight . . . is that one sees oneself with total intimacy and at the same moment as though one were someone else. "Immersed in the stream of consciousness, one can never achieve the second part of this illumination."[28]

Having recognized these elements of Snow's literary critique, however, it must be pointed out that stream of consciousness and interior monologue techniques, as well as psychological insight or introspection, have been the sources for serious misreadings of Snow's aesthetics.

This is a delicate point, for while Snow argued against the fiction of Joyce and Woolf, he praised as great novelists such masters of the interior monologue as Tolstoy, Dostoevsky, Balzac, and Proust.[29] Snow knew well that Proust was a master of analyzing that truly modern condition of "lost time," but Joyce analyzed this familiar Proustian ground of the "present moment" with considerable immediacy—and yet Snow found the result almost incomprehensible. Snow defended this position in the following way: "Anyone who has read novels between 1920 and 1950 can recognize this moment-by-moment technique. In reality, it is not so much a technique as an attitude of mind, which suggests that a writer can only learn anything of life *through the immediate present*, i.e., he should confine his art to what he can see and hear or . . . to the solitary moments of free association. No attitude could be more sterile. It is not in the least how one learns about life in actual fact."[30] Here, Snow seems quite content to restrict his commentary to the level of technique alone. But even beyond this, his inconsistencies are notable. As Frederick Karl has pointed out, when one tries to apply the realist ideas of the authors whom Snow admired, one finds that they do not fit with Snow's perspective at all. As ideas, the Russian realists' views were almost the opposite of Snow's. For example, Tolstoy advocated an almost total rejection of administration, bureaucracy, industrialization, and ambition—that is, almost all of the values that Snow accepted, assessed, and promoted. Similarly, Dostoevsky had apocalyptic visions in which humanity found salvation through Jesus Christ, but Snow and his characters were aggressively atheistic. However, Snow ignored these inconsistencies between his evaluations of literature and his own output. To a degree, Snow's distaste for Joyce is more understandable. Whereas Snow found meaning in the world at large, Joyce confronted the intensely immediate moment. In a sense there would seem to be nothing more obvious or tangible than the present moment. And yet as Joyce's work articulately revealed, it eludes us completely. All of the sadness of modern life lies in that one observation. In the course of a single second, all of our senses register a swarm of events, sensations, and ideas. And yet to the degree that Joyce's literary technique was able to seize that moment for inspection, it brought us directly into contact with the possibility that our quest for the self may ultimately end not in resolution but in paradox. More particularly, the more powerful the "stream of consciousness lens" of Joyce's literary microscope,[31] the more elusive the self and its uniqueness appear to be. "Beneath the great Joycean lens that breaks the soul down into atoms, [the more we realize that] we are all alike," that our uniqueness cannot be fully grasped by the interior life. This view—which is really an essential element of the existential phenomenology—is what Snow will not agree with, for two reasons.[32] First, the belief that individuals cannot be unique removes all hope for the betterment of humanity. The belief that cognition, thinking, or rationality cannot provide the vehicle for this betterment only traps humanity in despair. Second, reductionist philosophies believe that—in science, for example—ultimate understanding rests in determining and analyzing ever smaller particles of matter. Antireductionists, however, recognize that even within an individual organism, a contradiction to the absolute nature of reductionist theory exists. Admittedly, in the area of scientific experience, a particular scientist's adherence to one theory or the other as a total philosophy is irrelevant. To be sure, reduction is a successful and vital feature of the scientific method. But as numerous philosophers of science have argued, reductionism can only be a method for research; it cannot succeed as a total philosophy. Snow argued strenuously that literary works of art and problems in literary criticism are reducible and must be examined in this light if they are to be understood. But Snow, like the antireductionists in science, saw reduction as totally inadequate from a philosophical perspective.[33]

As Snow suggested time and time again, the ultimate success of a literary work is connected to its moral fiber. Having said this, however, opens the door to numerous interpretative difficulties. Many of the growing number of post-1945 realist literati spoke of the need to reconstitute British life and politics in terms of morality. Thus it is not surprising to find that Snow—as a member of this community, and despite his own dislike of moral appeals—did make occasional references to the need for "moral fiber" in both life and literature. However, rather than take such rare citations as they were intended, critics eager to suggest possible grounds for an intellectual reconciliation between Snow and Leavis (by symbolically closing, in their minds at least, the gap between "two cultures") have accepted the moralistic language used occasionally by Snow at face value, leaping to the conclusion that the real differences between Snow and Leavis were in fact quite small.[34] Using an article that was written by Snow on America's deplorable "sex-obsessed novels" of the 1950s and 1960s as the sole support for this thinking, these critics have cited but one passage: "No culture is healthy if clever writers fluctuate uneasily between the unreadable and the obscene." This statement, it is argued, is one a Leavisite could have made or agreed with easily. But this view, taken in the context of Snow's conceptual outlook, is superficial on many grounds. First, to Snow, claims made on behalf of morality or a moral tone are "vaguely absurd." Second, in Snovian terms, moral fiber is more of a reference to a typically English "stiff

upper lip"—used in support for postwar reconstitution of the everyday—than an appeal to divine intervention. And third, any serious
differences between the literary outlooks of Snow and Leavis are to
be found not on the moral plane but in the nature of their literary
imaginations and their relationships to social change. As this level
of abstraction, Snow can correctly be seen as something of a technological utopian who is strongly opposed to Leavis's Blakean romanticism. But Snow's occasional references to moral quality are
solely reflections of his realist framework. They are not grounded in
any elaborate philosophical tradition. Indeed, it can be argued that
his "moral" reaction is part of the larger, postwar English wave in
which amoral aestheticism was roundly discredited.

When World War II was over and a new literary atmosphere began
slowly to emerge in Britain, a group of writers that included C. P.
Snow, William Cooper, and Pamela Hansford Johnson set out to
fairly systematically (and in the end, very influentially) establish a
tone for the postwar novel. As with most movements, the tone was
experimental—except this experiment was a revolt against experi-
mentalism. As William Cooper put it:

> During the last years of the war . . . [C. P. Snow] and I, not pre-
> pared to wait for Time's ever rolling stream to bear Experimental
> Writing away, made our own private plans to run it out of town
> as soon as we picked up our pens again—if you look at the work
> of the next generation of English novelists to come up after us,
> you'll observe we didn't entirely lack success for our efforts. We
> had our reasons for being impatient. We meant to write a differ-
> ent kind of novel from that of the Thirties and we saw the Thir-
> ties Novel, the Experimental Novel, had got to be brushed out of
> the way before we could get a proper hearing. Putting it simply,
> to start with: the Experimental Novel was about Man-Alone; we
> meant to write novels about Man-in-Society as well. Please note
> the "as well"; it's important. We have no qualms about incor-
> porating any useful discoveries that had been made in the course
> of Experimental Writing; we simply refused to restrict ourselves
> to them.[35]

Thus what emerged in this "reaction against experiment" was a preferred tone of neutrality that in fact amounted to a disagreement
both about literary forms and about the class origins of writing
in Britain. The experimental novel and the literary *avant-garde*
had been largely identified with the Bloomsbury Group. The "new
writers," including Snow, sought to assert different social and cul-

tural origins for their work. Their new fiction was as much a class
revolt as a formal revolution. It signaled a retreat from a good many
well-established literary assumptions and allegiances. It found a
usable past in the main line of English writing by looking back to
George Eliot and Charles Dickens. It reactivated the spirit of social
attention, and it spoke the language of consensus. Its impact was
considerable.

But while Snow was aware of the ground swell of sympathetic
criticism that supported him and his colleagues from the late 1950s
onward, this did not cause him to lighten his attack on modernist
fiction, nor did it encourage him to move on to new lines of criticism. As he said, "There are a dozen or more promising novelists
in England—Doris Lessing, William Cooper, Emyr Humphreys,
Francis King, Kingsley Amis, J. D. Scott, Brigid Brophy, John Wyllie
are some of the best. . . . Not one of these . . . shows any interest in
the sensibility novel . . . several of them have explicitly and roughly
savaged it. . . ."[36] However, the fairly widespread emergence of this
reaction against modern literature, plus Snow's new opportunities
to travel to the United States and Canada in the decade following the
Rede Lecture as a celebrity *cum* scholar-in-residence, did encourage
him to turn his attention away from modern novelists to an extent
and to comment more on modern critics.[37]

As he explained, from about 1925 to 1945 the new novels were
taken for granted. But as these literary forms began to lose the interest of the reading public, literary critics ("coroners," to use Snow's
language) began to declare the death of the novel. The gap between
an increasingly specialized "art novel" and the reading public was
growing. There were plenty of books being written, published, and
read, but they were not the same novels that the literati were talking
about. "Many plain people were just plain baffled. They did not have
the patience to follow the course of the aesthetic war but when
asked to read wedges of moment-to-moment sensation, they pas-
sively went on strike."[38] In Snow's view, this situation extended well
into the 1960s and was fostered by academic critics of literature.

During Snow's many visits to North American universities, he
grew increasingly disapproving of the new criticism. He came to
view the new academic critics—with the notable exceptions of Alfred Kazin, Harry Levin, Leon Edel, and Lionel Trilling, whom Snow
deeply respected, and all of whom shared at least a modicum of admiration for Snow's writing—as groups of unwitting accomplices in
the decline of the novel. Snow saw the lesser critics as mimicking
the faults of the modernist writers by studying literature as if it was
no more than verbal structure. He saw them as waiting for meaning

to be automated and split so that they might reveal the literary se-
crets with the same "authority over nature" as scientists. Snow
never argued that the activity of these academic critics was useless.
He only argued that their types of literary criticism were far better
suited to the consideration of novels whose ranges are deliberately
narrow. According to Snow, this kind of criticism is unable to adequately evaluate such "real heavyweights" (as he liked to refer to
them) as Balzac, Tolstoy, Dickens, Dostoevsky, or Proust. In the case
of these writers their work is too elusive and too big in their art to be
handled by such techniques. Modern academic critics do not have
the required equipment to handle *War and Peace*, one novel that
many—including Snow—consider to be among the greatest works
of fiction ever written. To be assessed properly, such a novel requires
an array of techniques.

Clearly, Snow's critique of criticism and the experimental fiction
is only partial and is ultimately dissatisfying. But insofar as it unre-
lentingly stems from a concern with the self and the modern condition, it does encourage us to explore his critical alternative—his realist's response.

As a close reading of Snow's fiction reveals, the importance of the
"novel as art" emerges out of its capacity to communicate. Thus, it
is necessary for all of the literary components to work in the same
direction. It is the main task of a writer and a complete work of
literature to marshall all of the constituent parts together—the fiction's structure, themes, heroes, and techniques in order to transmit
the vision of life as completely as possible. It is on general terms
that Snow viewed the experimental novelist as investing too heavily in a notion of the novel as being simply an arrangement of words.
Meaningful literature cannot be valued only on the grounds of
whether particular arrangements of words can be an exact corre-
lative for a highly personal version of experience. In this type of
literature—literature obsessed with an aspect of private life—it
matters little if this vision can say anything much about the outside
world, or whether it can say anything about objective truth. To
Snow, this aesthetic view is both silly in the trivial sense,[39] and absurd. "It is rationalized into thinking which shows the characteristic of bad thinking, of a complicated rococo, and often subtle in its
decorations, but naive at the core. The basis for the rationalization
is, of course, a naive comparison with non-representational graphic
art: and its result would be to make the novel not less significant,
but also not more. . . ."[40]

To argue that characters, scenes, structure, and themes cannot be
separated from an author's intention and that they can have no

meaning apart from the words is, in Snow's framework, nonsense—a solipsism.[41] As science has revealed, the self can never again be conceived of in egocentric terms. Nor can it ever claim to be the sole source or object of knowledge. But in Snow's mind, the Moderns' refusal to recognize or acknowledge this connection between life and art was effectively dishonest. It represented a "syndrome of attitudes," which was, at its roots, a pure social reaction, and which comprised "the romantic conception of the artist, the alienation of the intellectual, the aesthetic of the anti-novel, the abdication of the generalizing intellect, the hatred of the scientific-industrial revolution, the desire to contract out of society. This syndrome is . . . visible in a considerable sector of advanced literature all through the first half of the century. . . . [There is a] connection which seems to be close, though not in individual practitioners inevitable, between this sector of advanced literature and extreme social reaction—not conservatism, but extreme social reaction."[42]

Perhaps the most extreme example of this is, for Snow, to be found in social and aesthetic exile. Of course one of the central themes of modern literature is exile. Certainly when one thinks of this, all sorts of names spring to mind. Ezra Pound was an exile all of his life. Vladimir Nabokov was an exile, albeit he was forced into exile. Joseph Conrad was a cultural exile in England. And James Joyce—who wasn't *really* in exile (in the sense that he picked a quarrel with Ireland, and nobody actually forced him out)—nevertheless gave "silence, exile and cunning" as Stephen Dedalus's motto. Other examples abound. Nevertheless, one always gets the sense with exiles that they are trying to deal with material or experience that cannot be expressed. They are always at the limit of the articulate—at the limit of the intelligible. They become marginal beings. And in so doing become quintessentially modern. However, insofar as "the exiled voices" became the dominant figures of this century's literature, many of the literary historians of this period have romanticized exile for its so-called liberating qualities. Snow didn't agree with this view for a moment—even though he, in a sense, exiled himself from mainstream society and subsequently spent a life "caught" between classes. He was ever self-conscious of his place in society. He wished to escape his past, yet he never wanted anyone to forget the difficulties and significance of his progress. As Snow simply put it, among the "disadvantages of exile is that particular kind of unselfconsciousness [that allows you to be self-reliant] leaves you. That the things that in your natural habitat are as easy and as unthought about as breathing, suddenly have to be thought about. And so, one of the many disadvantages of exile is that you lose a degree of freedom, you lose a chance to be unselfconscious in places where you would normally be so."[43] Certainly, social and aesthetic exile did seem to give modernist writers a sense of exuberance—a freedom of a certain kind. But in the end it was always circumscribed by something that enabled them to look at others who did feel at home with a kind of resentment. This single, and ultimately depressing, element of exile is one with which Snow was concerned, as the "separateness" that such a sensibility implied can, in the end, only inhibit the communication of shared experiences. As Raymond Williams noted, a weakness of the literary exile stemmed from his or her tendency to separate "feeling" from "thought." This coterminously leads to the separation of the public and private spheres as well as of consciousness and the unconscious. But while this is an inevitable outcome in Williams's conception,[44] it is highly undesirable and avoidable in Snow's.

However, given all of the above, perhaps what is most problematic for Snow regarding experimental literature is not that it is experimental *per se* but rather that—given its hegemony over the creative or social sensibilities of the period—it represents and promotes a view of progress that is fatalistic and passive. This perception is ultimately corrosive. Nowhere is this better seen than in Snow's response to the popular modernist claim that "a work of art is irreducible." According to this notion, "a novel which is a work of art exists only as a structure of words, independent of the writer's intention. From the structure of words, the 'characters', 'scenes', must not be separated, for they have no meaning apart from the words. . . ."[45]

With one word—"silly"—Snow dismisses this view and in so doing begins to build his own alternative literary framework. This alternative was to be an aggressive realism in which the connections between past, present, and future were always evident—even in the face of modernity. His focus was on literature as a form and on science and politics as major forces of modernity. His voice always recognized the weight of modern times, but he nevertheless championed the individual as the ultimate shaper of change.

All of Snow's fiction is made up of stories that thread processes of connection between the past and the future. In his novels, not only do we find families, generations, and the recurrence of experience, but we encounter time and memory as crucial elements as well. Snow does not simply construct "the architecture and edifice" of our time, but he makes these themselves matters of speculation, as indeed has been done in a great deal of the major fiction of our temporally disoriented century.

But there is no doubt that Snow's *Strangers and Brothers* sequence is significant. It has made a bid to be regarded as one of the great documentary and recapitulative works of a century that is not so easily susceptible to documentation. Snow's realism has succeeded at a time when realism itself has hardly seemed possible. As such, Snow's edifice represents one of the more ambitious ventures of contemporary British fiction. From *Strangers and Brothers* (later renamed *George Passant*) in 1940 to *Last Things* in 1970, Snow told us a tale that reached across some sixty years of British social, political, strategic, scientific, intellectual, and emotional history. It was also a story of modern time and memory. It is in these terms that Snow's fiction is—as he insisted of other major fiction—reducible.

A work of art, and especially a literary work of art, "is, in almost every kind of way, reducible. . . . In fact, if one did not [reduce them] it would not be possible to discuss [such work] at all."[46] As the cases of Tolstoy, Balzac, and Trollope (to use Snow's preferred examples) illustrate, writing deliberately and unavoidably includes a discursive theory of history, and as such it cannot be treated as a self-sufficient verbal structure in any sense that has real semantic or social meaning. Snow's own *Strangers and Brothers* sequence of novels exemplifies this perfectly. Throughout the eleven novels, Snow is concerned with time and history, but not as a treadmill or *un roman fleuve* as in Anthony Powell's *A Dance to the Music of Time*. Snow's series traces the course of our modern era in a straightforward fashion. *Strangers and Brothers* deals with the period 1925–1933; *The Consciousness of the Rich* covers 1927–1936; *Time of Hope*, 1914–1933; *The Light and the Dark*, 1935–1943; *The Masters*, 1937; *Homecomings*, 1938–1948; *The New Men*, 1939–1946; *The Affair*, 1953–1954, *Corridors of Power*, 1955; *The Sleep of Reason*, the 1960s; *Last Things* concludes the series in the late 1960s. Although Snow may sometimes take the reader back in time, we always move forward—we are always moving toward the discovery of some larger insights into the nature of our era and ourselves.

Snow may have quarreled with modernism, but he greatly admired Proust. However, his admiration was less with the Proust of formal and aesthetic sensitivity than the Proust who could construct, through the operations of memory, the great social edifice of French life. He also admired the Proust who could pursue and develop his theme throughout a lifetime. But where Proust's is a fiction of consciousness, Snow's is a fiction of history—both public and private. His is the history of one man who constitutes the history of a culture. Memory is a mode of response and retrospect that links the origins and background to future events and possibilities and to the great changes of the modern world. As such, embedded in Snow's history is a tacit critique of modern civilization.

The sequence,[47] which closely parallels the life of Snow, takes the form of a biography of Lewis Eliot—later Sir Lewis Eliot (though unlike his creator, he never achieves a barony). He is the son of decent working-class people in the Midlands; his birthplace is recognizably Snow's Leicester, and his date of birth is around 1905. He enters a divided world—the nature of which is suggested by the book and series title, *Strangers and Brothers*. Eliot has a deep and intuitive understanding of his brother (Martin), and of two friends who stand in a kind of fraternal relationship to him. Others are strangers, external phenomena to be recorded and coolly observed. As the series develops, and as Snow himself gains more insight into the workings of the world, this basic relationship expands and comes to stand allegorically for the relationship between society—its institutions, motives, and customs—and the individual who, although a stranger in any technical sense, still shares the same ambitions, drives, and hopes, and experiences the same private experiences, as any other person. The recording and commenting side of Eliot is not all we are allowed to see of him. He is an emotional man, though he tries to keep his emotions under control. He suffers in his first marriage to a neurotic, upper-class wife who is likely to damage his career. He is dedicated to a brilliant scholar, Roy Calvert, who is manic-depressive. Death, tragically, ends both relationships: his wife commits suicide, while Calvert is killed in an RAF bombing raid over Germany. About the loss of Calvert (who was modeled on Snow's close Cambridge friend Charles Albury) Snow wrote with a particular bitterness—a bitterness echoed by many who lived through the war and who saw the loss of friends and promising individuals.

Eliot's career flourishes, and as an external lecturer in a Cambridge college, he comes into contact with the world of academic politics. With the outbreak of war, he temporarily becomes a civil servant to assist in the war effort. He meets the woman who is to become his second wife. Her father is a successful artist—a painter who is contemptuous of, or indifferent to, the attitudes of society. At this point in Snow's epic tale, one of the imponderable events against which the world of reason cannot legislate descends upon Eliot and his new wife. The illness of their first child suggests a spiteful revenge on them for having lived as lovers (defying social convention). But as the mysterious power of illness lifts, their relationship is left more firmly cemented than before.

Professionally involved in the relationship between science and government, and particularly in developing a nuclear deterrent for

Britain, Eliot shares the growing sense of horror of many of his scientific friends. He sees his brother give up a promising career in scientific research because of his opposition to atomic warfare. Eliot then enters into the "corridors of power" (to use a phrase coined by Snow) and examines the closed politics of decision-making committees. The passage of Sir Lewis through this high-level wonderland reveals to him a dark and inexplicable division in society.

On one of his returns to his boyhood town as a student's representative in a legal case before the University Court, Eliot and his own teenage son visit his father in the house in which Eliot grew up. But the old man's life seems untouched by the successes of his two sons. Eliot seems only to be able to observe his father's life as one might see a boat from a shore. But there is comforting nostalgia for Eliot as he is involved with a group of militant students, one of whom leads Eliot into a labyrinth of horror and murder through which he must pass, incapable of either influencing events or of resigning from them. Eliot is thus brought face-to-face with the limits of reason and control.

Snow's series ultimately comes to a conclusion—Eliot leaves politics, faces his relationships with his family, and confronts his own existence as well as his past as his heart stops for a number of minutes during an operation. Eliot examines his life's potential, his relationship with others, and life's meaning. He tries to do so without mercy, and in so trying, he achieves a sort of freedom that resonates throughout the series. Thus Snow's sequence is clearly a history of our time as told by an individual who holds all of the earmarks of our popular idea of a modern hero. Snow's chief character, Lewis Eliot, and those around him are scholars and professionals in those areas that affect us the most on a day-to-day basis. But more than this, the series is also a thoughtful examination of some of modernity's deepest themes. Rather than simply being a passive recitation of insignificant events, Snow injects an articulate and analytical mind into the scene, actively interpreting events both for himself and for his readers.

Often, Snow's Lewis Eliot is center stage. Occasionally, he is what Malcolm Bradbury has called a "wise ghost" lurking on the edge of others' lives, always ready with a thought, an observation, a solution or compromise.[48] He begins his journey through the pages of *Strangers and Brothers* in the streets of a lower-class provincial town (recognizable as Leicester), looking in on the lit and warm windows of real life. He ends it, in *Last Things*, only just surviving the novel and telling his tale with the raging impotence of old age. But in between, there can be no doubt that he is one of the most ubiquitous and prolific narrators, bringing us through twentieth-century British social history, and maintaining his own intimacy with many of the larger events and daily choices of the struggle of modernity. For example, in *The New Men* he is at the birth of the British atomic bomb; in *Corridors of Power* he is involved in the aftermath of the Suez Crisis; and in *The Sleep of Reason* he is involved in a court case closely resembling the Moors murder trial. Each of the eleven volumes in the series has its own distinct subject of concern, but the sequence is linked, not just by a common narrator but by a belief that this narrator is intimate with the very nature of our time, with our history—a history constructed not only out of Eliot's ascent through the social order but through the movement of a certain kind of decent, optimistic, rationalist mind toward preeminence in public and private affairs.

As Malcolm Bradbury has said, *Strangers and Brothers* is told like "a Victorian novel and written in much the spirit of a Wellsian one. Snow conducts the sequence in an efficient, almost timeless, prose which is highly discursive. The entire narrative clearly depends on a strong autobiographical content and a reportorial social attentiveness which acts as an invitation to look at the record." In many ways, Eliot seems to function "as a diarist for Snow himself while at the same time engaging in the fictional function of effective dramatic presence at the significant junctures of history. Indeed in some sense history must be that which is near to him as he must arrange to be near to history. As such, he is one of our larger men of history. The curves of both modern history and his life seem connected. The world is made for us to feel young and optimistic when he is; important and wise when he is; old and distant when he is."[49]

As the observant narrator, Lewis Eliot's manner is emotionally flat, often indifferent (his is not the world of fantasy or imagination), increasingly pompous, and finally irascible. He is a public man who has some sense of his own weaknesses, and the tale gives him some insight into both himself and his limitations. For the most part, he is without irony. He portrays a critical intelligence and yet seems to have a sense of decency in human affairs; however, this is somewhat ambiguous, for it is not simply a perspective but a social commodity that enables his success. His famous gift for compromise does tend to make him dull, but it also opens all doors to him. This is both socially and narratively convenient. He is in every sense a modern realist who has found his way to the places where reality does its daily work, in that realm he calls "the world"—meaning the public world of social life, power, political influence, and responsibility.

As many of his critics have pointed out, there is much to the real

world that is left out of Snow's world. But his world is presented in a
way that is so familiar that we think we know it already. It is presented to us with a low-key discursiveness that may leave much un-
said and a lot more unfelt—but how well we know it. This gives the
impression, as much as realism does, that it is all virtually uncon-
structed, that it partakes of the pure contingency of life. But the
truth is that it is *highly* constructed according to a clear rationality
and historiography.

Snow's tale is the story of the "new men," who have new ways of
thinking, who bear the radical wisdom and ethical anxieties of science as well as the liberal program whose task is not just research
and discovery, but reform and social amelioration. It is the story of
rational social development, the kind that a lot of scientific thinkers
during the 1920s and 1930s saw as being a real possibility: people
would make a decent and humane society out of their capacity to
mediate their own survival, and their own sanity. To Snow such
hope means freedom from limitation and possessiveness.

Snow's technical alternative to the radical modernist novel is
modern realism. Realism has always had the advantage of being at
home amid the social institutions of its day, and of operating necessarily both in the aesthetic realm as well as in the cognitive and political realms. Indeed, realism is often touted for its capacity to represent totality. In its pure form, realism is a strategy that seeks to
situate individuals within the entire historical dynamic of their society. Viewed from the perspective of participants, yet structured by
the omniscient historical understanding of the author, the best realism presents history as a process that is revealed in the specific—
but generalizable—logic and experience of groups and institutions.

Thus, modern literary realism can be a liberation and an emblem
of the richness of the world just as much as it can be a restriction or
a prison. As such, realism leads a double existence—working simultaneously inside literature and in the "real world" of the everyday.
Literary realism has no special vocabulary or syntax of ideas. No
style and technique is exclusively its own (although transparency of
language, style, and technique *is* something of a prerequisite). What
unites the two parallel realms of meaning is realism's representa-
tional quality. Literary realism designates more of a condition than
a content. It refers to both a way of thinking about the world and
a way of expressing it. Thus, it should not be surprising that modern realism works most effectively when it maintains the middle
ground between life and art. Indeed, it should not be surprising that
there is an area in which realism is most fully at home: where human relationships are formalized or protected against the caprice of

solipsism—in the social institutions of the age. The failure of the critics to recognize this has been problematic for the popular reception of Snow's literature. For the transparency of his prose has too often been mistaken for being a simple representation of life rather than an interpretive craft.

To the extent that realism has no contribution to make to a model of reality, Snow must be considered a neorealist having no consistent political line to advocate—now being subversive, now conservative. As we shall see in chapters 5 and 6, Snow's politics float along a continuum of postwar liberal thought that is tied to no political party or platform but that is relentlessly loyal to the radical scientific commitment to a redefinition of the self.[50] The object of Snow's aesthetic interest is unabashedly the real world. Its subtle intention is to instruct, while its objective is unashamedly to delight. It is thus no coincidence that when asked "what do we read novels for?" Snow answered unequivocally that we read them "for various kinds of pleasure."[51] (Ironically, Snow never allowed himself to see that such writers as Joyce could also be read for entertainment.)

But insofar as Snow qualifies as a realist or neorealist, his choice of subject does not represent the charming realism of the eighteenth and nineteenth centuries, as some have suggested (even though his form is clearly cast in those molds).[52] His is more a realism that aggressively attempts to reflect the totality of modern technological society. However, the selection of realism as an interpretive strategy is not unproblematic. Indeed, as Frederic Jameson has detailed, literary realism and literary modernism have long shared an opposition to each other. "The division of these two starkly antithetical tendencies (form-oriented versus content-oriented . . .) is dictated by the attempt to deal adequately with modernism" rather than the other way around. The disturbing element about transparent literary realism as a technique to approach something of a totality seems to be that whenever you search for "realism," it vanishes.

This is not surprising, as this is what realism does best. But what is more helpful is the observation that the strategy itself is highly ideological. It recognizes that the strategy is inseparable from the development of capitalism and the quantification of the market system, and that it is linked to the bourgeoisie as its product.[53] As a result, realism—and certainly Snow's realism—may be too closely tied to the interests of a decaying bureaucracy to be able to objectively critique those elements of modernity's social anomie and fragmentation. But what Jameson offers in realism's place is a narrative that avoids modern social content as a way of managing or containing it, of secluding it out of sight in the very form itself. Nevertheless, it is clear that the debate between literary realism and modernism loses its interest if one side is programmed to win in advance. To understand the struggle of modernity, we need both sides. We are, after all, inexorably children of tradition and modernity.

Numerous critics have heard Snow claim that his is a realism for "the post-atomic age" and have taken for granted that he had not moved beyond the bases upon which he attacked radical modernist literature. In other words, critics have assumed that his was a political utopia featuring a Heroic Age of science at its core. A more perceptive and helpful view would recognize the impact that the second scientific revolution of quantum mechanics and the atomic bomb had on Snow's thinking. As he stated on numerous occasions, the year 1945 represented a quantum leap for humanity to a new level of technology. Snow asks the obvious question: "Is the atomic age going to make things worse for Mankind and for novel-writing?" To this he answered:

I do not believe the worse is likely. . . . The bomb has staggered scientists with a moral shock from which the best and most sensitive will not easily recover. Up to 1945 the climate of science was optimistic. Now that unquestioning optimism has drained away from most of the scientists I know. Technology is successful, they feel. As for science, they do not go in for facile despair, but there is a weight on their brows. And that mood brings scientists and novelists closer together . . . and the new humility of the scientists has in turn given the novelist new confidence.[54]

In terms of the implications of this technological awareness on the novel, Snow showed himself to be both more aware and better equipped than others. To some extent paralleling the concerns raised by such social critics as Theodore Adorno and Walter Benjamin,[55] Snow acknowledged that in an advanced technological society we will "edge closer to the position where . . . private novels [are produced], with a readership of one, which alone are treated as Art [while] popular novelists give up the struggle for any glint of truth and get read in millions at the price of surrender to the mass media, . . . film and television. It is arguable that such a polarization is the fate of all art in an advanced technological society. [And if] it happens, and it may happen, we shall have committed cultural suicide."[56] But such a scenario is avoidable, in Snow's view, if we foster a novel form that "has its roots in society."[57] "The novels of the atomic age must mount "a new attack on the relations of men to their environment," which is the "highly articulated complex of our technological society."[58] Only then will we, and the novel, "breathe freely." Only then will a reconciliation between modernity's public and private selves be possible. But—as Joe Needham reminded Snow in 1934—to achieve this requires a clear-minded social-political outlook as well as a series of complementary critical and literary techniques. Together, these could promote an "active insight into the atomic age."[59]

Clearly, Snow had the necessary assembly of talents for this task. "Snow . . . augmented the traditional realism of the English novel—realism in the line of Trollope, Thackeray, George Eliot, Galsworthy, and Bennett—with the technical enrichments this century has brought to the novel. . . ."[60] Among these talents was an emphasis on direct experience, first-person narrative, psychological depth, and social extension. Together, these permitted Snow to link the private (cognitive and emotional) and the public (political) elements of the contemporary human condition. Thus, beyond the purely historical portrayal of time presented in Snow's sequence, Snow's prose draws considerable energy from the modern social setting of his fiction. Snow never forgets that novels, especially "serious" novels, have a primary purpose of gaining knowledge of other people as well as of ourselves.[61] As Pamela Hansford Johnson put it, the greatest realist (and here she includes Snow without reservation) "elucidates for man not only his neighbour but himself; by increasing the self-knowledge of the reader he changes him on the surface perhaps imperceptibly, but inwardly with a completeness."[62] In order to achieve this in his novels, Snow uses a device called "introspective insight" through which he seeks to link the worlds of life and literature. "The essence of introspective insight . . . is that at one and the same time one sees oneself with a total intimacy and at the same moment as though one were someone else."[63]

This technique is essential to Snow's literature, for it allows him to probe beneath the continuum of feeling and enquire about motivations, ambitions, moods, and actions. Although it is different than the introspection used by such realists as Tolstoy or Dostoevsky, Snow's technique for introspection achieves much the same effect; that is, it makes for a complex and enriching interaction between the individual personages and their complex social ranges.

Snow's plots are explicit and his language is conversational. Narration and dialogues are purposeful and external. Since, for Snow, human loneliness and death are two immutable realities, he rejects the interior monologues of much radical modernist writing. To Snow, a "psychic odyssey" (such as that found in Joyce's *Finnegans Wake*) is at best irrelevant, and at worst almost obscenely personal.

In contrast to this, Snow's world is always observable, and when the situation dictates that evidence or time cannot be present, he uses Proustian recall. But far from being a convenient trick of an unaccomplished author, it serves as a learning device for Lewis Eliot while providing an effective bond for the novels in the series. Snow's language is that of analysis and commentary. But to many, this feature represents a weakness of Snow's fiction. As an early critic of Snow's work has written, "Snow . . . wants to show man functioning in the larger world, not man praying or playing but man working and making, *homo faber;* and yet, he also wants to see why that particular man acts that way—what his motivation is, what his causal psychology is, what he really is. These ambitions should bring Snow back to the inner man in a much more profound way than he is willing to go. . . ."[64]

The themes in Snow's literature are science and politics. This in itself has necessitated the adoption of a decidedly "non-stream-of-consciousness" approach, for as Snow describes it, trying to express motivations or experiences in science through interior monologue "would result in the equivalent of a series of equations which were meaningful only to scientists. The problem would be a serious one of communication." Similarly, Snow claims that, stylistically, politics is both "easier and harder." While the communication problem is not the same (i.e., verbal symbolism) the complexity of power relationships between people in organized society is itself a technical problem. "One cannot write about politics without constant call on causal and introspective insight . . . so one cannot use a technique like stream-of-consciousness which [*de facto*] rules them out."[65] In verbalizing the relationship between power networks and social settings, Snow argues that "one needs every aid within the writer's power to dissolve or disguise the complications. . . . There is no single aid so useful as the reflective intelligence."[66]

However, the themes of science and politics of which Snow writes are only his "thematic epidermis"—the more obvious skin of his literature. They provide the vehicles, in effect, for his realist interests. As he says, from the beginning he knew approximately the deeper themes he was going to write novels about. "[The] position seemed to me something like this: I was interested in the individual human condition and the social condition. I was interested in the power relations of men, and the progress of individual lives in time: and I wanted to show that such human beings, no better, no worse than they are, are all we have to make society of."[67]

In order to try to achieve the artful balance between the self and society; between the competing claims of individuals and groups;

and between the action and backgrounds that have in fact defined the modern condition, Snow wrote directly of those areas in which literary realism has always felt at home—that is, in the social institutions of our time. But so common is our experience of the dehumanization and bureaucratization of institutions that we have largely lost our understanding of their *raison d'être* and what realists have sometimes called "their charm." Throughout nineteenth-century realist fiction, for example, the stock exchange, government offices, municipal administration, Church, and army most often served as the background to individual action. Such writing thus embraced the claim of early sociologists that the individual self, in any living sense, was inextricably involved in a social whole. They were establishing a unity and a truth that realism—including Snow's realism—has never ceased to take for granted. Thus, by focusing on the twentieth-century university, government office, law office, and research lab—all against the backdrop of recognizably contemporary events—Snow's fiction is classical in literary terms and modern in its selection of social sites. His settings are all identifiable, familiar, and symbolically charged.

But of all the elements of Snow's literature, it is his use and development of character that truly define him. Indeed, as Pamela Hansford Johnson wrote in the year of their marriage, "Character in Mr. Snow's novels is by far the most important element, and he allows nothing to obscure this."[68] Like his settings, Snow's characters are all familiar, and almost all are cast in professional roles: lawyers, professors, clerics, scientists, politicians, industrialists, and physicians. Snow was thereby able to unobtrusively examine—by necessity—tensions felt within modernity by juxtaposing professional norms or values with issues relating to responsibility, power, and ethics, as well as tensions arising from conflicts in self-definition. The actions of Snow's characters clearly establish them as members of both formal and informal groups filling a variety of roles ranging from leaders and group members to individuals. But if taken in a narrow view, Snow's characters could be criticized for representing only the technocrats and the intelligentsia. However, the problems of both society and the individual are so powerfully conceived of and animated in these professions and sites that making them partially transparent can be—and is, in the case of Snow—highly rewarding.

The unifying techniques and themes of Snow's *Strangers and Brothers* series are at least partially realized through repetition and parallel action. This can be seen in his treatment of the major theme of politics. *Strangers and Brothers*, like *The Sleep of Reason*, begins with legal hearings and ends with trials. *The Affair* is an academic hearing in the same setting throughout as *The Masters*, which also is concerned with a heated election. Elections also occur in *The Light and The Dark, Homecomings* (Gilbey's demise and the rejection of George Passant's permanent civil-service status) and *Corridors of Power*. Although these elections all take different forms, they all require some form of voting, decision making, or similar political activity. There is, as in all the novels, a great deal of formal and informal dining, walking in parks or by rivers, *tête-à-tête*, and caucusing. The same characters weave in and out of the series. George Passant, for example, who is seen as an ebullient idealist in the opening book, is seen as spent and debauched in *The Sleep of Reason* at the end of the series.

Although one of the major themes—that of science—occurs throughout the *Strangers and Brothers* sequence, in (for example) *The New Men* and *The Masters*, nowhere is it presented more effectively than in *The Search*—a volume that precedes, and that is not included in, the sequence of novels. The book is about the struggles, disappointments, and successes of a young scientist. It is largely autobiographical and presents a foreshadowing of the style and technique that sustain *Strangers and Brothers*. The novel concerns Arthur Miles, a scientist who searches for an understanding of himself, of his relationship with others, and of the conflicts that arise when the ideals of science—those by which he has organized his life—seemed to be betrayed. It is in some ways curious that the successful character of Arthur Miles—a scientist—was abandoned by Snow in favor of the lawyer, Lewis Eliot. Snow had no background in law but clearly understood scientific research. Upon careful consideration, however, it can be seen that Miles was in effect too close to Snow's own persona—so close, in fact, that Snow's artistic range would have been severely restricted had the Miles character been continued as the basis for a series. Snow himself understood this and noted that, despite the high praise for *The Search*, it was "a false start."[69] However, by adapting a profession of which Snow didn't know the details, he was able to get at his concerns in a much less encumbered way.

Much has been made of the autobiographical character of the Snow novels. But rather than detract, Snow's close observation of individuals who are intimate actors in the corridors of power has only lent greater credibility to Snow's exercise. Never does the character portrait become so photographic that art gives way to journalism. But the list of "models" that Snow used is most interesting. Many of Snow's friends at Cambridge served for the principal, partial, or composite sketches of his fictional characters, as did some writers, industrialists, and politicians. Among the scientists were G. H. Hardy, J. D. Bernal, and Frank Bowden; among the academics were Sir J. H. Plumb and Herbert Howard; the writer William Gerhardi and the First Lord Beaverbrook were also among Snow's models.

In addition to the characters themselves, Snow cast quite a number of predictable modern types. For example, Horace Timberlake is a 1930s industrial philanthropist whom Chrystal successfully courts on behalf of the college. Lufkin, the wartime industrialist, is Snow's midcentury millionaire, capitalizing largely on the wartime situation to gain from military-related contracts. The gregarious Schiff represents financial success during the 1960s, largely through international portfolio management. There are academic types as well: the paternalistic Brown, the aloof and assured Crawford, the scholarly elitist Gay, the unpopular G. S. Clark; the out of touch Shaw; and the opportunistic Lester Ince. Although an atheist, Snow also included a number of clergymen: Lawrence Knight is the country parson; Ralph Udal is a scholar-minister looking for a good living; Despard-Smith is the resident theologian in Cambridge—a bitter, old man; and finally, there is the socially involved Godfrey Ailwyn. While the clergymen are not reprehensible, they are certainly lacking in convincing religious faith. Contrary to the dominant criticism, Snow's characters do mature, and their attitudes (whether or not they are in tune with the times) clearly signal an evolving history as they come to grips continually with the various challenges of our highly organized technological society. Given that Snow's novels fully realize more than forty characters, this is in itself a considerable achievement.

These types are animated directly by Snow's use of a first-person narrator. Throughout the *Strangers and Brothers* series of novels, this narrator is Lewis Eliot. Eliot appears in eight of the novels as the camera eye and in three as the autobiographical first person. Through this narrator device, Snow has effectively chosen to subject his characters to direct observation and analysis. Thus, it is the job of the narrator not only to act himself but to interpret the psyche as it manifests itself in external action. This technique has been identified as a "more social, objective and public approach to character"[70] and thus is Snow's attempt to address what Lukacs highlighted as the central aesthetic problem of realism: to provide an adequate presentation of the complete human personality in a work of art. However, there have been criticisms of Snow's first-person narrative. Bernard Bergonzi sees Snow as failing in both his roles as observer and autobiographer.

With the camera eye method the narrator has to see and record everything important that happens: if he is describing a small and enclosed world this need not present any difficulties, but the larger and more varied the society, the greater the danger of manifest contrivance on the author's part in order to have his narrator in the right place at the right time. With the autobiographical method, where the narrator is much more at one with what he writes about, this difficulty may not arise: unable to describe naturally and convincingly his own deepest emotional experiences.[71]

In the observer, or camera-eye, novels, Bergonzi finds it remarkable that—as in *The New Men*—Eliot is privy to so much information in so many locations. He also finds it extraordinary, for example, that the senior Mr. March would make Eliot such a confidant. To Bergonzi, this is simply not convincing. However, perhaps Bergonzi has paid Snow a great compliment without realizing it, for he has confused the reflection of the thing with the thing itself: he writes as if Eliot were controlling himself and does not consider manipulation or re-creation by the author.

Other critics of Snow have also noted his use of the first-person narrator, but one—Helen Gardner—inadvertently highlighted the core element of Snow's literary realism. In making the case that Eliot's world was "grey and drab," she also highlighted the point that one of the reasons Snow's novels can be so readable and have so much to say about the contemporary scene is that he presents a "hero of our time . . . one of the indisputable men of the twentieth century . . . a born administrator . . . successful and important, but not, of course, famous."[72] For Snow, true heroism exists not in the salient moments of history but in the minute and mundane decisions made by everyone on a daily basis. Moreover, if Ms. Gardner finds Snow's world grey and drab, perhaps it is because—to so many people—the world *is* grey and drab.

It is through an expression of what some would call "intelligence" or what Snow would call "reason" that many of the anxieties of modernity can begin to be dealt with on a personal level. The point for Snow is not that the narrator should announce the truth as though he knew it all along. It is far more important that the narrator (in the case of the novels) and individuals (in direct social contexts) should become sensitized to the experience of thinking about a problem. Thus, a narrator can become directly involved in the process of discovering. Snow does this in a back-and-forth movement of reporting and reflection, an ongoing dialogue between the self and society, between the text and the world. As we shall see, this element of praxis is a particularly important one for establishing Snow critically within a modern context. Indeed, his typical characterization conforms more to a definition of character as that which defines itself by *what* it thinks and what it thinks *about.*

In Snow's series of novels, planned to cover more than half a century of English life, he created one of the most remarkable series of portraits of our time. Character and understanding for Snow are both to be discovered directly through a process of living. What he does through his fiction is try to express all of these qualities in a coherent whole reflecting his views and interests in science, politics, and the modern age. The artistic design *Strangers and Brothers* suggests a resonance between its constituent parts and the whole. The techniques, plot, language, themes, sites, and characters all strive to convey this unity—this paramount interest in the self—through the intermediary of a narrator who is always involved in the action. "The inner design consists of a resonance between what Lewis Eliot sees and what he feels."[73] Snow's art is a direct daylight art. The transparency of his fiction permits the reader a glimpse into the major institutions that make our society work. The active intelligence of the narrator encourages us to think for ourselves, to actively seek our individual totalities, and to become our own New Men. His work appeals directly through the mind and less through the senses. In order to understand the role and form that reason takes in Snow's struggle of modernity, it is crucial to grasp the breadth of his realism. This is the subject of the next chapters.

5

THE UNNEUTRALITY OF SCIENCE

El sueño de la razón produce monstruos.
(The sleep of reason brings forth monsters.)
—FRANCESCO JOSÉ DE GOYA [1]

THAT THERE IS a direct relationship between Snow's conception of reason, his philosophy of science, and the radical High Science he was to find at Cambridge is clear. Indeed, the case can be made at several levels that it was science, as one of modernity's most powerful driving forces, that ultimately provided Snow with many of his basic values and insights, which were to inform his own search for totality and balance in modern life. Ironically it was also his Cambridge science experience that was to mark Snow as something of a perennial outsider; the angst it resulted in was to initiate and enforce his need to search for totality. Snow's status as a provincial lad at an elitist university, as a doctoral student near to—but not in—the great labs, as a rather mediocre researcher and teacher in a profession where only brilliance counted, and as a writer among scientists all contributed to his alienation as an individual. Nevertheless, science, scientists, and rationally thinking individuals were all critical features of Snow's personal and literary attempts to reconcile the public and private spheres, strongly attesting to the importance of his Cambridge science experience. Examples abound.

As I will discuss at some length in this chapter, it was science that gave Snow his earliest sense of intellectual power and excitement. At the same time, it was science that gave him his first model or stereotype of "social greatness" and of the trappings that science and society could confer on an individual. Later, it was science that provided the vehicle through which Snow could defy traditional class barriers of English society and leave provincial Leicester by taking a higher education, going to Cambridge University as a student, Fellow and Tutor, and becoming a member of the bureaucracy in metropolitan London. It was the rigor and social cohesion of scientific research at a time of social turmoil and political collapse that was to imbue Snow with an acute sense of what a more stable democratic structure based on science could look like. It was through his involvement with the left-wing political factions of the 1930s scientific community that Snow gained a liberal, if somewhat utopian, view of the social function of science. Thus it can hardly be said to be an overstatement to assert that science is a pivotal element to any understanding of Snow. However, in so saying, we also raise important questions about scientific knowledge and Snow's position as a scientific realist. Did Snow believe in the immutability of "scientific facts," in their status as value-free and absolute truths, or in the evitability of scientific progress?[2] Such might be asserted if one were to read his Rede Lecture as being a simple expression of scientism,[3] or if one were to read Snow's *The Physicists: The Generation That Changed the World* as an uncritical tribute to that profession. Such readings, however, would badly underestimate Snow's complex perspective.

While there is no clear correlation between literary and scientific realism, it can be said that both perspectives share an aversion to absolute or dogmatic positions and a preference for "transparent" or apparently nonintrusive methods. And yet "realist" perspectives are highly constructed. Strictly speaking, typical representations of scientific realism can be thought of as follows:[4] the descriptive terms of a scientific theory typically refer to objects, quantities, and so on in the external world; and theoretical statements are true if what they state about these objects and quantities is in fact the case. "When the scientific realist claims that theoretical terms "refer," he or she means that the terms in question refer in a straightforward, literal sense. For example, terms like *electron, positron,* and *quark* refer, according to the realist, to existent subatomic particles with certain mass, charge, and spin. This is in contrast to the position taken by the more extreme forms of empiricism, such as positivism."[5] In a sense, scientific realists never know if a scientific theory is true. However, their philosophy is the only philosophy that does not make the sheer success of modern science seem to be a miracle. As John Forge has outlined:

> One function that is fulfilled by theories, and which was largely overlooked by traditional positivists, is the prediction of previously unknown phenomenon, such as the prediction of the positron by Dirac's theory of the electron. That novel predictions should fall out from theories interpreted as merely economic bases for generating statements describing previously known

phenomenon is indeed, seemingly, miraculous. However, if theories are taken to describe actual regularities in the world it is quite conceivable for these to become manifest in hitherto unknown and unforeseen ways. Also, reference to these regularities can explain more mundane and everyday predictive successes. So argues the scientific realist.[6]

Thus realists are only rarely sceptics when it comes to science. They believe that science does describe the natural world rather accurately. They agree that it might be otherwise—that their theories may be false. But this openness serves primarily to underline the significance of the successes they attribute to science rather than dismantle it.[7]

However, as Roy Bhaskar points out in his *Scientific Realism and Human Emancipation*,[8] there are many grades of scientific realism, and the attributes just outlined tend to define tenets of a "strong" realism.[9] The realist program that most closely describes Snow can best be thought of as being a modification of this. As I will argue, while Snow clearly did believe in the independent existence of the natural world, he also came to fundamentally understand that scientific theories were mental constructions. As such, they might be (and probably were in any deeply meaningful sense) false. Thus for Snow, "truth" was a metaphysical concept that bore no meaning in absolute terms. Indeed, to try to impose truth claims on science or on the social world seemed to Snow to be vaguely absurd. By relieving the burden of pursuing such a notion, Snow was freed to respect science as an activity that was uniquely successful in its ability to advance and bring with it "progress," through a combination of mental work, social organization, and collaboration. This modified version of scientific realism then defines what Snow would have viewed as being the kernel of the "scientific method." Science, in these terms, outlined what Snow would have called "reason."

In many ways, Snow's conception of reason actually previewed what was to become a dominant view of scientific change in the modern philosophy of science. This view, which is most cogently forwarded by Thomas Kuhn in his 1963 classic, *The Structure of Scientific Revolutions*, outlined the close linkage that exists between cognitive and social factors in the development of scientific theories. In Snow's language (which is evident as early as 1938 in *Discovery*, as well as in *The Two Cultures, Science and Government*, and *Public Affairs*) the excitement of a second scientific revolution—in this instance, the major scientific revision of electronic structure proposed by Schrödinger, Dirac, Pauling, and Heisenberg—was to be found in the resolution of anomalies and puzzles that were developing in the early years of the century's normal science. In Kuhn's terms, a field of science is cognitively dominated by "paradigms" that are accepted, almost without question, by the scientists working in that area. These paradigms are jealously guarded, socially protected, and passed on to the next generation of students through teaching and research supervision. The core element of this paradigm is a well-established and seemingly comprehensive theory or set of theories. Closely associated with this set of theories are research methods and problem-solving techniques. Most research is directed toward investigating "puzzles" that can be identified but not fully explained within the dominant theoretical framework. As the research advances, however, various "anomalies" become evident. The revolution in physics and chemistry around atomic structure was one frontier that Snow was not only aware of and excited about and had explained in Kuhnian terms; it was also cognitively and socially important to him. In the course of these puzzle-solving activities, some anomalies are resolved, while others undergo a cancerous growth that threatens the integrity of the paradigm itself. Eventually a rethinking, or gestalt shift, shows that the data can be reinterpreted in terms of a rival theory, the acceptance of which creates a new dominant paradigm that embraces the facts in a more comprehensive manner. A new "normal" science is born. Kuhn has acknowledged that the language he used in the second scientific revolution was openly discussed in the 1930s,[10] and thus it is no surprise that such "Kuhnian" terms as "revolution," "paradigm," "puzzle," and "anomaly" are found regularly in Snow's writings.

In very general terms, Snow clearly recognized his debt to science and to the radical scientists at Cambridge, as indeed much of his literary output directly attests. Recall, for example, the central place that Snow gave to the "scientific revolution" in his Rede Lecture and the relationship between science and government in his Godkin Lecture; or note the pivotal role that scientists play in ten of his seventeen novels;[11] or simply take heed of the sentiment he expressed throughout his last book, which was a tribute to physicists.

However, to move beyond this superficial recognition of the importance of science in Snow's life and to arrive at a clearer understanding of the exact nature of this influence is not, in itself, unproblematic. The principal reason for this is the existence of an obfuscating mythology concerning Snow that uncritically accepted that, as a scientist, Snow was at the very center of what he fondly called the "Elizabethan Age of Science"; that Snow was a physicist who worked at the Cavendish Labs under Rutherford; and that Snow was a member of Cambridge's scientific inner circle, the Kapitza Club.[12] To be sure, these are images that were fostered by Snow himself. But the net result has been that Snow's scientific career has itself been made "golden" by uncritical readers, with a subsequent authority being conferred on Snow and all he wrote. Remarkably little attention has been paid either to the accuracy of these images and their importance for Snow's thinking or to the quality of Snow's own scientific research.[13]

More accurate, but still only partially understood, images have Snow as a member of the "Visible College" made up of Hardy, Bernal, Blackett, and Julian Huxley, which concerned itself with politics and the modern social function of science; as a cofounder, with Bernal, of the Science of Science Society that operates today as the International Science Policy Foundation; and as an occasional member of the London-based "Tots and Quots" dining club convened by Sir Solly Zuckerman to discuss government science policy.[14]

Clearly, Snow was deeply influenced by individuals within both the radical and reformist factions of the Visible College, notably Bernal, Hardy, and Huxley. Equally clearly, Snow shared many of the same concerns and intellectual outlooks. For example, his expression during his Rede Lecture of the benefits of the second scientific revolution that included food, health, and automation exactly echoed the arguments of Bernal's 1939 *Social Function of Science*. At the same time, his insistence on creating change from within social institutions is a view that is very much at the heart of the reformist's credo. And furthermore, his disagreement and debates with the Republic of Science school—particularly with distinguished X-ray crystallographer and philosopher Michael Polanyi,[15] who fervently argued on behalf of the objectivity and social neutrality of science, and the government of science by scientists only—clearly aligned Snow with both elements of the 1920s and 1930s "social relations of science movement."

But beyond this, what were Snow's views on science, scientific knowledge, and the scientific community? In Snow's view, what should the role of science in social change and government be? And how did he link scientific knowledge and social responsibility? Clarifying these questions is the purpose of the present chapter.

It was in 1914, at the age of nine, that Snow experienced the intellectual spark that was to drive his life: science. In his words, it was "the first excitement that knowledge gives."[16] Indeed, the young Snow was indirectly coming into contact with the first phase of the second scientific revolution that is often associated with Thompson's atomic model (1900), Einstein's papers on relativity (1902–1905), Rutherford's discovery of the atomic nucleus (1900–1911) and Bohr's model of the atom (1912). This was a profoundly private experience for the young Snow, as it injected him with a clear sense both of individuality and of contact with an unfolding, exciting world. This was a potent combination that Snow would never forget or separate.

The world into which Snow stumbled as a boy was a world of profound revolution. He recorded his recollection as follows:

> I had got hold of a bound volume of Arthur Mee's *Children's Encyclopedia*. It was a dark afternoon and I was sitting by the fire. Suddenly, for the first time, I ran across an account of how atoms were supposed to be built up. The article had been written before Rutherford had discovered the nucleus, although by the time I read it the nuclear atom must have been well known. However I was innocent of all that, I had never seen the word "atom" before; this article explained that its descriptions were only a guess, that no man knew the truth, and yet it seemed to open up a new sight of the world.[17]

For Snow this article, which was in a section called *The Child's Book of Wonder*, crystallized what would lastingly become his core understanding of "rationality" or "reason" by saying that "though so much of [the descriptions in] that article could not endure, it gave me the first sharp mental excitement I ever had. Somehow it gave me the heightened sense of [both] thinking and imagining at the same time."[18]

The Snow household was filled with a wide range of books and periodicals,[19] and it was the early exposure to science that was to most stimulate Snow. But Snow's childhood interest in science was not solely the result of private "book learning." It was also strongly encouraged by his father. Though not in any way trained in science, William Edward Snow took his son's interest in science seriously. Acting partially out of a late-Victorian belief in "self-help" and partly out of a deeply hierarchial understanding of Britain's classed society, "W. E. Snow, Fellow of the Royal College of Organists," was able to keep Charles's spark alive by helping him build small cardboard telescopes and by talking of the "great men" who had studied and advanced science—the names of Newton and Priestley were often whispered into Snow's young ear. Snow alluded to this in his highly autobiographical novel *The Search* (1934), which opens with the young hero, Arthur Miles, stating:

It must have been a Sunday night, for my father and I were walking. . . . This particular Sunday night was warm and twilight . . .
the sun had just gone down behind the river, and—in the yellow
sunset sky there was a sickle of new moon, and high over our
heads a sprinkling of stars just coming dimly out. We stopped
and looked. My father said: "I wonder if they're what we think
they are? Stars! Stars like this!" He waved vaguely. "People think
we know about them. I wonder if we do." I gazed up at him. "I
wonder if we *can*," he added. I didn't know what he was thinking. All of a sudden I felt that all the things around me were toys
to handle and control, that I had the power in a tiny, easy
world. . . . The night had taken hold of me. I wanted to do something with those stars. I did not know what, but I was elated.
Their beauty stirred me, but it was not only that. . . . "I'm going
to find out all about them." . . . "Perhaps you will," [Snow's fa-
ther] reflected. We began to walk home. "A lot of people have
tried, you know," he said doubtfully. "Sir Isaac Newton—and Sir
Robert Ball—and Sir William Herschel—and Sir Oliver Lodge . . .
Very great men."[20]

As Snow continued to read all that he could on science, that first
sense of creativity, imagination, and power continued to be fanned
as images of what it meant to be a scientist—of what it meant to be
a "great man" and of what "progress" meant—began to take shape.
He began to look forward to his introduction to formal school
science.

This was to come at the Alderman Newton School for Boys, the
buildings of which are still standing in Peacock Lanes, Leicester.
Snow attended as a student until 1921 and later as a lab assistant
until 1924.[21] However, Snow's first exposure to "school science"
proved to be, as is often the case today for far too many students, a
dulling and unexhilarating affair.

I had looked forward to my first day of science lessons; and when
they came I was puzzled and disappointed. . . . When I saw [the
chief science master], I was not sure whether it could be he.
Even to a boy, eager to be impressed, he was not an impressive
man. . . . He taught us in an indifferent, uninteresting way; during that lesson, and the rest of the term, we did nothing but
stand in the laboratory and heat little pieces of wood and similar
things, and tiny portions of powders from bottles on the benches,
in tubes. . . . He told us to notice what happened. . . . I studied
the tubes very carefully. For the first few months I still thought I

must be missing something. This business couldn't be as point-
less as it seemed. But no one explained what I was doing. It just
became a drill, like any other drill, one of those inexplicable
pieces of school routine, a good deal less interesting than the
French verbs I was beginning to learn in the lesson before we
went to the laboratory. School "science," I decided, was something quite different from my own exciting private science, my
world of space and stars.[22]

Indeed, the apparent teaching strategy for science (which continues
to hold considerable sway) gave Snow a severe distaste that was to
stay with him throughout his life and that was, in part, to lead to the
criticisms he leveled against education in the Rede Lecture. As he
wrote, the dominant educational philosophy stated that if "you
want to interest your pupils, you can put them in the position of the
original discoverer. Put them in the position of the discoverer! The
pedagogic nonsense of it all! When you think of the chances and
stumbling, the flashes of insight and the sheer mistakes, that have
gone into every discovery since science began!"[23] Nevertheless, despite the contradictions that Snow met between his private science
and school science, he was able to keep his interest, hope, and ambition alive.

Snow was a bright, all-around student. He achieved an average
grade of 508 out of a possible 560—the lost marks being in wood-
work and gymnastics. His basic intelligence and temperament were
sufficient to put him on the first-class honors list when he took the
school's 1921 Oxford Senior Local Examinations[24] in English, history, geography, French, mathematics, religious knowledge, and
chemistry. He achieved a distinction in physics.[25]

In order to have achieved this, Snow's experiences in taught science were clearly not always disappointing. At one point during his
middle years at Alderman Newton, his usual routine in science class
was disrupted in such a way that it finally matched the private science he had been cultivating on his own:

"We're not going into the laboratory this morning," [the science
master] said. "I'm going to talk to you, my friends. . . . Forget
everything you know, will you? That is, if you know anything at
all." He sat on his desk swinging his legs. "Now, what do you
think all the stuff in the world is made of? Every bit of us, you
and me, the chairs in this room, the air, everything. No one
knows? Well perhaps that's not surprising, even for nincompoops

like you. Because no one did a year or two ago. But we're beginning to think we do.[26]

If you took a piece of lead and halved it, and halved the half,
and went on like that, where do you think you'd come to in the
end? Do you think it would be lead for ever? Do you think you
could go down right to the infinitely small and still have tiny
pieces of lead? It doesn't matter what you think. My friends, you
couldn't. If you went on long enough, you'd come to an atom of
lead, an atom, do you hear, an atom, and if you split that up you
wouldn't have lead any more. What do you think you'd have?
The answer to that one is one of the oddest things you'll ever
hear in your life. If you split up an atom of lead, you'd get pieces
of positive and negative electricity. That is all matter is. That's
all you are. Just positive and negative electricity. . . .[27]

And whether you started with lead or anything else it wouldn't
matter. That's all you'd come to in the end. Positive and negative
electricity. How do things differ then? Well, the atoms are positive and negative electricity and they're all made on the same
pattern, but they vary amongst themselves, do you see? Every
atom has a bit of positive electricity in the middle of it—the
nucleus, they call it—and every atom has bits of negative electricity going round the nucleus—like planets round the sun. But
the nucleus is bigger in lead than it is in carbon, and there are
more bits of negative electricity in some atoms than others. It's
as though you had different solar systems, made from the same
sort of materials, some with bigger suns than others, some with
more planets. That's all the difference. That's where a diamond's
different from a bit of lead. That's the bottom of the whole of
this world of ours.[28]

That morning's lecture provided all the added impetus that Snow
needed. From that moment on, he was able to direct his energies
through more clearly distinguished institutional paths.[29]

With his formal education completed at the age of sixteen, Snow
remained at the school for three more years (1922–1924) as the
school's laboratory assistant. This was taken up subsequent to a suggestion made by H. E. "Bert" Howard, who had joined the Alderman
Newton staff in 1922.[30] As Howard made clear to Snow, by staying
on at the school in this capacity, he would be able to prepare himself
for the Intermediate British School Certificate (IBSC), which was
then a prerequisite for admission into the external science degree
program of London University. This seemed, to Snow, a most appro-

priate thing to do, for although he knew from a very young age—certainly before age sixteen—that he wanted to be a writer, he was pragmatic enough to realize that science would give him "a nice way to earn a living."[31] "It was [both] the easiest way to a more congenial life, for a time," and the way to escape "the discontented life" of Leicester.[32] Thus the timing of Howard's suggestion was fortuitous as, prior to 1921, there was no opportunity for a university education in Leicester.

These extra years at the school clearly were not easy for Snow as he was growing impatient to leave Leicester and get on with a career. Howard was influential, however, and Snow stayed. The time was made more tolerable by late-night chess games, cafés, long discussions of literature (Snow read and reread Dostoevsky, Tolstoy, Proust, Balzac, and Wells), and considerations of what the future would hold for a provincial lad with a science education. This time was well spent and passed quickly for Snow.

In 1921, however, as a memorial to those from Leicestershire who had died in the war, a university college was opened in Leicester in the disused Leicestershire and Rutland County Lunatic Asylum. The syllabus and examinations of the college were set by London University.[33] In 1925, Snow was awarded a scholarship on the basis of good IBSC examination results and was thus able to complete a general B.Sc. However, given that the college only appointed its first physical science lecturers in March 1925, Snow, in effect, had to complete the majority of his degree work alone. He was examined on the subjects of mathematics, chemistry, and physics but received little tutoring from the faculty.

The two new lecturers in Leicester were Louis Hunter, who was a hydrogen bond specialist and who was appointed to teach chemistry, and Alexander "Sandy" Menzies, a spectroscopist who was appointed to teach physics.[34] After his years of studying and working as a lab assistant, Snow now was keen to pursue research, and so neither Hunter nor Menzies had much difficulty in convincing him to stay on for the additional two years in order to take his Honors B.Sc. in chemistry. In making this commitment, both Hunter and Menzies were well aware of Snow's reputation as a lab assistant. As the science master at Alderman Newton had warned, Snow's idea of dismantling equipment after a lesson was to open a top drawer just below the equipment and, stretching his arms all around the apparatus, sweep it into the awaiting drawer. Thus Snow had, at an early age, become renowned for his lack of ability in practical experimental matters.[35] Consequently, Hunter was to reminisce that Snow had been one of the worst students of experimental chemistry he had ever met. Further evidence of this deficiency is provided by Snow's brother, Philip, who wrote that Snow's "slender fingers and flipper-like hands could not assemble equipment. An external examiner for London University told me that he had marked an experiment by students who had to prepare a dye stuff, malachite green, from supplied chemicals. It was normal, at the end of the experiment, for hands and fingers of all the students to be covered with the dye: Charles managed to emerge distinctively with the addition of a green face and green hair."[36] But despite this weakness in experimental chemistry, Snow succeeded in taking a first-class chemistry degree from London University in 1927 as an external student.[37]

Following this, Menzies, one of the first physicists in Britain to take up Raman spectroscopy in 1928,[38] convinced Snow to specialize in spectroscopy, which was then one of twelve M.Sc. subjects that London University allowed external students to study for. As Menzies's very first research student, Snow studied the Raman effect and investigated the absorption of light by molecular films of cinnamic acid, as well as their absorption spectra and chemical constitution.[39]

Although Snow received no honors for his work—due, according to both Menzies and the historian W. H. Brock, to the fact that he was the only external M.Sc. candidate in all of England in that year—he did receive his M.Sc. in 1928. Out of this work came the first of Snow's more than twenty published scientific papers: "Band Spectra of Molecules without Unused Valency Electrons" (1928) and "The Relation between Raman Lines and Infrared Bands" (1929),[40] this latter article serving as an important bridge for Snow between Leicester (and his work with Menzies) and his new research at Cambridge.[41] London University examiners awarded Snow a Keddey Fletcher-Warr Studentship worth the substantial sum of £200 per year for each of three years (1928–1930) so that he might pursue further research. Snow's chance to leave Leicester had come. However, the studentship was normally tenable only at London University. Menzies (who had been a Fellow of Christ's College, Cambridge) argued to the examining board that Snow should be allowed to continue his research in spectroscopy and that the best place for this was not London but the Department of Physical Chemistry at Cambridge. Once the London committee had acquiesced to this idea, Menzies then had to convince the Fellows of Christ's College of this idea. This was not an easy matter because of the lateness of Snow's application and the nature of the request. Both caused a small row among the Fellows. Nevertheless, in the final analysis Snow's application was accepted, and he went up to Cambridge as a research student in October 1928.[42]

From this it is clear that Snow's exposure to Cambridge's legendary "corridors of scientific power" owes just as much, if not more, to Sandy Menzies as it did to Snow's own intellectual abilities and hard work. Although Snow was finally on the verge of realizing the dreams that he and Bert Howard had put in place and worked toward, he was also permanently leaving behind both his childhood era of private science and his provincial class status. A new and foreign world awaited.

It was with a sense of warmth, awe, and impending power that Snow entered prestigious Cambridge University in pursuit of what was then the rare Ph.D. in physical chemistry. The awe with which Snow did so was genuine. Literally overnight, he had left his provincial middle-class world, which he understood and which largely defined his sense of self and security, for the privileged and elitist world of Cambridge. In so doing he established himself as an outsider. He had also gone from a world in which there was little in the way of research or tutoring into an institution that had, by all accounts, one of the highest concentrations of research in physics and chemistry. In addition, here was the research, and the researchers, of which Snow had been reading as a boy. Indeed it was here, in Snow's own areas of atomic and molecular structure, that research would alter the very nature of our understanding of ourselves and the world around us. As Snow later came to realize, the discovery of the atom finally put an end to the scientists' "affectation" of separating human concerns from scientific truth.[43] Evidence of the juxtaposition to the private science of his early years was now all around Snow as the names and voices of Sir J. J. Thompson, Lord Ernest Rutherford, Professor Peter Kapitza, J. D. Bernal, P. M. S. Blackett, John Cockcroft, James Chadwick, and Paul Dirac all could be heard in the courtyards! Great names and exciting ideas! "It was, perhaps, the most brilliant period in Cambridge intellectual history. When you think of the people who are about . . ."[44] Indeed, when Snow later associated the second scientific revolution with the year 1925, he was not making an outlandish claim. While we often think of the Einstein papers (1905), the Bohr model of the atom (1910), and the Rutherford model (1912) as signifying the dawn of modern science, Snow's perception very accurately aligns with a number of powerful breakthroughs. In 1923, for example, the Compton effect was discovered, as was the "de Broglie wavelength." But more importantly, the theory of quantum mechanics was introduced in 1925 with its foundations being developed with great rapidity during the next few years. These were largely introduced by Heisenberg, Born,

Schrödinger, Bohr, and Dirac. Cambridge physicists were deeply involved in these discussions.[45] In this kind of environment, who could blame Snow for dreaming of greatness and wishing that he too would become a Fellow of the Royal Society?[46] But in the interim, there was much work to be done. Snow was determined to be part of it all, even though his ambitions were temporarily tempered by a provincial young man's awe.[47]

Snow felt certain that, as Bert and Sandy had repeatedly told him, "one can not have a scientific career without going to Cambridge."[48] This "Mecca, Westminster and Rome; this was the greatest scientific meeting place in the world."[49] He recalled the feeling of preparing to meet these men and ideas: "[It] was an exciting time . . . for the first time in my life I was meeting very clever people.[50]

"I remember reading the University Calendar, learning the names of the professors, looking them up in the *Who's Who* and in the indexes of the modern textbooks."[51] He was not disappointed. He was introduced not to the world he dreamt of but to the real world of science. As a result, Snow's childhood view of the immutability of scientific knowledge and the inevitability of scientific progress began to be significantly revised. Moreover, the private world of science which he had associated strictly with books and ideas and only rarely with scientific discussions was suddenly replaced by large, busy and fully staffed labs, a host of possible mentors to choose from with their conflicting ideas, and an array of research students with whom to share one's excitement and thinking. Nowhere else in Snow's writing, and perhaps in all literature, is this realization portrayed more vividly than in those two sections of *The Search* entitled "The First Friends" and "Effect of a Revolution."[52]

Referring to his earliest Cambridge classes, Snow fictionally evoked the revisions that he faced as a student in his growing realization of the apparent contradictions that he was coming to see were a necessary part of scientific thinking. These revisions were to initiate the transition Snow made from being essentially a private "positivist" scientist to the more public world of a realist. The first of several transitional blows came from a professor.

[The professor of physics] was a plump man with something of a presence; most of his lecture was read from notes, but at times he looked up and spoke to us with a slightly pompous affableness. "We're beginning to think—" he said once, and told us about the modern development of an idea, and I had the thrill of being intimately in touch with the hub of the world. He men-

tioned the nucleus and said, "Rutherford has suggested a constitution for it, but I'm not sure that he's right." Before that, I had
never imagined that these new concepts were anything but unanimous; I had heard of controversies in the past, but the science I
was studying seemed without people or contradictions.[53]

Thus Snow came quickly to understand that science is both cognitively and socially constructed.

A second blow came from fellow students against the potential
ethical and political blindness of science.

When Sheriff or I assumed, as we so often did, that science was
inevitably going to change the future, and that we were optimistic because of it, Hunt protested:

"I can't understand the way you two *believe*."

"Don't you see," Sheriff would break out, "that science has got
the future in its hands? It will make people live longer, give
them leisure, give them power—why, we shall soon have Nature
at our mercy. Isn't that enough for you?"

There was a pause. Hunt was always a little slow at finding his
reply. And then:

"It's not. We shall have a fine healthy population, maybe—and
give it some wholesome exercise now and then by making it run
away from poison gas.

"But I'll grant you everything will get more hygienic every
year. We shall pull off a gigantic piece of plumbing. Do you think
that's enough for me? Do you want me to have a mystical belief
in a super-plumbing organization?"

Sheriff got nettled.

"One can make anything ridiculous by reducing it to its lowest
terms."

"And anything romantic by raising it to its highest."

"Romantic be damned!" Sheriff cried.[54]

This position certainly reflected the extreme view of many of
Snow's colleagues but was not one to which he subscribed. He was
far too sceptical and pragmatic to give credence to such a view—
although this kind of exuberance made up, by his own calculation,
something like 2 percent of his temperament. Indeed, Snow would
have eventually agreed much more easily with the argument made
by Jacob Bronowski that those "who think that science is ethically
[and politically] neutral confuse the findings of science, which are,
with the activities of science, which are not."[55]

A third blow, again from students, came against the epistemological certainty of "scientific facts."

"The people who have the power in their hands. Look at them. They're not like you, Arthur. They're not wider than the average. They're infinitely narrower. Like this Austin of yours. Like clever children with an aptitude for mechanical toys."

"That's not fair," I said.

"It's fairer than your picture of bright clear minds—and everyone else in the darkness. . . . all those words . . . you haven't got a monopoly on the truth."

"In a way, I think we have."

Hunt smiled, a little annoyed. "God, you're as arrogant as the rest. How?"

I spoke quickly; I had thought this out:

"We make experiments and we get results and we infer that there are such things as atoms. Then we work out that if our atoms are right we ought to do more experiments and get certain definite results. We try it: and our atoms fit the facts."

Hunt paused. "Your atoms are just a guess that works. They're not the truth."[56]

The epistemological frailty of science was repeatedly driven home, even if only tacitly. The normal science of lab routines plus the late nights of studying, arguing about theory and formulas, bore the lessons of realism in science.[57] Snow referred to this himself in the guise of Arthur Miles in *The Search*, using an allusion to Heisenberg's uncertainty principle.[58] In drafting a compromise position between Hunt and Sheriff, however, Snow reiterated the impact of the scientific revolution that he was participating in as a student, as well as its nature.

It is rather difficult to put the importance of this revolution into words. In fact, it is important because it cannot be put into words. However, it is something like this. The relation between the choice, the chooser, the external world and the fact produced is a complicated one, and brings us before questions of relativity and epistemology: but one gets through in the end, unless one is spinning a metaphysical veil for the sake of craftsmanship, to an agreement upon "scientific facts." You can call them "pointer readings" as Eddington does, if you like. They are lines on a photographic plate, marks on a screen, all the pointer readings which are the end of a skill, precautions, inventions, of the laboratory.

They are the end of the manual process, the beginning of the scientific. For from these pointer readings, these scientific facts, the process of scientific reasoning begins: and it comes back to them to prove itself right or wrong. For the scientific process is nothing more or less than a hiatus between pointer readings: one takes some pointer readings, makes a mental construction from them in order to predict some more.

The pointer readings which have been predicted are then measured: and if the predictions turn out to be right, the mental construction is a good one. If it is wrong, another mental construction has to be tried. That is all. You take your choice where you put the word "reality": you can find your total reality either in the pointer readings or in the mental construction or, if you have a taste for compromise, in a mixture of both.

The scientific revolution that began in 1925 was altogether a matter of mental construction.[59]

Thus the "real" science that Snow was coming to know was a mental construct full of people, politics, and contradiction. Indeed, Snow's language shows clearly that he was aware of the thinking of the day. For example, as A. S. Eddington wrote in 1930: "The philosophic trend of modern scientific thought differs markedly from the views of thirty years ago. Can we guarantee that the next thirty years will not see another revolution? . . . [By] dogged endeavour, [Man] is slowly and tortuously advancing to purer and purer truth; but his ideas seem to zigzag in a manner most disconcerting to the onlooker."[60] Here, in what Snow came to see as the liberal-democratic model of rationality, lay the source of science's power. Among its facets were curiosity and concern about the world around us, reasoned and open (public) inquiry, and responsibility. This realization clearly gave a new dimension to Snow's scientific thinking, and at times it left him with an exhilarating and intoxicating sense. His description of scientific progress clearly illustrates both this realization and its aesthetic pleasures—again echoing that first excitement that knowledge gave to him.

Before, a great many pointer readings had been necessary for us to use the mental construction of atoms like solar systems—the Atom which [had first] fired my imagination when I was a boy. These atoms, of course, were never objects in the sense that a pin is an object: they were—mental objects, transcendental objects, bridges between one pointer reading and another. And if we went from our pointer readings and constructed our atoms and made them obey certain rules, then we could prophesy a lot of other pointer readings. As mental constructions, our atoms worked fairly well. But not well enough. Too many pointer readings were left unexplained, and even such explanations as there were had about them a queer arbitrariness, a lack of neatness, which left most of us dissatisfied. For nearly all scientists feel, rather than think, that our mental constructions should have a sort of economy which produces an aesthetic response.

During the time between the end of the war and the beginning of the scientific revolution, there was none of this economy. The mental constructions were affairs of patches, expediency, makeshifts and hope.

Then almost simultaneously a few men began to think along different lines to the same end. The model atom was not good enough. So let us, they said, get rid of models altogether. Let us stop thinking of these transcendental objects as though they were ordinary objects we can see and feel. Instead of the transcendental objects, we will have mathematical expressions that will take their place. They will be "atoms"; but now we will describe them in a definite mathematical way, instead of trying to make pictures with our sense in regions where the senses cannot enter. These new mental constructions are the most economical that can be made between pointer readings; the idea had an austerity that went home to a certain type of mind at once. And it worked. It worked like no other in the history of science. As soon as the model atom was thrown away and the new mathematical constructions made, atomic science fell into order straight away. At the beginning, to perform operations, one or two rather obscure mathematical techniques had to be unearthed. And then paper after paper came out in the German and English journals; anomalies ceased to be anomalies . . . facts which had puzzled us before now fitted in completely. . . .[61]

It was because of recollections like these that Snow was able to freely and honestly exclaim throughout his literary career, from the Rede Lecture to *The Physicists*, that "we are living through the greatest of scientific revolutions."[62] "We're lucky to be alive just now. . . . Coming into things like this. Coming into science at this time of all times. It's the renaissance of science, it is the Elizabethan age—and we're born right in the middle of it. Lord, we shall have lots of fun!"[63]

And yet, it could also be a time of deflation and anger, as Snow recalled:

> Suddenly, I heard one of the greatest mathematical physicists say, with complete simplicity: "Of course, the fundamental laws of physics and chemistry are laid down forever. The details have got to be filled up: we don't know anything of the nucleus; but the fundamental laws are there. In a sense, physics and chemistry are finished sciences." It is two hundred years since Newton talked of our being like children who pick up pebbles on the beach. This man who spoke of "finished sciences" was Newton's successor. As I heard his clipped, impersonal voice saying what to him was an evident fact, I realized for the first time, how far science had gone. We were not picking up pebbles from the beach any more; instead, we knew how many we should be able to pick up. They had found the boundary to our knowledge; some things would remain unknown forever; one of the results of this new presentation of matter was to tell what we could not know as well as what we could. We were in sight of the end. It seemed incredible to me, brought up in the tradition of limitless searching, mystery beyond mystery, the agrophobia of the infinite. I resented leaving it. I gazed at the speaker's opaque brown eyes, angry with him for the insight and the vision that made my own belief in a hazy, unending progress seem, even to myself, both tawdry and second-rate. I wanted him to be wrong. Yet I could see what he meant.[64]

Thus, between the charged, all-embracing climate of Cambridge and the powerful juxtapositions of insight and emotion that were to cascade from his first fireside exposures to the real world of scientific research's most exotic frontiers, the character of Snow's outlook was revised in a way that served to deepen his commitment to his realism. This fused with his own natural enthusiasm and hopefulness and buoyed him through difficult moments. The sobering contradictions and struggles of science that he encountered as a student served not as a depressing counterbalance that fostered an ideological belief in science's special epistemological status (Snow was far too sceptical for such a belief) but rather as a powerful amplifier to the tough-minded pragmatism that already underpinned Snow's character.

With these combined revisionist forces, Snow was enfolded in Cambridge's scientific culture. He turned his attentions (for the time being) to his own research. As he said, while keeping the frailty of facts and the excitement of intellectual rigor in mind, "details of the future kept running through my mind—[when] I could begin [my] research. . . ."[65]

Although Snow worked near the Cavendish and Dunn labs, he never actually conducted research there.[66] Indeed, his home for two years was a bench in the Physical Chemistry Laboratories on Free School Lane, which are now part of Pembroke College.[67] These facilities were quite new when Snow entered them in 1928 and were becoming renowned in their own right for the high quality and wide-ranging research carried out there.

Despite the fact that the professor of physical chemistry at these labs was Martin Lowry—whom Snow described as "a very clever man who had never been accepted in Cambridge . . . and who had, with a certain kind of obstinacy, got stuck with researches on optical rotation that didn't attract many pupils"[68]—and that the titular, administrative head of the lab was the rather dour Sir William Pope, these laboratories nevertheless took on an exciting tone that was commensurate to what Snow expected of Cambridge. Of particular interest to Snow was Eric Rideal, an eclectic researcher who had been appointed in 1920 to the then newly endowed Humphrey Owen Jones Lectureship in Physical Chemistry.[69]

By 1922, Rideal and his entire research team had joined the Lowry labs. According to one of Rideal's closest and most long-standing research associates R. W. G. Norish, "the atmosphere [during this period] was a lighthearted one, and Rideal was bubbling with ideas, good and bad, but [he was] not strong on experimental detail, leaving the working out of his ideas to the (hopeful) ingenuity of his students. . . . Rideal would come round the lab most days to talk in a very airy and stimulating way, and *if one could separate the good from the bad*, one got on quite well"[70] (emphasis added). A research student with Snow, Philip Bowden, agreed and wrote of Rideal that "all those who have worked with Sir Eric Rideal agree about his gay and infectious enthusiasm for scientific work and about his conviction not only that all problems are soluble but that it will be great fun solving them."[71] During these years leading up to Snow's arrival, Rideal developed an outstanding research school, which included electrochemistry, photochemistry, and spectroscopy.[72] As a result, the chemistry research students at Cambridge—including Snow and Bowden (with whom Snow would soon collaborate)—had a natural attraction to Rideal. It seems likely that the Professor Desmond of Snow's novels is Rideal. Rideal's broad-based tutelage was just the place to go. Snow soon became aware of this and noted that "Rideal was willing to accommodate research on any topic from pure physics to biology, and his sub-department accordingly became a kind of hold-all for anyone who thought he had a decent problem."[73] In practice, however, Rideal's research program was never as ad hoc as this might suggest. Snow came to appreciate, as others already did at Cambridge, that Rideal's reason for encouraging such diverse research was not his "consuming desire to understand the nature of chemical reactivity" as Brock has suggested but rather his impetuous interest in the noninvasive analysis of chemical structure. He was always willing to try any new analytic tools. Indeed, Rideal's strength seems to have been his enthusiasm on the broad front. It was said that he could answer any question on any area of physical chemistry. This may also have been his weakness, for many have alluded to his superficial tendencies in that research students who were looking for guidance had to carefully fumble through a hundred of Rideal's research suggestions in order to find ten useful ideas.[74] Nevertheless, he was responsible for producing some fifty professors and fourteen FRSs. If Desmond of *The Search* was truly Rideal, then Rideal could (and often did) disclaim ownership of any ideas that did not pan out. Snow was left "red-faced," as a result, with his N_2O analysis and his photochemical studies of biological molecules. However, because of Rideal's enthusiasm and eclecticism of research, Snow was to find in him an excellent match, not only for his own research, which floated within that poorly defined world of 1920s and 1930s physics and chemistry, but also for his intellectual temperament and style, which was never to really accept intellectual barriers. This refusal to accept intellectual bounds was a characteristic that was ultimately to bring Snow to leave science. In a particularly revealing passage from *The Search*, Snow wrote of Arthur Miles (i.e., himself) that "Arthur plunges . . . they're almost the complete successful life plunges. . . . But the scientific plunge couldn't last, because, you see, Arthur never lets himself quite go. There's always a piece of him detached and wondering 'Now why am I doing this?' He plunges and asks. Most people only plunge or only ask. But if you plunge and ask and can't answer the question—well, the plunge ends . . . [that has] prevented him from believing anything; but the ability to plunge has made him know what it's like to believe something. He's been able to go into things—up to a point. The detached part of him has got in his way. . . ."[75] More will be made of this later.

In a rather obscure essay on the nature of chemical research being done at Cambridge that was published in 1933, Snow analyzed with considerable acumen the directions in which chemistry was moving, including the increasingly close relationship that chemistry and physics would need to develop.[76] "Chemistry," he began, "is essentially the science of molecules." A primary tool for unraveling these molecular structures was spectroscopy, which Snow likened to "solving an immense and rather tedious crossword puzzle," the process being "laborious in the extreme to perform (*albeit*) exciting and invaluable in results." Arguing strongly that the future of chemistry rested with physics, he was optimistic that "a physical invasion" of the electronic states of complex organic molecules would soon be possible, and he gave examples in support of his view from the work of Rideal and his pupils. Interestingly, Snow did not refer to any of his own work, which—by the time of the article—consisted of seventeen scientific papers written either in solo or in collaboration with Rideal and Lowry, as well as with other research students.[77] It is intriguing as well that Snow's argument concerning the future closeness of physics and chemistry was to foreshadow a talent that he was to display rather prominently later in his career: notably, his ability to write of scientific detail in clear prose that was accessible to the layperson and his ability to identify areas of scientific importance at an early age, as he was to later do with genetics and biochemical research, operations research, and cybernetics.[78]

Largely as a result of the highly autobiographical nature of *The Search*, it is often assumed by readers of Snow that he, like his character Arthur Miles, was a crystallographer and that he had built an X-ray spectroscope.[79] But for no particular reason Snow changed this small detail. He had, in fact, built an infrared spectroscope with A. M. Taylor.[80] Clearly Snow knew a good deal about crystallography and knew some of the top practitioners of the time, such as W. L. Bragg (later Sir Lawrence), who convinced Snow—one night on a cold and damp train platform—to leave Cambridge in 1940 in order to become the technical director of the Ministry of Labour during the war,[81] and Bernal, who also had an important impact on Snow. However, if our examination of Snow's career were to be restricted to his fiction and his more publicly accessible writings, all we would find would be a few very superficial and cursory statements on the content of crystallography. For example, Snow superficially defined it in an interview: "Crystallography is the study of crystals." Somewhat more usefully, Snow wrote in *The Physicists* that

> crystallography had always been off the mainstream of modern physics. It deals, not with the structure of nuclei and atoms, but with the geography of atoms—the position of atoms in solid matter, and recently, and far more difficult, in liquid matter also. Crystallography is not only an elegant study, but one with multifarious uses. However, the nuclear physicists didn't consider it

touching the core of physics. [With the exception of Bernal] Rutherford didn't permit it to enter the Cavendish. It might be slightly more acceptable than spectroscopy, Kapitza remarked, but both were like putting things into boxes, or perhaps a form of stamp-collecting.[83]

He further explained:

W. L. Bragg . . . , whom everyone agreed was a scientist of the highest class, had devoted his life to [crystallography]. So did another man of great gifts, J. D. Bernal. Although chemists and geologists had been looking at the exterior form of crystals for centuries, Bragg and Bernal could bring a twentieth century technique to bear on the fundamental atomic structure of crystals. The key was X-rays. X-rays are radiation, light, but with a much shorter wavelength. X-ray wavelengths—at around a ten-thousand-millionth of a metre—are very similar to the spacing between atoms in a crystal. When X-rays shine on a crystal they penetrate it. But some are reflected back from the different layers and rows of atoms, and the reflected patterns are not easy to read. It requires an experienced judgement, or complex computer programmes that have only been available in the past few years. But in principle, all the information is there, cryptically, in the pattern of reflected X-rays.[84]

But beyond these, the few general references to his own research that do exist are vague and share only a repeated allusion to the "tedious," "difficult," or "laborious" nature of the work. A hastily added yet obligatory mention of the ultimate value of going through such a process was also typically included.[85] If we note Snow's repeated description of the work in these rather dismal terms, and at the same time his own reputation for being a poor experimentalist plus his desire—recognized since 1921–1922—to become a novelist, then important questions regarding Snow's impression of his own research and future prospects as a scientist invariably arise.

By turning our attention to Snow's scientific papers, some of these questions can be addressed. Before this, however, a number of preliminary observations can be made. First, it can be noted that Snow's total scientific output spanned the period 1928 to 1935. Second, it can be said that this consisted of twenty-six papers.[86] Seventeen of these (65 percent) were collaborations, while nine (34 percent) were written solely by Snow. Of the collaborations, a quarter were written with research supervisors (notably Rideal and Lowry), while the remainder were written either with colleagues or with Snow himself acting as the senior researcher and writing with students. Some of these collaborators would go on to become extremely successful researchers in their own right: most notably in this regard, Sir Eric Eastwood (FRS, who was to become, in 1962, the director of research at English Electric while Snow was their director of scientific personnel); and Philip Bowden (CBE, FRS, Fellow of Caius College, professor of surface chemistry at Cambridge, director of English Electric from 1953 to 1968, Snow's lifelong friend, and the man who appeared as Sir Francis Getliffe in Snow's novels).[87] A third introductory point is that all of Snow's articles appeared in such recognized and well-regarded journals as the *Proceedings of the Royal Society,* the *Transactions of the Faraday Society, Nature,* and the *Proceedings of the Cambridge Philosophical Society.* Snow also wrote two chapters for the 1933 edition of F. W. Aston's classic text *Mass Spectra and Isotopes,*[88] and a 1933 chapter on "Chemistry" in Harold Wright's *University Studies Cambridge.* In addition, although it was not standard procedure during the 1930s for journals to have articles carefully peer reviewed, Snow's papers were all "communicated" by credible researchers, including both Rideal and Lowry.[89] Indeed, one paper acknowledged the assistance of Patrick Blackett. A fourth and most significant preliminary observation concerns Snow's field of science. Clearly his interests were in the area where physics and chemistry overlap, but his insistent identification with physics was obviously more a matter of choice than of strict fact. More specifically, even cursory examination of Snow's scientific publications reveals that his research was not in crystallography but rather in the related field of molecular spectroscopy.

Snow's scientific research all dealt with aspects of the interaction of molecules and electromagnetic radiation.[90] As J. C. D. Brand has noted, they fall into three main, chronologically distinct groups. These might be described as Snow's periods of research into (1) infrared vibration-rotation spectra of di- and triatomic molecules (1928–1930), (2) the photochemistry of large molecules (1930–1933), and (3) the electronic spectra of solids and gases (1932–1935).

Snow's first contributions to published science were in 1928 and were based on his M.Sc. work. However, his first contribution to a high-level science meeting came in September 1929 at a meeting of the Michael Faraday Society held in Bristol. The topic of the conference was "Molecular Structure and Molecular Spectra." This meeting was, in fact, very well timed as applications of the new quantum theory to physical chemistry were just appearing.[91] Indeed, as C. V. Raman himself pointed out at the meeting, the 1928 discovery of

Raman scattering[92] had opened up a completely new means of studying molecular structure.

By 1929, the only infrared spectra for which extensive rotational analyses had been completed were those of the hydrogen halides in which intervals between successive lines in the rotation structure are large and readily resolved. However, the spectra for polyatomic molecules were far from understood. Snow's papers on the fine structure of carbon monoxide (CO) and nitric oxide (NO) were landmark contributions and put him ahead of all competitive researchers in this area. Snow's collaborators were E. K. Rideal, F. I. G. Rawlins, and A. M. Taylor.[93] Rideal's interest in the infrared was new and was, in part, stimulated by Taylor, who was a visitor to Cambridge from the Applied Optics Institute at the University of Rochester, New York. It is worth noting that after his collaboration with Snow, Rideal dropped this line of investigation into the infrared entirely.

Snow's paper described work that had, for the first time, achieved a resolution of rotational structure in the fundamental bands of CO and NO—molecules whose reduced mass is substantially greater than that of diatomic hydrides. To achieve this resolution Snow and Taylor constructed a simple prism-grating spectrometer[94] that was of proven design and that was comparable in performance to other high-resolution instruments in use at that time.[95] The Snow-Taylor instrument involved a single infrared beam with the sample material and reference cells exposed alternately. The sensitivity of the instrument was adequate to resolve the detailed features of the fundamental bands but not sufficient enough to determine more than the general outlines of the overtone bands.

Although acceptable for CO, the resolving power of the Snow-Taylor spectrometer could not handle the more complex NO spectra. CO was shown, by Snow, to consist of the P and R branch energy levels only; however, NO proved to be the first and for many years the only example of diatomic molecules of an infrared spectrum in which a Q branch energy level is present between the P and R branches. The importance of this observation was that it confirmed Mulliken's prediction in his molecular orbital theory. This was, in fact, the first time that infrared rotational analysis was used to confirm orbital symmetry.

The difficulty in dealing with NO, as was anticipated by the theory of Hill and Van Vleck,[96] is that it is made up of two almost superimposed components that each have slightly different rotational constants. No instrument in 1929 could have resolved this structure; but Snow, Rawlins, and Rideal must have been unaware of the

Hill–Van Vleck work, for they would surely have noted the absence of this Hill–Van Vleck splitting. Ten years later, when the double band of NO was finally deciphered, the authors of the analysis commented that the "existing measurements of the fundamental [by Snow, Rawlins, and Rideal] were made with insufficient dispersion and sensitivity for precision measurements."[97] Brand has remarked that this comment "is less than generous." However, it is hardly a pejorative statement but is rather a neutral explanation. In spite of some difficulties among the CO and NO analyses that formed the core of Snow's Ph.D. dissertation, these have become landmark papers in the field—bringing Snow closest to the crest of a breaking wave of scientific discovery. They had the desired effect of helping Snow achieve a Cambridge College Fellowship and of launching Snow into his professional scientific career. However, his future work was not to be quite as successful. Indeed, his tendency to rely on negative evidence plus his impetuosity (what Brand has called "the dark side of ambition") landed at least four serious scientific blunders on Snow's doorstep.

In 1929, Snow wrote a paper entitled "The Relation between Raman Lines and Infrared Bands." This was communicated to the *Philosophical Magazine* by Rideal. In this article Snow discussed the compatibility of Raman and infrared spectroscopy. However, in what is a rather general and inconclusive analysis, Snow made the startling claim to have observed infrared absorption by N_2 and O_2, which "while not definitely proved is more than a possibility." By today's standards, this claim sounds preposterous, as neither molecule exhibits an electric dipole. In fact, it seems certain—as Brand has pointed out—that Snow's "observations" were caused by uncompensated residues of CO_2 and H_2O in the spectrometer. However, Brand's criticism is a shade too heavy, for at that time, no possibility could have been ruled out. Nevertheless, Snow's speculations were mistaken, and he should have been suspicious of any absorption in the same region as CO_2 or H_2O. But Snow never checked—revealing what was to become a problematic flaw in his experimental method. But (perhaps more surprisingly) Rideal never checked either. As Snow's supervisor, it is remarkable that he ever sponsored such an extravagant claim by a student who was only in his first year of doctoral research. Thus the adequacy of Rideal's "Desmond-like" supervision must be seen—at least in part—as contributing to Snow's negative experiences in science.

This incomplete understanding of theory was to manifest itself in another paper from this phase that set out to establish the structure of nitrous oxide using infrared and Raman spectroscopy. The basic questions Snow had to tackle were, Is the molecule symmetrical (NON) or unsymmetrical (NNO)? and Is the molecule bent or straight? During this research, Snow was in touch with E. F. Barker of the University of Michigan and was well aware that the vibration-rotation spectrum of carbon dioxide had proven that its structure was symmetrical: O-C-O. In this analysis, Snow reported the fine structure in the N_2O IR spectrum—the first researcher to do so. But in his analysis Snow unequivocally claimed the structure to be linear-symmetrical NON, thus specifically ruling out the linear NNO or "bent" NON possibilities. Within a year, however, Barker (at Michigan) showed the structure to be linear NNO[98]—a demonstration we still rely on today. The significance of this event in Snow's career requires a more technical analysis into the problem of negative evidence.

The assignment of observed bands to particular vibration modes is never easy. Variables to be manipulated include the wavelengths of the center of each band, their intensity of absorbance, their overall envelope shape, and the comparison of the presence or absence of each band in ordinary IR and in Raman IR. Brand has shown Snow's minor errors in assigning each mode whether symmetric, asymmetric stretching or bending, fundamental or overtone, combination or "hot." In themselves these errors are forgivable; even today, comparable misassignments are made at an equivalent frontier of research. However, these errors pale in significance compared to Snow's gigantic gaffe when comparing the IR and Raman data. For it is this primary reasoning that decides whether the molecule is NNO or NON.

The rule of mutual exclusion, as it is now called, allows a simple test of symmetry. Although Snow and his contemporaries would not have used these words *per se*, their knowledge of theory is correct by today's standards, and this rule can be seen as an easier way of expressing this knowledge.

Thus the rule states that if a molecule has a center of symmetry (e.g., OCO), all Raman active vibrations are IR inactive and vice versa.[99] If there is no center of symmetry, then some (but not necessarily all) vibrations may be *both* Raman and IR active. If ever one fundamental band is found to exist in both IR and Raman at the same frequency, the molecule cannot have a center of symmetry.

Snow was led astray by two errors—one of his own and one from the paper written by Dickenson, Dillon, and Rasetti, which reported that "only one Raman line was found; this was rather weak but sharp. The frequency shift was 1281.8. An infra-red absorption of this frequency would lie at 7.8 mu; we are not aware of data showing any band at this wavelength. However, the least approximate agreement of the frequency measured by us with the difference between the frequencies corresponding to the prominent absorptions given by E. V. Bahr as occurring at 2.86 and 4.49 may be significant."[100] Actually there is another Raman line at 2224 that, if known, would have given the game away. The point here is that Snow bought the Rasetti work "hook, line, and sinker." Rasetti said that there is no IR band at 1282. Snow's instrument could not reach down below 1400 because the grating became ineffective in that region. He did a quick scan, ". . . a search with a prism [NaCl] instrument up to 15 mu [i.e., down to 700 cm^{-1}] [that did] not discover any more strong bands." Was this error comparable to the technical assumption made by a research assistant in *The Search*? It would have been easy for Snow to check that his small spectrometer was adequate by running CO_2, which absorbs in that region. But he didn't, and the false, negative result stood. Snow continued to follow Rasetti's speculation that the Raman line is somehow derived from the difference between the 2223 and the 3487 bands (note $3487 - 2223 = 1264$, *not* 1282).

It had taken the unlucky combination of both these experimental errors for Snow's analysis to be wrong. If either one had not occurred, Snow would have got the right picture. Snow had reported a very strong band at 2223. If Rasetti had reported the same band in the Raman, the rule of mutual exclusion would have ruled out the symmetric NON structure. Alternatively, if Snow had picked up the 1285 IR band with his own prism spectrometer, he would have matched it to Rasetti's 1281 Raman band, and again the NON structure would have been ruled out.[101]

Barker's paper of a year later gives us several clues as to what went wrong. First, Barker showed very clear spectra (he was renowned for his superior gratings). In this case, the resolution was more than adequate to pick out lines separated by only 0.8 cm^{-1}. Snow's published spectra of the strongest band is incomprehensible, and with the benefit of hindsight, the numbers he quoted in the published table were totally wrong. He reported peaks with an average separation of 2 cm^{-1}. One can only surmise that he was looking at either noise or, more probably, optical interference bands from nonparallel surfaces of the NaCl discs in the spectrometer.

However, Barker was kind in the paper that demolished Snow's work, giving Snow partial credit for being involved in the reasoning that led to the correct NNO structure. As he wrote: "During the course of the investigation our observations were submitted to Professor Dennison, and he first suggested this interpretation, which is apparently the only consistent one. We understand that the idea originated in a discussion between Dennison and Snow on the subject of the N_2O spectrum. . . ." Later in the paper Barker acknowledged that "Snow has kindly informed us that his computations using our three fundamental frequencies reproduce the specific heat curve very accurately." Barker's work not only had better resolution but also extended to the higher wavelength, and he picked up the 2224 IR band that ruled out the NON structure. The case was closed.

Snow was clearly moving in the right circles. One can imagine Dennison, who was mentioned above and who was five years older than Snow, debating the issue with Snow in Cambridge. Dennison, the American prodigy who had worked with Bohr, Heisenberg, and Schrödinger, was well known in the Cavendish. Earlier in 1927 he had been asked to give three lectures. Finding himself short of material for the third, he resolved the orthoparahydrogen specific-heat problem that had eluded the theoreticians—one of the highlights in his illustrious career.[102]

The immediate criticism of Snow's paper on N_2O was to be the first exposure to public criticism of his logic and judgment, and on the evidence of such novels as *The Search*, he was not to forget the unpleasant feeling that this represented.

Snow's research into photochemistry, which was to amount to the biggest embarrassment in his young scientific career, was undertaken with Philip Bowden—Frances Getliffe in *Strangers and Brothers*—in 1932–1934. Snow had just published the mystery novel *Death under Sail*, and it was during this period that Snow wrote and published *New Lives for Old* and *The Search*. The purpose of their research was to study the structural rearrangements brought about in large biologically important molecules by the absorption of light quanta. (We must not forget that it was the stated objective of Arthur Miles in *The Search* to apply crystallography to biological systems.) Neither Snow nor Bowden had any previous experience in this area. The research program was based on the "dual premise that (i) the ultraviolet and visible absorption bands of large molecules could each be attributed to local sub-groups, or *chromospores*, and (ii) physiological activity, when present, similarly resided in a particular sub-group of the molecule as a whole."[103] As a consequence, or so Snow and Bowden thought, it should be possible to link physiological activity to a particular absorption band. More particularly, they believed that they could destroy the biological activity of a vitamin by irradiation in an appropriate band or induce physiological activity of an inactive precursor by a photochemical rearrangement using light of a correctly chosen wavelength. "At the time, vitamin molecules were at the threshold of structure determination by standard methods of chemical degradation, but no vitamin had yet been prepared in the laboratory from physiologically inactive material."[104] Snow and Bowden hoped in effect to leapfrog this process through photochemically induced partial synthesis. It is likely that the idea for this line of experimentation came from J. D. Bernal, whose own work on the photorearrangement of crystalline vitamin D was published at almost the same time.[105] In part, Snow's enthusiasm in this work was connected to his enthusiasm for the new quantum theory.

> The idea had an austerity that went home to a certain sort of mind at once. And it worked like no other idea in the history of science. As soon as the model atom was thrown away and the new mathematical constructions made, atomic science fell into order straight away . . . it was convincing beyond the quiver of a doubt . . . it was fairly easy to see how the new ideas would include a theory of crystals. I could imagine the sort of explanations which would soon clear up most of the problems of quantum mechanics, the first suggestions on crystals and molecules were beginning to come out. I could see, in the near future, these new methods restating my own work. . . . And my ambitions, I thought, my plans [would lead to] attack on the structure of biological molecules. . . .[106]

Rideal, who had achieved an outstanding success by applying surface chemistry to biological systems, was now trying to replicate this success by applying spectroscopy to biological systems.

Snow and Bowden published their preliminary work in a letter to *Nature*.[107] In so doing, they acknowledged the "generous co-operation" of such individuals as Sir Frederick Gowland Hopkins and J. B. S. Haldane. Unusually, Hopkins, who was then president of the Royal Society and a pioneer of vitamin research, also sponsored a press release in the *Times* under the title "Birth of a Vitamin." As Brock has pointed out, "the event was a 30 day wonder," attracting considerable positive attention from industry and the press. The journal *Industrial and Engineering Chemistry* wrote that "production of Vitamin A on a large scale and its manufacture in foods, such as bread and cereals, may be expected if recent British experiments are confirmed." The *Chemical News* wrote that "by arranging for the exclusion of the radiations which destroy the vitamin and free passage for those which create it, further yields should be obtained." The *Lancet* and the *British Medical Journal* both reported that "they believe they have produced vitamin A artificially." However, within weeks their work was publicly criticized by two senior authorities on the organic chemistry of vitamins. The work of Snow and Bowden, according to this assessment, was completely wrong on all points that were essential to the argument.[108] In a devastating letter published in *Nature*, (later Sir Ian) M. Heilbron and R. A. Morton of the University of Liverpool totally dismissed the claims of Snow and Bowden. They were in a very good position to do so as they dominated this field. Their demolition was done on many levels. To begin with, the method used by Snow and Bowden was not new. Indeed, "the technique (the study of spectral absorption curves, and irradiation with light of selected wavelengths) is familiar and has already been applied in vitamin studies." Morton himself had used spectral analysis of vitamins as early as 1928. Additionally, "the idea of experimental method as a key to several vitamins seems to underestimate the differences between organic compounds of widely varying constitution." This is the scientific equivalent of acknowledged experts saying that Snow and Bowden "didn't know their organic chemistry."

More serious criticism of Snow and Bowden's work was addressed regarding each of vitamins A, B, C, and D. Of the vitamin A experiments, for example, Heilbron and Morton wrote that "from the published spectrograms their product is obviously coloured and in all probability contains unchanged carotene, so that the relevance of the promised biological assay does not emerge, since it has been fully established that carotene is converted *in vivo* into vitamin A." This is the scientific equivalent of acknowledged experts suggesting that Snow and Bowden "didn't know their biochemistry."

Of vitamin C, Heilbron and Morton state that "Drs. Bowden and Snow state that when they are able to record the absorption spectrum of pure vitamin C, they will be able to test its identity with either initiated narcotine or hexuronic acid. This is so true as to be obvious."

Closing their response, Heilbron and Morton write simply that the claims of Snow and Bowden "have no precise meaning."[109] Once again it is important to step back and analyze this disaster from today's vantage point. It would be trite to categorize biology and biochemistry as encyclopedic in magnitude and complexity, but Snow and Bowden showed little comprehension of their scope. However, at that time, intellectual territory was not as guarded as it is now.

They just needed a "guide" to show them around the geography and to protect them from pitfalls along the way.

In retrospect it is still a major regret in modern chemistry that simple photochemical reactions have not worked out in a way that might have seemed possible in principle. Most chemical reactions are initiated thermally. That is, heat is applied so that molecules are made to go faster and in so doing to collide with each other, in the expectation that on average the right "bits" will break off or the right fragments will attach themselves. Of course, inevitably, the molecule breaks in the wrong places; thermal degradation gives unintended byproducts. A more efficient way would be to cut the bonds exactly where you want. No molecular-sized "scissors" are available, but if we shine light of exactly the right frequency (this was achievable before lasers only by filtering out the "wrong" frequencies) we should in principle be able to make a particular bond in a molecule vibrate so energetically that it could break clearly at that point.[110]

Attention was quickly focused on Snow and Bowden. The controversy is recounted by Brand's comments on the experiment that claimed to convert beta carotene into vitamin A.

Beta carotene, the molecule responsible for the color of carrots, is abundant and available so that its conversion into the vitamin would have been of considerable importance in the pharmaceutical industry. Bowden and Snow claimed that the conversion took place when carotene was irradiated in a hydrocarbon solvent in an atmosphere of nitrogen. In dismissing this claim, Heilbron and Morton pointed out that Vitamin A is an alcohol—a property established in 1931, the year preceding the Bowden-Snow experiment—and so could not possibly have been produced from carotene under oxygen-free conditions. The argument was unanswerable, as Snow later conceded: "we thought we could produce certain vitamins by using . . . light, but that wasn't right." Now we know that Vitamin A is formed from carotene by enzyme action but not by irradiation.[111]

Snow and Bowden were thus careless and once again had not done their homework; they were unaware that in 1931 the chemical constitution of vitamin A was virtually settled. Snow must have been horrified that his blunder was committed in full view of the president of the Royal Society. Referring to this period of his life Snow wrote, "I was extremely miserable. Everything, personal and creative, seemed to be going wrong."[112] The trauma of these errors of judgment was represented clearly in *The Search*. Asking "what am I to do?," Miles (i.e., Snow) received clear advice.

> "That's quite clear." Macdonald lit his pipe. "You've got to re-habilitate yourself. Which will take a longish time. You've got to accept the assistant directorship if they offer it to you. . . . You've got to work absolutely steadily, without another suspicion of a mistake. You've got to let yourself be patronized and regretted over. You've got to get out of the limelight. Then in three or four years you'll be back where you were; though it will be held against you, one way or another, for longer than that. It will delay you getting into the Royal, of course. That can't be helped. You'll have a lean time for a while; but you're young enough to get over it."[113]

Bowden, of course, took the advice, rebuilt his career, and became a very famous FRS.[114] Snow—embarrassed, hurt, and dejected—did not. But by 1935 he knew that he would have to leave science.

During this same period, Snow wrote articles in such periodicals as the *Cambridge Review* and carried out work with Rawlins on the visible spectra of transition metal complexes. Their hypothesis was that the spectral bands of complexes correlated one to one with the transitions of the free metal action in the gas phase. This basic idea commanded considerable attention at the time; however, Snow and Rawlins (who had published previously in the field) gave no indication of having known the frontier work in this field that had been done by Hans Bethe,[115] or by Sauer,[116] or had they seen the implications that these papers later were to have in terms of spectral analysis. In Brand's view, "it is difficult to believe that the failure to mention [this] work is simply a lapse of courtesy: instead, it appears to represent a careless indifference towards the work in other laboratories. . . ."[117]

Another form of spectroscopy in which Snow did research was conducted near the ultraviolet spectra of ethylene and certain of its relatives. This work was done with Allsopp and Eastwood. While in retrospect the tone of the research results can be seen to be somewhat hesitant, this is understandable, since no one had attempted to analyze rotational substructure in the spectrum of a molecule of such size and complexity before. Nevertheless, despite their hesitation, the methods that they pioneered in this work remained current for several years.[118] In the context of its period, this was probably

Snow's best work. It showed more judgment, patience, and imagination than any of his previous work. Of course, we must not forget that a considerable portion of the credit may well belong to Eastwood, whose later accomplishments were considerable. In a footnote to their paper, Snow and Eastwood suggested possible future work[119] that could have been quite significant. But they did not pursue this line of work, and Snow was to leave primary scientific research altogether. In the end, Snow knew privately that his scientific career was a failure; he knew that he would have to leave Cambridge. As he wrote in *The Search*, in "a sense, I myself have lived by my wits since I was eighteen; a failure in an examination, a bad start in research, a mistaken choice—and I should have been a schoolmaster all my life."[120] This, to Snow, meant failure. And thus once he had become "a schoolmaster"—a Tutor at Cambridge—coupled with his scientific research experiences, he knew he had to leave science behind.

Thus in sum, a number of things can be said of Snow's scientific research. He did perform some good science; however, he was far from being the "brilliant physical chemist . . . whose work on photochemistry in the solid state could easily have opened up for him a new field of research," as Bernal said during the "Two Cultures Debate" in 1962.[121] But Snow knew this. As he said, "I was not good enough." "I should have made quite an adequate scientist, but not a great one." "I should only have been happy in Cambridge if I was an academic of the class of [Bernal, Rutherford, Kapitza, and Hardy]—which I should never have been, even if I had tried."[122] Certainly he was well thought of by such eminent personalities as Blackett and Gowlin-Hopkins, but this was more for his affable nature, overall intellect, scepticism of dogma, and his ease around powerful or important people than for his prowess as a researcher. Clearly, he was a competent technician, as he would have needed to be in order to be awarded a Cambridge doctorate. But importantly, and equally clearly, an overall assessment of Snow's research reveals that his work was uneven, that he was impatient, that his judgment was sometimes impaired by his attraction to the idea of making a major contribution to science, and that he would never have been a major scientific force.

As to why he was so anxious to associate himself with the Cavendish instead of being satisfied with being simply a "physical chemist" from Cambridge, the answer is most assuredly buried within the powerful cognitive and subtle political values espoused by that scientific community that Snow was to admire. Cognitively, many Cambridge researchers felt that even if they weren't working under

Rutherford, they were at least playing a part of the second scientific revolution. As Snow said not long before his death, although he didn't work at the Cavendish, he knew that it was an important time and he regularly went to the Kapitza Club meetings. They were exciting.[123] Socially, Snow knew that he was an outsider to the Cambridge class structure. By affecting an association with the Cavendish he was privately convincing himself that he belonged, that he *had* left Leicester. And politically, Snow was well aware that "the general atmosphere [of Cambridge at the time] was vaguely liberal, [and] strongly international."[124] Moreover, the friends whom he "idealized" (from Hardy whom he met in 1927 to Bernal whom he met in 1928; from the Huxleys whom he met in 1929 to Blackett whom he met in 1930, along with Hogben, Crowther, and Gregory) were all quite far to the intellectual left, but not the trade union left.[125] Snow was also on the left of the Labour party, but he was always less adamant about mass movements than his friends.[126] These influential scientific friends kept hoping that Snow would see "the light and really throw [his] weight in [to the political reformation of the interwar period,] but [he] never did."[127] While Snow saw the left as the only practical option at the time, he was also "genuinely sceptical" of anyone resembling an ideologue. But a more important explanation of Snow's scientific affiliation related to his early impression of the progressive nature of modern physics versus the supposedly unprogressive character of chemistry. This point was driven home by Bernal, underscored by Hardy, and fictionally recollected by Snow in a conversation between Arthur Miles (i.e., Snow) and Leo Constantine (i.e., Bernal).

"Why is chemistry the most conservative of sciences? Because it's got no mathematical basis," he said promptly.

"You mean," I said, "that there's nothing to test the new ideas by? And the old ones have all the force of tradition behind them. Back to Kolbe, as it were?"

"Any science without mathematics is bound to be conservative. Physics is just the opposite. New ideas get a hearing. I'm a physicist by temperament myself, you know. Only I didn't get a mathematical training."[128]

This was Snow talking candidly of himself, although what he was describing was certainly no "revolution" in any Kuhnian sense. Moreover, the work of such figures as Bohr had—through spectroscopy—begun to effectively marry chemistry and physics. Snow, it can be said with some certainty, was a physicist by temperament—

trained (to some degree) in advanced mathematics by G. H. Hardy. In Snow's eyes, physics was both scientifically and socially progressive. This was reflected repeatedly in such novels as *The Search.* For example,

> When Sheriff or I assumed, as we so often did, that science was inevitably going to change the world, and that we were optimistic because of it, Hunt protested: "I can't understand the way you two believe." "Don't you see," Sheriff would break out, "that science has got the future in its hands? It will make people live longer, give them leisure, give them power; why, we shall soon have Nature at our mercy. Isn't that enough for you? . . . We're getting the power, and that's making our civilization the first stable one there's been. It's because it's the first civilization that has got hold of science—not enough yet, but enough to give it power. Call it plumbing if you like, but it's making us unique. And as well as that, we've got scientists: the first collection of people in the world who've been trained to be honest and detached about the things they see. They've vowed honesty and detachment, and that's something staggeringly new."[129]

Beyond this, through extensive tutoring by Hardy during 1929–1930, Snow learned the necessary advanced mathematics to "understand more physics than most physicists."[130] Thus, in Snow's own mind he was clearly—and without any doubt—one of the generation that changed, and would continue to change, the world.

None of these observations regarding the limitations of his scientific career would have come as a surprise to Snow. Indeed, in later life he insisted that "by vocation I was a writer."[131] In an occasionally enlightening series of interviews conducted in 1978, Snow affirmed that as a teenager he was convinced that, one day, he would be a novelist; that there was never any burning desire to become a scientist—rather, that it seemed the easiest way of making a decent living in the 1920s, and of escaping the economic climate of provincial Leicester. Science was something that came easily to him. But in retrospect he knew that he could not have stayed on at Cambridge. "[Going to Cambridge as I did] was a nice way to earn a living in the thirties; out of what I got from various sources, about £1200 a year, I lived like a well-to-do bachelor. . . . I knew I was going to write."[132]

Furthermore, and contrary to the still dominant perception of many of his readers,[133] Snow's literary career does not in any way represent a radical break with science, or a crisis period in Snow's professional life (even though professional crises were reflected in his writing). We know that from the earliest period, while still at the University College in Leicester, Snow's interests were diverse and he was clearly not intending to pursue science as his career. Writing was always to fill this bill. As a teenager, and well into his Cambridge days, Snow had taken an active part in debating societies, had done a considerable amount of writing for such school periodicals as the *Newtonian* (1923–1925) and the *Luciad* (1926–1928), and had in fact written his first novel (*Youth Searching*), which was never published. (The sole two copies were destroyed by Snow and his girlfriend at the time.)[134] Therefore, we can surmise that when Snow left Leicester in 1928, he had no real intention of pursuing a career in scientific research.

We can further assume that when Snow wrote *Death under Sail* (1932), *New Lives for Old* (1933), and *The Search* (1934), these were not just the result of a casual pastime carried out between scientific experiments. Rather, this was the real Snow, doing what he always intended to do. Although his intellectual excitement over science was real and sincere, he was much too preoccupied with people and the world around him to be able to focus entirely on science. Although he was never to officially break with science—gaining considerable authority and self-definition by identifying himself as a scientist as late as 1978 while speaking at the University of Texas at Austin—there can be no doubt that he did migrate away from it. In so doing, he began to sense the extent of his own marginality: as a provincial lad at Cambridge, as a mediocre scientist amongst brilliance, as a writer amongst scientists, as a scientist unknowing of (or excluded from) the Cambridge literary circles. This recognition would, in time, resolve Snow's optimism into a darkening vision that would leave him feeling out of touch with the modern world.

Nevertheless, there can be no mistaking that science—that is to say scientific knowledge, the social style of its community, and its relationship to society—deeply influenced Snow's values and lifelong realist's outlook. By the time Snow's training in science was complete, his personal form of literary, scientific, and political realism had become importantly coextensive. How Snow conducted this translation of his early observation that scientific facts were the result of mental and social constructs into his view of the importance of science was significant indeed. This is particularly true as it illustrated his affiliation with the "social relations of science movement" while at the same time demonstrating clearly his differences with that faction.

While colleagues such as Bernal and Huxley argued about the importance of science in society, Snow adopted a subtly different approach and quietly argued instead on behalf of the importance of science to the individual. The distinction for Snow was an important one. To speak of "society" was too macro a concept, Snow felt. It carried with it too high a level of aggregation to be able to usefully make initial observations. And as a political concept, it led too often to a confrontational style which was unproductive.[135] To someone such as Snow whose own successes had come by studying the fundamental units of matter (atoms and molecules) and by working as an individual within the power centers of social systems, such advances as we can make in life could only be thought of at the level of the individual. For example, it is here that political change can be made; it is here that people live, think, and experience; it is here that any direct meaning or knowledge of the world can be held; and it is here that science can have its greatest impact. Snow expressed such ideas in terms of the second scientific revolution (i.e., 1900–1925).

In an unpublished series of notes for talks he was invited to give at the Massachusetts Institute of Technology and at New York University, Snow wrote succinctly that "the scientific revolution is already performing, and has in fact partly performed, a structural transformation of modern democracy and of Man's idea of himself."[136] By this latter note, Snow meant nothing unduly complicated but intended, quite bluntly, to question what we—as individuals—are like, how far removed from the rest of animal life we are, and in what sense are we responsible for our actions.[137]

In posing these questions, Snow could be perceived as asking what were, for him, uncharacteristically philosophical questions. However, while the questions raised are undoubtedly subtle, Snow—in posing them—never left his basic realist framework. His reasons for raising them were due to his sense that in "modern," "advanced," or "urban" society,[138] which he defined as those societies in which "most people have enough to eat, . . . [where] there are houses to accommodate them, where—by and large—they are almost completely literate, and where children have some education,"[139] there was a growing sense that "civilization is slipping backwards."[140] This, he noted, often translated into an inarticulate anti-science sentiment. But this was the wrong response to our technological world and was based on false hopes. What Snow offered in his discussions of science was "a bit of non-utopian thinking."[141] What he delivered in practice was a modified version of the radical social function of science rhetoric recited in his best Bernalian voice. Although this was not to reflect Snow's most creative and unique contribution to the modernist debate, it did serve as the basis for his distinctive brand of realism. But in sketching out his *prima facie* argument, Snow defined his basic elements simply and conventionally: science was "the attempt to understand the natural world," and technology was the "attempt to alter and control the natural world."[142] However, in setting up these categories, Snow failed to critically examine either the usefulness or integrity of the categories themselves, or their implications for social development. From time to time, Snow would become vaguely aware of these shortcomings, but this only resulted in him burying his assumptions or building arguments that did not directly depend on them.

Snow's flawed assumptions arose out of a common, still popular, but only partially useful distinction between science and technology. "That is a deliberate choice. I could have said applied science, but increasingly I have come to think that that is misleading. The relation between [science and technology] is extremely complex. . . . In some domains the two activities fuse and the frontier between them disappears. In others the separation is complete."[143] This distinction was made for essentially two reasons: first, in order to redress what Snow recognized as "a profound confusion in the popular mind"; and second, to underscore his conviction that science holds a special and irrevocable status in human activity. Both stances are flawed. "In the West, one meets quite a strong wave of feeling which is called for short-hand purposes anti-science. . . . It is most active among people living exceptionally comfortable lives in the material sense. . . . 'Anti-science' is a protest against the possibilities of nuclear war, the dangers of pollution of the atmosphere, the hazards of nuclear waste, the devastation of the countryside, the inhumanity of motorways. . . . Of course it is not really anti-science. It is anti-technology."[144] But in so saying, Snow was attempting to protect the sanctity of science by clinging, definitionally, to two artificial categories. To anyone familiar with science policy trends, as Snow was, terms such as "science" and "technology" can only be of use in the broadest sense. Closer examination of the research function reveals, far more practically, a blurred continuum of activity, as is represented by basic and applied research, experimental design and development, process and product innovation, technology transfer and diffusion—each one of which is, in itself, definitionally problematic. This recognition is now widespread.[145] Today all research is still an act of enlightenment. However, as governments continue to insist on the importance of the market-organized research system, researchers and research administrators have had to learn to adjust to the commodification of science. Snow knew this but chose not to admit it—preferring to recall what he remembers as the "Golden Age" of science. To Snow, in this weakened line of thinking, "science as science doesn't present any practical problem. It is international as no other human activity can be. Nearly everyone would agree that it is worth doing. It is one of the beautiful things that humans can do."[146] And why? Because, he argued: "no one can deny its progress. . . . No sane and informed person doubts that our scientific picture of the world is richer and more accurate than it was fifteen years ago—and that in fifteen years time it will be richer and more accurate still. The *certainty* of progress freshens the air which scientists breathe. . . . [It] assures them that they are not wasting their lives."[147]

Thankfully, Snow was not to build these assumptions into his larger framework, although trace elements of it are frequently encountered. Much more important to Snow was his overall view of the significance of science. Speaking of the ancient past, Snow reflected: "The revolutionary changes in human life have all been technological. . . . Agriculture was somehow happened upon 9 to 10 thousand years ago. . . . It meant the beginning of what we term civilization. Human life didn't change much for the overwhelming majority of the human race until only a few generations ago. Then there was a quantum jump . . . [and men] learned to develop machines and make industrial products on a mass scale."[148] These changes were, "on the whole, technological as opposed to scientific."[149]

"The first industrial revolution was largely the result of clever craftsmen; people with the mechanical gift; people who knew the material; people . . . who weren't scientists in any sense. . . ."[150] However, we are currently going through another change that has far greater implications for the way in which we think and live, and which Snow foresaw. This change "springs, not from technology but, from science. . . . [The] really exciting things which are about to happen to us now are coming from science into hardware in an astoundingly short time."[151] These were to come from quantum physics, molecular biology, and computing science. And as Snow perceptively understood, these changes would have a far greater impact than any conscious political decision, for these changes would directly affect human beings' changing idea of themselves.

In a very basic sense, Snow saw science as being responsible for dismantling our long-standing anthropocentristic beliefs, and for giving us a clearer (and still evolving) sense of who we, as individuals, are. This has taken time but has been a great lesson in humility that has deeply affected our common wisdom.

Men in the Renaissance didn't realize that their own conception was changing. A few were saying that man was the measure of all things. [This was] a great piece of vanity but [was] nevertheless the first clear statement of individualism. . . . In the same fashion, our successors may possibly look back upon us and detect, as we can't, that something new was stirring. Something which would in time make human beings think more gravely, more stoically, about their condition, wouldn't make them exuberantly happy but might give them a solider place on which to stand.

Men have looked at the stars from the dawn of history, have wondered, and have often felt awe. Three hundred years ago Pascal, one of the most introspective of thinkers, said "the silence of the infinite space terrifies me." Now the development of cosmogony has told us much more, and more exactly, about the infinite spaces. Our planet is one insignificant speck going round a minor sun. There are billions of such suns dotted round a universe so enormous as to be unimaginable. There are, no doubt, very large numbers of planets similar to the earth—though not quite so many as one would have thought. Life, human life, may be a bizarre chance, but statistically it seems as certain as statistical thought can take us that similar life, the same kind of bizarre chance, must have happened a good many times elsewhere. The trouble is, we may never know. The distances are so vast that even messages are unlikely to reach us, if such are ever going to be sent. My own guess is that we shall go on living in isolation and ignorance, not knowing what other kinds of intelligent life are like. And our life will go on until finally the sun has the fate which we can observe happening to other suns. This is an extension of those features of the human condition which existentialists refer to as absurd. But that is a literary flourish. This is the only life we know, and human beings will go on enduring it and sometimes enjoying it.

Yet this certainty of our cosmic insignificance is a very long way from the time when we were assured that the earth was the fixed centre of all around us. No sensitive person could now say that man is the measure of all things. A lot of our conceit has gone. Insensibly now more quickly, our idea of ourselves is changing. Much of this change, spelled out to us [by science] is not entirely comfortable. And yet, in the long run, it will be to the good. The great shocks to human confidence have come through the demolition of false hopes. The idea of man as a special creation was another edifice of conceit, and when that was shattered much security went. People had to search for another place to stand. Our idea of ourselves has now changed enough for us to find a stable place to stand.[152]

But insofar as science has revised our conception of where we are in the universe and of who we are genetically, a change of greater proportions affecting the role or place of the individual in society is also being effected by science. Some of this change will be perceived as being either good or evil. Through the continuing rapid development and diffusion of computers, for example, it may well emerge that none of us will need to sign or have checks in the near future. To many this kind of change will be positive. At the same time, it is possible that we will have computers that can take account of what each of us is doing. It may track all of our income and all of our expenditures; it will make doing income tax returns much easier while making the avoidance of income tax very difficult. In this sort of case, convenience is riding on the back of very serious questions about technology and individual rights to privacy, but always there are the good and evil aspects. Nevertheless, in the view of many technology and labor theorists (which Snow anticipated) it seems "inevitable that perhaps 10% of the population (of the advanced industrial nations) is going to work much harder and 90% is going to work much less." The serious implications of a society based on "non-work" are manifest.[153] Speaking to a reception at the British Embassy in Washington, D.C., in 1966 and encapsulating what was, for him, the necessary condition that accurately defined the active and socially meaningful individual—the modern individual—Snow noted:

I believe that it is good that people should in fact not have to work like beasts of burden, as we must remember that all men have worked (except a tiny fringe who are not statistically significant) since the species first developed. This, I believe, is a good thing and a much greater thing than the disadvantages that I am now going to annunciate. But there are disadvantages. It is all very well for us. We have anterior resources. Most of us like the jobs we are doing, and although we have to work too hard we can put up with it. But imagine what a large population is going to be like if in fact work, which was once the purpose of life, is taken away from you. Now purpose is the salt of life. Most people are unhappy if they are not given it. I can't help thinking that here, before it happens, we ought to be using every scrap of imagination to imagine this gigantic biological-sociological problem which [we] are going to be faced with soon. . . . [For example,] I believe that some of the American and British pre-occupation with sex is precisely because the purpose of life has tended to disappear. You must have some existential moments by which to pass your time. I believe that a kind of boredom and despair even may come upon people if we cannot find any live-able and purposeful non-work for people to do. I believe that non-work . . . is going to be one of the great problems of the next generation. . . . [This, plus] the lack of identity that people are likely to feel. . . . [If] in fact the computers [along with molecular biology and physics] are really at work, and if you really are part of an enormous mechanism, then I suspect that it may be true that the individual personality will seem less important; the individual will, the individual responsibility, may get danger-ously less.[154]

But this is no reason for despair. Indeed, quite the contrary is true.

Science and technology embody elements of both good and evil. They bring great benefits, but have a knack of unexpectedly stabbing you in the back. This is true even of what seems to be the most be-nevolent of technologies—medicine. "This is a technology which spreads most quickly over the planet. The length of a human life has increased dramatically since I was young. Fewer children die in in-fancy. No one with a spark of human feeling can doubt that those are great [and] good things. No decent person could wish they hadn't happened. Medical technology more than any other has been kind to the human race. And yet of course those blessings are also respon-sible for the growth of the world's population which may undo all we are trying to achieve."[155] Here Snow did not even touch on the im-portant questions raised by contraceptive technologies or the moral-ity of sustaining human life by technological means, but they are clearly not questions for the faint of heart. These types of questions, which surround and press in on us daily, present the greatest chal-lenge to our intellect and our will. This in itself is cause for great excitement, as it imbues us with an urgent sense of purpose and identity. Although it is true that "we can only do little things . . . that is no reason for not doing [that which we can do] as strongly as [possible]."[156] In so doing—in attempting to define and redefine what it is to be human—we cannot deny the existence of technol-ogy. "Technology, properly used, is the only weapon . . . at hand."[157]

It is this qualifying phrase—"properly used"—that is of particular importance here and that runs as a central thread in Snow's thinking since, at least, 1938. Because of the peculiarly scientific character of

our age, Snow reasoned, "scientists are the most important occupational group in the world today. What they do is of passionate concern to the whole of human society."[158] And hence "in a time like
this, scientists would be less than human if they did not consider
their responsibilities."[159] These responsibilities are especially great
because most decisions in an open society are made as a result of
closed politics and not by open groups of people. And for those most
vital of decisions—by which Snow meant those decisions by which
we live or die—the process is becoming infinitely narrower. "It does
not seem that there are any advantages other than speed. The possibility of errors in judgement is greatly increased. [And] what is
worse, the spread of indifference, of a kind of 'contracting out' of the
whole world of decision-making, has spread widely through society.
This is part of the despondency of our time. . . . Isn't it possible that
the computer age will add to the bad effects of [decision making]?
That is, the number of people who are going to be informed about
decisions is going to become still smaller?"[160]

Thus, with regards to the reality of science—its community,
knowledge, and rigor—Snow posed what is by some estimates the
ultimate question: "How are we going to restore a widely-based individual judgement?"[161] He was sure that it could be done. But it
will not be based on false hopes. As we have already said, the *findings* of science are ethically neutral—or as Snow would awkwardly
say, "non-moral" or "morally un-neutral." It is true that published
research results can be used for good or evil. But the *activity* of science is far from being morally neutral, as questions of practical ethics always lie in what to do next. Research that is yet to be completed, or that is yet to be undertaken, cannot be undertaken
without a commitment of will and resources. The population at
large, including scientists themselves, must firmly come to know
this. As Snow phrased it: "Science can no more prevent itself producing poison and high explosive than a cure for diabetes or the
steam engine. . . . It is admitted that much research is directed consciously and entirely towards producing means of destruction.
Whether an individual scientist takes part in such a work is a problem for his own conscience."[162] But, in speaking of the imminent
outbreak of World War II, Snow drove his point home:

Any utopian solution, in which it is hoped that science or scientists will not co-operate in war, can be rejected as a dream. But
that does not eliminate the responsibility of scientists in trying
to prevent war. . . . Living in a world of crisis [scientists] have
been compelled to learn that war is a symptom of society's

sickness, not a single phenomenon on its own account. To understand the causes of war, in order to prevent it, we must understand society itself: in particular we must understand the change in the world since . . . science enabled the whole scale of industry and organization to change. . . . Until that change is understood, and until those powers of . . . science are directed consciously to the benefit of the people of the world, human life will be a precarious business at best.[163]

To this end, Snow conceived of a modern realist mechanics for the human condition at the fin de millennium. At its center was the credo of Richard Gregory, G. H. Hardy, and J. D. Bernal to which Snow was exposed at Cambridge: "We must know as much of the social relations of science as we do of science itself."[164]

"Science [can no longer be] very remote from human intricacies, human problems. . . ."[165] But animating this view—in addition to the understanding of the emergence of science as a qualitatively different engine of change in both the public and the private spheres— was Snow's privileged focus on the individual over society and on the need for *purpose* in life, an appreciation for the force of *will* in society as well as for a sense of rational judgment and responsibility. Even though Snow had left scientific research by the late 1930s, science had provided him with all of these elements and had immeasurably improved his life. As he said of his own life, science "had been more important than money, love, or security. . . .[166] And as such—as Snow sought a balance between his own public and private personae—he began to realize how the ideas and practice of science had led him to ideas of the importance of personal politics in modernity's public affairs. In examining how social change could be generated by rational individuals, Snow developed what could best be described as a pervasive and highly individual "politics of reason." But nowhere is Snow's political perspective seen more clearly than in his literature.

6

PERSONAL POWER
AND PUBLIC AFFAIRS

Men must know that in this theatre of man's life it is reserved
only for God and his Angels to be lookers on.
—FRANCIS BACON

We live, as we dream—alone.
—JOSEPH CONRAD

IN WHAT IS STILL an influential depiction of "the political novel,"
Stendahl wrote that "politics in a work of literature is like a pistol-
shot in a concert" (something loud and vulgar that cannot be ignored). However, insofar as this is true, then Snow's work must be
seen as something of a departure, for at no point in his writings—all
of which deal with overtly modern and political themes—is the
reader distracted by the stark intervention of partisan politics, nor is
the reader forced to cater to the thoughts of an ideologue.[1] Politics is
too sustained and too subtle a theme in Snow's fiction and nonfiction for either of these.[2] Politics, in Snow's thought, is transparent
yet ever-present. It is the medium of the struggle of modernity, of
aesthetics, and of rationality. Indeed, Snow's sense of the political in
fiction leans more toward the definition of the political novel provided by Morris Speares.

In Snow's fiction we find novels of ideas, involvement, and of direct observation. They record the character and the significance of
social change in a scientific/atomic age. They gauge the tensions
and the shifts that occur as a result, especially within the establishment, all so that the implications of these changes for individual life
and the social form can—at least—be better understood and—at
best—be acted upon or used.[3]

In many ways it is a pardonable error to assume that since Snow
spent a total of twenty-two well-placed years in the service of the
British Government, and since his novels parallel modern historical
events,[4] his work must therefore be directly and obviously political.
But this would be a gross overstatement. It is true that Snow did actively pursue a firsthand experience of politics. As he himself said in
the preface to The Realists, such "experience can only be learned

first-hand."[5] Indeed, it was this desire to gain firsthand knowledge of politics that brought Snow, in March 1963, to ask Maurice Edelman, a member of Parliament, if he could "prowl around the House [of Commons]" so that he might "get it right" in writing *Conscience of the Rich.*[6] He once again alluded to his interest in the political disposition of modern society when he wrote in a personal note to Prime Minister Harold Wilson upon his resignation from the Ministry of Technology in 1966 that "you have given me a most privileged ring-side seat." Certainly Snow's pursuit of direct experience was in part driven by his literary requirements. But this was also driven by Snow's considerable ambition, by his desire to permanently escape his own social history and boy-from-the-Midlands social background, and by his attraction to—indeed by his sheer fascination with—society's corridors of power. But beyond these, Snow rarely— if ever—directly discussed matters of politics, even though he could be heard, as late as October 1970, addressing local Labour party meetings in London.[7]

In part, Snow's avoidance of formal ideology and political criticism is traceable to the fact that he was bound to the service of the British government during 1940–1944, 1945–1960, and 1964–1966. This required that he not directly discuss matters of politics. As he put it in *Public Affairs:* "I had been thinking about [politics] for a good many years . . . but I hadn't been free to express myself in public. This was because . . . I had been a public servant. . . . I was bound by the obligations and conventions of the public service. It is an old, and on the whole valuable, convention that one doesn't make statements which bear directly on politics. . . . [Anything I have said in public has been] within the rules."[8]

Learning, and then playing within, the rules of modern society was a very important part of Snow's worldview, and identifying the rules was a central aspect of Snow's political realism. As such, a close reading of Snow's work reveals, not a close documentary of Whitehall but rather an articulate view of social change within mass society in which his nonutopian notions of "the good life" and "the good person" inform each other. In so doing, Snow never adopted the position of a political theorist in the manner of a Raymond Williams, a George Orwell, or a Frank Raymond Leavis. Indeed, evidence suggests that Snow's knowledge of formal social and political theory was almost nonexistent, and that his reaction to the "English Dreamer" ideas of Leavis and T. S. Eliot[9] was strongly intuitive. Indeed, as a study of Paul Boytinck's authoritative bibliography reveals, Snow chose to review hundreds of books dealing with fiction, science, history, and history of science, but only twice—in the case of Raymond Williams's *Culture and Society* and Jean Paul Sartre's *Iron in the Soul*—did he review anything remotely associated with the social or political theory of modern society. Nevertheless, it is clear that Snow was very much engaged in his own coming to terms with the broad political realities of the twentieth century, and in attempting to say something publicly (through his literature) about these realities.

Perhaps nowhere else is Snow more firmly anchored as a political realist than in his own operative definition of politics as "the power relationships of men in organized society."[10] In so saying, he can be clearly identified with the traditional concerns of political realists— the art and transparent exercise of power, and the balance of power between private and public spheres. As those caught in the struggle of modernity already know, this does not come freely—as Snow emphasized and as we shall discuss. One person's freedom or responsibility is the next person's prison. But Snow the liberal political realist did not wish to celebrate power. Rather, he meant to approach an understanding of it so that it could be used in the service of individuals.

More specifically, Snow sought (and, for himself at least, found) degrees of freedom within the confines of social institutions and responsibility. Yet he was never to forget the essential tension that exists between freedom and responsibility. His vision of "the good society" reflected these values as the values of a vibrant civilization—independence, intellectual freedom, and individuality.

To liberal political realists such as Snow, the world must be seen as a thoroughly human place in which skillful people can—and must—work to create an open society. The realist also never believes that the state can ever provide or establish the conditions for goodness. It can only promote the conditions for happiness. Insofar as this is true, political realists hold a deep-seated belief in the possibility of social reform; but the responsibility for this change must rest with individuals, while the form that change takes must be defined by the parameters of existing social institutions. Thus it is not surprising that Snow rejected proposals for radical social reform that came from the English Dreamers, as Snow refused to entertain any critique that sought social change on the back of an antithesis of scientific-industrial society. Nevertheless, Snow was well aware of the growing tensions of the modern Metropolis, and through his framework, he did try to comprehend "the growing moral discontent of the West"[11] that modernity implied.

Like many other critiques of the modern condition, buried deep within Snow's assessment lie strong conceptions of progress, rationality, and history; but for Snow, conceptions of history leaned less toward Walter Benjamin's notion of "revolutionary nostalgia" and more toward Stendahl's *"promesse de bonne heure"* (promise of a good age). This tendency's animating character is most visible through his fiction—through Snow's New Man.

But this is not to suggest that his assessment of modernity was fixed or static. Indeed, the optimism that Snow derived from his progressive images of science and that typifies his early to middle years underwent a decisive transformation over time and left Snow with a darkening vision of society. As Saguna Ramanathan has noted,[12] the combination of science, aesthetics,and politics that had once given Snow his sense of vigor, insight, and public attraction had, by the end of his life, diminished in their capacity to explain the modern world. We will briefly discuss this aspect in the following chapter. For the moment, however, it is important to understand Snow's perspective on the public sphere.

Snow rejected any assessment of modern public affairs that failed to comprehend the nature and growing influence of science. By ignoring science in this way, the successful mediation between the individual and society could not be effected. Snow's views of the importance of science should be clear. As we have seen, Snow argued that "the scientific revolution is already performing, and has in fact performed, a structural transformation of modern democracy. . . ."[13] As a result of this simple fact, Snow argued, science must begin to be taken into account in any realistic attempt to progressively comprehend the nature of our contemporary condition. He underscored this view on numerous occasions saying, for example, that "whatever happens to us, our fate in the next fifty years depends on how far society can adjust itself to the new power science has put into its hands. . . . Our culture will be a very mandarin affair unless it includes a knowledge of the most important single force in human affairs."[14] But nowhere did Snow make a more articulate presentation on this theme than in his *Science and Government* and in the preface to his 1971 book *Public Affairs*.

When Snow's three Godkin Lectures at Harvard University on November 29, December 1 and 2, 1960, were published in April 1961 under the name *Science and Government*,[15] they engendered a discussion that—while not as heated as those that surrounded the Rede Lecture—was nonetheless immediate and that seemed to have far-reaching importance for the futures of advanced Western nations. This was largely due to the fact that it touched on the national policy questions that had been recently and urgently brought to the fore by such events as the launching of *Sputnik* by the Soviet Union in

1957. Moreover, it was recognized that what Snow had to say dealt with the fundamental choices that nations had made in the recent past and were sure to make in the future: choices such as those taken in England and the United States in 1940–1941 to work on the fission bomb, or that taken in 1945 to go ahead and use the fission bomb, or the choice taken later in the 1940s to make a fusion bomb, or those taken in the United States and the Soviet Union regarding intercontinental missiles. In the Harvard lectures, and in order to discuss the current affairs of immense public import, Snow explored the relationship of science and scientists to the functions of government during World War II. In so doing, he proposed several considerations for the future role of science both in periods of crisis and in healthy democracies generally. In the course of Snow's lectures he clearly demonstrated why the *New York Times* had dubbed him a "story teller for an atomic age." Even at this level, the link between Snow's nonfiction and fiction cannot be broken.

The tale that Snow tells in *Science and Government* focuses on two men and two choices. The men are Sir Henry Tizard, FRS, and F. A. Lindemann, who as Lord Cherwell became "the right-hand man and grey eminence of Winston Churchill. . . ."[16] Close friends since 1908, Tizard and Lindemann were to become bitter enemies by the 1930s. As the head of a government committee set up at that time to study air defenses, Tizard was in the ascendancy of his career. Indeed, Snow claimed that without Tizard, Britain would never have developed radio detection finding (RDF), which later became known as radar (*r*adio *d*etecting *a*nd *r*anging), in time for the August–October 1941 Battle of Britain. But in May 1940, when Churchill became prime minister and Lindemann became his scientific adviser, Tizard was quickly relegated to a comparatively minor scientific-military function.

The most important row between Tizard and Lindemann came in 1942 on the subject of strategic bombing. In that year a paper was issued by Lindemann (who was now a cabinet member) claiming that the British bombing offensive must be directed essentially against German working-class homes. Although the ethics did not seem to bother Tizard, Snow asked: "What will people of the future think of us? Will they say . . . that we were wolves with the minds of men? Will they think that we resigned our humanity? They will have been right." Tizard and his allies were more concerned that Lindemann's calculations of the effect of such bombing were overly optimistic. He claimed, in fact, that Lindemann's claim that a total concentration of the bombing effort would destroy 50 percent of Germany's houses was five times too high. Indeed, P. M. S. Blackett claimed that it was six to seven times too high. Tizard pushed the minority view and argued that a different strategy needed to be developed. Within the prevailing atmosphere, which had the "faint but just perceptible air of a witch hunt," he was regarded as a defeatist. Lindemann won the debate and strategic bombing was "put into action with every effort the country could make."[17]

Lindemann's policy was a failure, as Tizard and Blackett predicted it would be. Indeed, postwar surveys indicated that the estimates used by Lindemann were, in fact, ten times too high! As Tizard wrote after the war: "No one thinks now that it would have been possible to defeat Germany by bombing alone.... The effort in manpower and resources that we expended on bombing Germany was greater than the value in manpower of the damage caused."[18] Tizard believed to the end of his life in 1959 that, had he been listened to, the war could have been ended earlier and with less cost. "As one goes over the evidence," Snow stated, "it is hard not to agree with this."

From this story, Snow extracted a number of warnings for the industrial nations to consider. No nation's government science is "freer" than any other's, nor are its secret scientific choices. "So we find ourselves looking at the classical situations of closed politics."[19] The relationship between Lindemann and Tizard is "the purest example of court politics"[20]—the attempt to exert power through a man with a concentration of power. Tizard's authority was over when he called on 10 Downing Street in 1940, and Lindemann—as Churchill's chief science adviser—"had more direct power than any scientist in history." Roosevelt also had a "court," but no scientist ever became as intimate with him as Lindemann had become with Churchill. Fortunately, Snow noted, Hitler kept his power all to himself. The relationship between Lindemann and Churchill—although noble and admirable in some ways—thus resulted in bad judgments in public affairs. "Bold men protested to Churchill about Lindemann's influence, and were shown out of the room."[21]

Although Snow conceded that there are no easy answers to the problems concerning the use of power in closed politics, he nonetheless believed that there are things that we must avoid in the future. He put these points quite simply. "I think most of us would agree that it is dangerous to have a solitary scientific overlord. It is specially dangerous to have him sitting in power, with no scientist near him, surrounded by politicians who think of him, as some of Churchill's colleagues thought of Lindemann, as the all-wise, all-knowing Prof."[22] Even if the adviser is a Tizard or a Blackett, a Vannevar Bush or an Allan Bromley, the obvious dangers outweigh the vestigial possibility of good.

Nevertheless, having said all this, Snow did believe that scientists should be allowed to be more active in all levels of government. At a somewhat superficial level, this position may seem paradoxical, but in reality it is simply a reassertion of Snow's emphatic belief in the responsibility of the intelligent, articulate individual to participate as fully as is possible in the shaping of society. Snow was also, of course, supporting the revision of the British practice of separating the science service from civil service within the government, which allowed scientists little migration into the mainstream bureaucracy during their careers. But more philosophically, at a time when society is clearly deeply troubled, the scientists, Snow felt, have something that society could make good use of—foresight. "I am not saying, of course, that scientists have foresight, and no one else has," but "science, by its very nature, exists in history. . . . Scientists have it within them to know what a future-directed society feels like. . . . Science itself, in its human aspect, is just that."[23] I have no doubt that Snow would have considerable difficulty in making such a strident claim today at a time when science has become tied to funding and missions that are influenced by the government or industry. But nevertheless, within the temporal context of these lectures, Snow's claim that bureaucrats, managers, and administrators have become masters of the short-term solution—that they had, in effect, created the need for scientists who could bring their gifts of foresight to problems of government decision making—fell on interested and receptive ears.

In an appendix to *Science and Government* published in 1962, Snow lightly extended his argument to say of the military-*qua*-nuclear threat that "the longer I think about the way decisions have been taken, are being taken, and will continue to be taken, the more frightened I get." We are forced to depend, "much more than is healthy for society, on the scientific judgement of a comparatively small number of men. . . . Whatever we do, [the narrow reliance we had with Lindemann] must not [be allowed to] happen again."[24]

Undoubtedly Snow's most succinct expression of the need for an understanding of the relationship between science and politics by both scientists and politicians came in 1971. In the preface to his *Public Affairs*, Snow summarized his concerns as follows:

1. We—that is, most of the people in the world—are moving into great dangers. One is the possibility of thermonuclear war. . . .

2. These dangers have been brought about by technology, or what we now call applied science: that is, our ability to understand, control and use certain features of the natural world. Technology has two faces, benign and threatening. . . .

3. The only weapon we have to oppose the bad effects of technology is technology itself. There is no other. We can't retreat into a non-technological Eden which never existed. We can't look into ourselves and take comfort from any doctrine of individual salvation. . . . It is only by the rational use of technology—to control and guide what technology is doing—that we can keep any hopes of social life more desirable than our own; or, in fact, of a social life which is not appalling to imagine.

4. This being so, people will have to understand what technology, applied science, science itself is like, and what it can and cannot do.

5. The scientific decisions made inside government are, and will be increasingly, of critical importance. Often they have been taken by inadequate methods, or worse than that.[25]

Of course, this view runs counter to the views of such dystopians as Jacques Ellul—who had published his views in 1964. Ellul denied that major transformations in politics, economics, culture, and ethics can have a significant impact on technology. Here particularly, Ellul argued that humans really have no free choice over whether technology grows or how it grows. As he said, "At the present time, technique has arrived at such a point in its evolution that it is being transformed and is progressing without decisive intervention by man." Underlying Snow's passages is a more complex perspective that Snow brings to bear on the changing character of public affairs, and the way in which science and personal involvement is infused into the process of social change itself. But in so doing, and as these passages suggest, Snow did not advance the views of technological utopians who see the cure to social evils lying in the need for more technology. While he did see the scientific breakthroughs of this century as having profound social, political, and personal impacts,[26] Snow was also very early in recognizing the now widely accepted idea that problems that are essentially social and political in nature cannot be solved through technology.[27] Solutions to such problems can only be achieved by active individuals who have a deep understanding of the changing character of the age.

This character, which also implicitly contains a revitalized and revised social contract between the individual and society, is distinguished by developments beginning in the modern scientific revolution. As Snow pointed out, these included electronics, atomic energy, automation, and cybernetics. "Materially," as he said, "our lives are bound by these developments."[28] Conceptually, as we suggested earlier, this is also fundamentally true.

However, Snow's conception is not unproblematic. Working on the basis of the Godkin Lectures and *Public Affairs* alone, we do not get a clear notion of the practical mechanics of Snow's views on science and social change. For instance, if we were to extrapolate from his view that scientific decisions should not be left to a very small number of individuals, then are we correct in thinking that Snow thought widespread scientific literacy and subsequent public participation in the policy process is a viable solution?

Although many have assumed that this is the case, Snow never went so far as to explicitly endorse this approach. In fact, while the level of scientific literacy in a population undoubtedly has important implications for science policy decisions in a democracy, the reality is that no individual today can hope to acquire and maintain a mastery of more than a very few political issues at any one time. Thus modern citizens who choose to follow political affairs opt for political specialization—that is, they select out of myriad issues those few in which they are willing to invest the time and money that is necessary to become and remain informed. The need for specialization springs from a combination of three basic forces. First, participation in the political process is but one of the many demands on the time of contemporary men and women. That many adults choose to devote a smaller share of their time to political affairs, in favor of more attractive and personally satisfying alternatives, can be seen in the steady decline of public participation in the political system over the last four decades. Even presidential elections in the United States, which command the highest level of the American public's concern and participation, attract a surprisingly low proportion of the eligible adults.

Second, the specialized information that is required to be knowledgeable about almost any given political issue is increasing rapidly. Issues involving science fall into this category, as do most issues on the national political agenda.

Third, as our national political agendas become increasingly complex, it is also increasingly difficult to identify science as a discernible issue. Science and technology have become implicated in a spectrum of public policy issues from acid rain to trade. Therefore, hoping that a public will become sufficiently sophisticated to both follow science and participate in those policy issues in which science is implicated is simply not realistic.[29]

All three forces work to narrow the political horizon, and thus deny—if this was indeed Snow's intention—the possibility of having a scientifically literate, publicly active population. However, on the other hand, if we were to extrapolate from Snow's view in the opposite direction and suggest that what he really proposed was a narrow concentration of power in the hands of scientists, then—not only would the whole point of *Science and Government* have been missed but—to so suggest would be to give Snow little credit for originality, as this is a theme that John Kenneth Galbraith dealt with quite extensively in *The New Industrial State* as did Thorstein Veblen more than fifty years before him (i.e., the rise of technological elites and the growing primacy of expertise in modern society). Clearly neither perspective is adequate in trying to appreciate Snow. Thus, in order to finally grasp the full character of Snow's perspective on politics, we must move beyond the Godkin Lectures and *Public Affairs.*

Snow said of his original conception of the *Strangers and Brothers* novel sequence in 1935 that "I had . . . a certainty of the major themes—in short-hand terms. . . . man-in-society (including politics, but somewhat more than that), [and] man-alone."[30] The distinctions between Snow's meaning of politics and that of other critics, all of which rest essentially on differing conceptions of the changing social contract between the individual and society, can be clearly seen.

As we have seen, Snow recoiled vehemently against the response to modernity offered by both Bloomsburian aesthetes and the English Dreamers. Snow also totally rejected conceptions of "mass culture" or "mass society." "Mass" notions were, in Snow's eyes, not only homogenizing culturally and erosive to the individual, but he also saw such conceptions as failing to realistically acknowledge the limited potential of individual action and as being acquiescent to the weight of an impermeable conception of "social structure." In rejecting the category and reality of mass society, Snow refused to accept—in a cynical fashion—the central themes of modernity: alienation and exile, even though the "stranger" of his sequence title was an intentional allusion to the modern alienated condition.[31]

This is not to say that Snow was blind to the problems of urban living. Indeed, Snow fully recognized the Metropolis as a site of angst and sympathized with the plight of the stranger in the modern world.

Nevertheless, Snow was not willing to relinquish his sense of social hope to angst. For Snow, the constructive potential of rationality was too powerful and too positive to ignore. As he argued—against both academic theorists and the condition that they describe: "Alienation is a smart verve word for a condition which is common among disaffected people anywhere. There are some people who will never comprehend their world; never be able to come to terms with it; never be able to get either the joys of fellowship or the joys of their own individual life. . . . I cannot accept this fashionable . . . despair."[32] To Snow, despair—whether it manifests itself at a private, social, or political level—is the most erosive of moods. It totally negates any possibility of progress or improvement. "Despair," as he put it, "is a sin. . . . It removes any chance of action, small as it might be."[33] Action based on despair is perhaps the most ugly manifestation of unprogressive behavior that displays the schism between the private and public persona. Speaking in 1970, Snow stated unequivocally that "if you are performing as an anarchist, on the good graces of your parents' income, or on the good graces of the water and electricity services, this is real hypocrisy. . . . Anarchy is not a respectworthy proposition. Or even an interesting one."[34] Clearly in such cases, Snow saw the working definition of modern society in these actions as being distorted by highly unrealistic depictions of contemporary social change, perhaps ideologically based, and dangerously romantic.

At no point does the *raison d'être* for Snow's analysis of public affairs lie directly in countering specific assertions made by various cultural critics. Snow was never so anchored in the present as to address his disagreements to such individuals.[35] His is, instead, a much more diffuse, difficult, and future-oriented *raison d'être* arising from his growing sense of the apparent abdication of social responsibility in Western society and the active general apathy expressed toward formal political influence by newly disenfranchised groups (such as students) as well as by growing numbers of the mainstream citizenry. (Indeed, it only becomes possible to clearly locate the sources of Snow's own angst *after* 1968, during which time the student protests, the counterculture movement, the Chicago Seven trials, and the apparently general collapse of social order all signaled to Snow a crisis in his own conceptual framework.) Speaking as an observer of the state of public affairs in the West, Snow—referring in passing to the second law of thermodynamics—suggested that "the depressed mood of the West may be a mixture of frictions, lack of decisions, self-woundings of a plural society; and the idleness and acedia, the gloomy apathy of affluence—all tending to maximum entropy or "mixed-upness." This is not the whole of our mood, and naturally it is not constant, but it is there somewhere in the hinterland of many minds, and it is enough reason to be depressed."[36]

However, in recognizing these problems, Snow nevertheless rejected the analyses of romantics or counterculture gurus. Snow's own response implicitly addressed each of the points highlighted by these thinkers. He recognized—at a deeply personal level—that aspects of human life appear to be tragic, such as the fact that *on mourra seul*,[37] but these are inexorable realities over which we have no control. We should only expend our energies on things that are within our power to change. As Snow said in *The New Men*: "To Martin it was jet-clear that, despite its joys, individual life was tragic: a man was ineluctably alone, and it was a short way to the grave. But believing that with stoical acceptance, Martin saw no reason why social life should also be tragic: social life lay within one's power, as human loneliness and death did not, and it was the most contemptible of the false-profound to confuse the two."[38] Snow's refusal to abandon social hope, progress, and social reform represents a steady commitment to cultural continuity and traditional wisdom (standing on the shoulders of others, as in science). But in so saying, it is important to recognize that these are not static or frozen in time—curios under glass. Instead, they are part of a dynamic, re-iterative process. They are powerfully augmented in an ongoing fashion by new knowledge and assimilated into new forms of social organization. Thus, what is truly tragic is if we allow ourselves to believe, even for a moment, that life is elsewhere—that we cannot affect the process of change. Putting it rather strongly, Snow believed that "if you don't live in society, you are a fraud."[39]

Snow believed fundamentally that the exploration of the individual necessarily means the study of human beings in society. Because he found that most, if not all, people can be understood adequately only if both the public and the private sides of their lives are examined, his analysis attempts to examine those interactions between people and society. In *Strangers and Brothers*, life is a continual balance between the necessities and demands of social institutions and the needs and potentialities of individuals. Snow saw human fulfill-ment—including his own—as coming through participation in society.[40] In Snow's series, then, it is not surprising that those who do not choose to live in a truly social life are anomalies—either world-renouncing saints (like Martineau in *George Passant* and *The New Men*) or neurotics (like Roy Calvert in *The Light and the Dark*, *The Masters*, *George Passant*, and *Time of Hope*).

In attempting to move toward a progressive understanding of contemporary public affairs and a realistic reconciliation of the private and public self, Snow's first concern was to examine the terms for a new balance between the legitimate claims for personal power. In order to do so he not only appealed to the level of theoretical abstraction that is often used to discuss the process of social change itself, but he also convincingly addressed the minutiae of decision making in both its corporate and moral dimensions.

Snow began by establishing the basic premises that he adopted, and that he maintained throughout his career. Principal among these is that the relationship between the individual and society is symbiotic. Extending the observation that there can be no disembodied social (or technical) change, social change was, for Snow, entirely the result of the actions of individuals. The oppressive weight of institutions, such as colleges, research labs, or government departments, is not (in Snow's view) intrinsic to the institution but is more the result of a power matrix of individuals, institutions, and their respective histories.

A second reciprocal premise is that, apart from a core psychological character and predisposition, an individual's existence is created within the flux of society that embraces the full range of experience—from the construction of our physical and political environments to the organization of our ideas.[41] Snow's belief in human sociality was well grounded, as human beings were seen as gaining significance principally through their mastery and manipulation of symbols, be they mathematical or linguistic. This understanding was very much one of Snow's generation and was represented by such diverse individuals as John Dewey, who observed, in 1900, that "the individual mind is becoming defined by the social";[42] and Lord Annan, who—discussing the rise of modern social science in 1959—noted: "Nothing marks the break with Victorian England . . . more decisively than modern sociology. . . . They no longer deal with 'the individual' as the central concept in terms of which society must be explained. They [see] society as a nexus of groups . . . [that is] determined [by] men's actions."[43]

Both of Snow's underlying premises are present throughout the range of his writing. However, it is only when Snow defines politics, as he did in 1961, that we can fully begin to discern the nature of his worldview. This definition—which equates politics with "the power relationships between men in organized society"—is the key to Snow's reconciliation between the public and private selves, and to its limitations.[44]

Snow began his conceptualization with a rather weak notion of "the individual" who, he says rather quixotically, is free. "Nearly all of us . . . feel in a queer sense free, if we are in a set of circumstances that we know, however depressing that set of circumstances may be. . . . [To] an extent, you're your own man. . . ."[45] The essential parameters of this condition are clear: "we all live our lives in terms of immediate existence; how are we getting on with our partners, what's happening to our children, what's happening to those closest to us, the state of our health, everyday success or the reverse—and so on." [46] However, these "atomized units of society" that Snow describes hardly seem capable of being either the basis for meaningful power relationships or the empowered rational actors who will achieve his vision of social reform. In order to bolster them, Snow elaborated somewhat by injecting both a realistic encouragement— "It is no use to project a future from a base of false hopes" [47]—and an acknowledgment of strong social constraints: "How free are you to choose your work? From day to day? From week to week? From year to year? How free are you to explain it? How free are you to say what you think about it? How free are you to earn your living through your work? In your own country, in other countries, anywhere in the world? These couldn't be more simple and matter of fact questions." [48]

Even these, however, fail to direct us. Indeed, the missing ingredient of Snow's reformist equation is the belief that "the moment you abstract man from society you don't make him any more interesting, you don't make him deeper, you make him more trivial." [49] Snow posed this proposition in a way that clearly appeals to the reconciliation of the public and private selves by asking, "In our world, can a man feel even remotely reconciled with himself unless he has tried to do what little he can in action?" [50] This apparently simple query is itself a derivative of an ancient piece of rabbinical wisdom that Snow first came across in the 1930s at Cambridge and that inspired both his actions and his approach to action throughout his life. It reads: "If I am not for myself, who am I? If I am for myself alone, what am I? If not now, when?" [51] However, it is through this sentiment that Snow importantly imbues his conception of "individual" with the quality of personal ambition. Personal ambition transforms our passive condition of "free will" into an active agent for change— or, what Snow called "acts of will"—through decisions. [52]

Taken together, it is these judgments that collectively focus all of Snow's social critique and creative writings into a central conviction that a person's relevance only becomes manifest when he or she is (a) actively engaged in a quest for rational control over the surrounding social world and (b) defined as a member of formal and informal organizations. Illustrating these principles we find, in *Strangers and Brothers*, George Passant asking the senior solicitor, "Did you make these people realize that I was acting as a private person?" To which he replies, "My dear Passant, you ought to know that one can't draw

these distinctions."[53] And in *The Search:* "Get an unimportant job—
and have an unimportant sort of life."[54]

Frederick Karl amplifies this point, saying that in his fiction
"Snow . . . wants to show man functioning in the larger world, not
man praying or playing, but man working and making, *homo
faber.*"[55] Commenting more generally—but at the same time recognizing the implied converse that in order to have an important life,
in Snow's social terms, you must get an important job—Jerome
Thale writes:

> Snow's fiction exemplifies the sociological truism that our sense
> of identity comes most strongly from our jobs. Lewis Eliot's
> work is at the centre of his personal life, and is the source and
> occasion of many moral crises which form his character. It is
> through work that he meets friends, and even his relations with
> his brother are strongly affected by their jobs. . . . As we see
> Lewis Eliot at the various stages of his career, we always know
> exactly where he stands in the professional hierarchy. . . . This is
> true even of the minor characters—they are identified in terms
> of their positions in professional and institutional hierarchies.[56]

In part this reliance on one's affiliation and place in the hierarchy
echoes Snow's fixation with his own ascendance through British
class society and with the difficulty of his rise. But also it represents
a realistic acceptance of the character of the modern working world.
However, in so doing it suggests, within Snow's conception, the sub-
servience of the worker to the dominance of the organization. Snow
paid tribute not to coal miners, secretaries, and clerks but only to
those who decide to become actively and rationally engaged in the
operation of public institutions. Professionals would recognize themselves immediately in Snow's work. For Snow, particularly in his
earlier period, the involvement of such people is the only progressive
route to social change.

Snow ascribed to the individual a moral responsibility—a redemptive role for curing the world of alienation. Again, however,
this is not the "radical transformative role of the intellectual" that
many have called for. Instead, Snow argued that one must constantly come to terms with oneself in every act. In so stating Snow
demonstrated his keen awareness of the fact that everyday life forces
choices. The fact that a person can actually recognize the choices
involved is, to Snow, an indication of maturity. Often the decision
itself is secondary to the realization that it has to be made. Accord-

ingly, the burden of decision is the sole heroism that humanity is ever called upon to bear. What Snow sought here—between his rational actor and modern society—was a fine balance indeed.

Snow's "heroism of decision" is effectively available to all members of society; however, it only becomes a constructive form of social change when it can be combined with a sense of duty to one's friends and to one's fellow human beings, and when it can be engaged within the important—that is, transformative—institutions around us.

For Snow, it was largely through professional occupations (or, at least, "professional-style" behavior) that a positive social and political position is gained. In today's context, this may seem rather commonplace. However, the rapidly growing "technocracy" was only beginning to become evident in Snow's developmental years. The period saw the growth of professions—most notably of professionalized scientific research. These trends did not escape Snow's notice and served only to reinforce his view of the formative powers of the scientific revolution. Clearly, as we now recognize, the professions have come to be rigorously institutionalized within the capitalist system, influence many of the important decisions made within the system, and wield a growing social power. Indeed, it is in many ways these professional technocrats who are actively engaged in the process of changing the forms and conditions of our organizations, our environments, and our consciousness. But in Snow's earlier and most optimistic period he had no doubts that he would himself join the heroic scientific profession and thereby gain influence and bring about change. Snow's hopeful self-assessments are typified in such conversations as those found in *Strangers and Brothers* in which Snow says, "I was making my way" or in which he himself is advised by the young, but established, local dentist, Arthur Morcom, that "I know that you want to help your friends from being kept under. But you won't have the power to do it 'till you're firmly established yourself. Isn't it worth while to wait 'till then?"

However, as Snow came to know in maturity, professional status does not in itself confer greater personal liberties, freedom, or influence. Indeed, in Snow's view, professionalism can—with the sole exception of the scientific professional—have an effect opposite to what is desired.

As Snow came to realize, the level of additional personal freedom that accrues to those with professional status is limited, and over time (as the individual moves deeper into the organization) this only becomes more so. While it is true that those in certain occupations, such as law and medicine (and here, Snow should have included sci-

they have done, how and when they please. They can handle the results of their work however they like. Unlike other kinds of creative person, they are not normally immersed in any kind of commercial complex. . . . There is another factor which separates the professional scientist decisively from the rest of us. Their skill is international in the fullest sense.[61]

Much of this statement is frozen in the Cambridge of the 1930s—before the involvement of government and industry in scientific research that we have today. Snow's view was in many ways congruent with the sentiment of the period. As Don K. Price wrote in his 1965 classic *The Scientific Estate*: "scientists, even those who have no other political interest, are interested in freedom. They are manifestly concerned for the freedom of their own research. . . . They like to believe that the inner spirit of scientific research is one of freedom, that the processes of scientific research require freedom, and that therefore the political influence of science must be in the direction of freedom—not merely for scientists but for Mankind."[62] However, what Snow clearly did not understand was the changing social contract that has emerged between science and politics. Science has, in effect, entered its "post-heroic phase."

As Thomas Kuhn has suggested, modern science has indeed become a profession complete with codes of ethics, behavior, hierarchies, social legitimacy, and so on. However, in so doing a sharp dichotomy has been made between "revolutionary" and "normal" images of sciences with the vast majority of scientific research now being comprised of normal, or routine, science. Clearly, while Snow's own research must be classified as being "normal," his public vision of science was "revolutionary." But today, such a clear-cut bifurcation may no longer be tenable. Indeed, while Snow recognized that professionalization could curtail personal freedoms, he could not bring himself to extend this understanding to the scientific profession itself. He retained his view of science as an open activity despite the fact that the professionalization of science was essentially the outcome of twin sources: that is, extrascientific pressures (demands from government, industry, the military, and so on) that were attempting to mold science to social need, and demands from within science aimed at developing broad-based social acceptance for scientific research and social influence for scientific knowledge. Thus what he did not fully appreciate was that the professionalization of science is itself a manifestation of the existence, at a deeper social level, of a principle of exchange that, it is often said, is the hallmark of modern industrial society. In the case of sci-

ence), are more or less free to choose to practice in o
(thus giving them a slightly wider range of freedom r
working lives), the impact of various mechanisms as
professionalism is highly restrictive. The effect of co
conduct, and practice—not to mention the responsibili
contractual obligation that a professional has to his
normalize and strictly monitor behavior. As Snow succ
evidencing his partial understanding of this, "profess
soon establishes a whole domain of acts you may not
things you may not do. . . ."[57]

Here Snow's assessment has the attractive air of
comes of a man who seems to understand the way the
He recognized that decision makers—that is, largely
persons who are in positions where some degree of p
acted out—rely heavily on traditional wisdom, and o
and rationality that their occupational backgrounds bri
Snow himself never became fully aware of the ideologic
science or of his own training. But increasingly, Snow
sion makers are having to deal with, and rely on, the f
nitive wisdom (which is part of scientific wisdom) in add
ditional wisdom.[58] Indeed, as we have seen, this was
point of *Science and Government*.

The observations made in Snow's Godkin Lectures ar
tractive, extending several of the positions made during
the relationship between science, government, and socie
place during the 1920s and 1930s. Lying beneath Snow
a vision for the future reform of political power. This
of Snow's privileged scientific profession. Exemplifying
Sheriff exclaimed enthusiastically in *The Search*: "We're
power, and that's making our civilization the first stable
been. It's because it's the first civilization that has got l
ence. . . ."[59] As Snow put it rather baldly, "The scient
sion . . . gives us what we can call a model of what concr
ter of fact freedom means."[60] For Snow, the reasons fo
quite clear.

By and large, the professional scientists have the possib
acting more freely than any other collection of human
this earth. Answering my simple questions, they can sa
as soon as they are out of their ordinary training or app
ship, that they can choose what kind of work to do. Th
jects for research are, at least in principle, at their own
posal. . . . Scientists are entirely free as a rule, to publis

ence, professionalization was a way in which groups with specialist expertise were able to obtain a degree of autonomy in return for delivering some other social good. This was an important development, not least because in adopting professionalization as a route to social legitimation scientists gave tacit acceptance to the application of the principle of exchange to knowledge. Perhaps, as Snow intuitively understood and illustrated in fiction, all industrial societies achieve cohesion by means of a more or less complex network of exchange relationships. But it cannot be denied that such exchange relationships have come to be very narrowly interpreted because of the general presence of an experience with the production and sale of commodities. As many scholars have already noted, the march of industrialization has been, in some respects, the march of commodification. In such a society even Snow's knowledge producers could not expect to be treated differently.

The limited recognition of the restrictions inherent in professionalization, and of their propensity to increase in weight and complexity as the system they support expands, forced Snow early on to realize that "most of the open decisions of society aren't made by single people . . . [but rather go] through the minds of very large numbers of people and [collect themselves] in points of decision-making."[63] In addition, Snow had come to understand that the decisions that mattered—the decisions that could affect the direction of social change—were not made in the open society at all but rather took place in the realm he called "closed politics."

On the occasion of Snow's Godkin Lectures, he outlined three forms of closed politics that are evident throughout modernity and the *Strangers and Brothers* series. These he called committee politics, hierarchial politics, and court politics.[64] Of committee politics, he wrote: "The archetype of all these is the kind of committee where each member speaks with his individual voice, depends on his personality alone for influence, and in the long run votes with an equal voice."[65] He defined hierarchial politics—that is, the politics of the chain of command, of bureaucracy, and of large industry—as follows:

> To get anything done in any highly articulated organization,
> you have got to carry people at all sorts of levels. It is their decisions, their acquiescence or enthusiasm (above all the absence of their passive resistance), which are going to decide whether a strategy goes through in time.[66]

This is a form of politics which has not yet received the attention it needs, if one is going to have any feel for how an elaborate organization is supposed to operate, but for how it does in fact. It cuts across all kinds of romantic stereotypes of official power. The top bosses of great corporations like General Motors or General Electric, or their English equivalents, could not act even if they wanted to, could not act by the intrinsic nature of their organization, like the proprietors of a small film company.[67]

The form of politics Snow called court politics is defined as "attempts to exert power through men who possess a concentration of power."[68]

The Tizard-Lindemann affair was, for Snow, a case in point of court politics. Lindemann and Winston Churchill "really did work together on all scientific decisions and on a good many others, as one mind."[69] Lindemann had no official position, and yet he made his unofficial position obvious "by holding his interviews in 10 Downing Street, or by threatening Churchill's intervention. Bold men protested to Churchill about Lindemann's influence and were thrown out of the room. Before long everyone in official England knew that the friendship was unbreakable, and that Lindemann held the real power. Before long also men had accustomed themselves to that degree of power and jumped up behind it; for an overwhelming majority of men find a fascination in seeing power confidently used, and are hypnotized by it. Not entirely through self-seeking, though that enters too."[70] Snow concludes:

> In all closed politics the three forms I have isolated—committee politics, hierarchial politics, court politics—interweave, interact, and shift from one to the other. This is independent of the objectives, which may be good or bad; it is simply the way men have to operate in order to get anything done at all. I do not mean that as satire. Satire is cheek. It is the revenge of those who cannot really comprehend the world or cope with it. . . . So far as I have been able to observe anything, this is how the world ticks—not only our world, but also the future world one can imagine. . . . It seems to me important men of good will should make the effort to understand how the world ticks. It is the only way to make it tick better.[71]

These ultimately are the themes animating both Snow's fiction and his New Man ideal: the individual; reason—based on international peer review, as well as critical and honest intelligence; personal power; ambition; closed politics; social reform. It is clear from Snow's impressive perspective that what he presents to the reader is not just an articulate examination of important modern British social history. He also succeeds in constructing what in some ways is *both* a classical *and* a transitional modern hero in the form of the "public men" he chooses to portray. He does so not because he feels he must counter the arguments of the aesthetic and political experimentalists but to help reveal the rational inner workings of the institutions that are most likely to be responsible for future social directions. As we have seen, in order to fulfill the demands of his chosen framework, Snow almost exclusively selected the university and research laboratory as well as the government department as his principal sites for the investigation of these themes. As he said (indeed as he said of all these sites): "a college is a society of men."[72] Animating these sites in a way not found in any other modern fiction is Snow's array of characters who are, almost exclusively, professionals—"public men" through whom social change *and* social stability are effected. Through these individuals, Snow portrayed the issues of our time, their struggle with modernity, and in so doing addressed—and attempted to reconcile—the private self with the public person.

The fictional character of this investigation lies in Snow's portrayal of real choices that must be made by individuals: for example, the ambitions of professionals who are faced directly with ethical choices (as in the case of Charles March who must choose between a life at the bar with a comfortable family fortune and life as a public physician with low wages and social esteem); or moral choices (as in the case of Martin Eliot who is a physicist working on the atomic bomb and who must come to political, practical, and personal terms with America's use of the weapon, and subsequently with the new image of science that the war has delivered); or personal limitations (as with the scientist Arthur Miles who—after years of dedication to the dream of running a research laboratory—abandons the dream because of an error of judgment in research); or with the limitations of others who are close to you (as with Lewis Eliot and his friends, Jack Cotery and George Passant, who irrevocably succumb to sensuality and idealism while Lewis helplessly watches on).[73]

Snow's first novel, *Death under Sail* (1932), brought critical attention to him as a novelist—as indeed it should have, as this novel is a fine exercise in the genre of detective fiction, but it was with *New Lives for Old* (1933) that Snow's concerns were really initiated. A rather heavy-handed science fiction tale of biochemistry, ageing, and the discovery of a rejuvenating agent, this book—which is obviously written in the style of H. G. Wells[74]—nevertheless contains an interesting reference to "consciousness," which was preoccupying Snow during this period—"consciousness of motive, awareness of one's emotions and those of the people around one, perceptions of the reasons behind the actions that human beings do."[75] The topic of the book may seem, by today's standards, stiff and farfetched, but it was sufficient to bring reviewers of this anonymous publication to identify Snow as "one of the cleverest of our younger scientists."[76]

The story concerns the discovery of a hormone that could rejuvenate the human race. It is also concerned with the ethical effect that the discovery had on its discoverers: the not insignificantly named Professor Billy Pilgrim and his young co-worker David Callan, and on their friends and colleagues. Among the major problems created by the fictional rejuvenation process was the discovery that the hormone is more effective in men than in women. Thus men seek out younger wives and lovers, and the family unit ceases to exist. As well, the rejuvenating process became class structured: the poor die at the age of seventy or so while the rich—by paying £1,000—live on. A social revolution ensues, and both Pilgrim and Callan struggle with the implications of their work. Foreshadowing the growing pessimism that descended on Snow in his later life, a character in the novel, the sociologist named Bock, writes in his notes—a document entitled *Statistics of the First Ten Years of Rejuvenation*—that "unless one realizes how unlike one, and how like one, other human beings are, then there's no chance of recovery from an inferiority which is the dominant note of most of our lives."[77] In the end Callan himself says: "I don't know whether science is important, or not, or anything. But if anything is important, then this work of mine [research] is—and if there is any hope for humanity at all, then science and art are the most important things that man can do."[78] The book illustrates unmistakably that the achievements of science have important social and political impacts and must therefore be governed by understanding and reasoned individuals.

Extending these preliminary examinations on consciousness and motivation in a science-influenced world, Snow explored the fictional world of personal power and decisions more directly in *The Search* (1934). The hero of this tale, who is in part based on Snow himself, is Arthur Miles. The story tells with great passion and energy the emergence of Miles's love for science.[79] The tension of the story becomes focused on his dreams for success in research (which include having a laboratory under his leadership at a very young age). This expresses the inner tension felt by all professionals of ability and ambition. While Miles sees his goal with clarity, he is fully conscious of the costs. Initially the cost is Audrey Tennant, a girl whom Miles probably should have married but whom, instead, he lost. A more important tension to Snow (and to Miles) is the ongoing need to reconcile ultimate truth (which is broader than scientific truth or knowledge) with human happiness. The power of the young intellects who are "finding their way" is made clear throughout. For example, in the midst of studying for exams and caught up in the excitement of the new physics, Sheriff confronts Miles.

> "The people who have the power in their hands. Look at them. They're not like you, Arthur. They're not wider than the average. They're infinitely narrower."
> "That's not fair," I said.
> "It's fairer than your picture of bright clear minds—and everyone else in darkness."[80]

The Search also provides Snow's first attempt to reflect directly on idealism and to reveal his awareness of the changing social organization of science that was taking place in the 1930s. Both of these come principally through the portrayal of J. D. Bernal in the character of Leo Constantine.

As we have already argued, Snow's view of idealism was that it more often than not provided "considerable heat but little light."[81] However, Snow was quick in the 1930s to acknowledge the wide continuum that idealism and intelligence could share. Elaborating on this, Miles characterized the personalities with which he would have to deal in matters of personal politics and human affairs as follows:

> These verities seemed to me to fall into two main types. Perhaps this was a shape I imposed for myself and corresponds to nothing real; but they are types observed often enough before in human affairs and I still believe that they are not entirely artificial. Applying them to scientific thinking, I should call the first the problem-solving type; minds which choose out of the world 'round them a certain piece of experience and drive through to an explanation. The probing, analytical and pragmatic minds, which at their best can reach the heights of Rutherford and Darwin. . . . In everyday affairs it is probably the commoner type of mind, and so the performances of its highest exponents seem familiar and easy to most of us . . . which means that we under-estimate them unduly on the principle that what is not mysterious cannot be profoundly admirable. The second type, the abstracting mind, of which Constantine is an example, gets perhaps more than its share of admiration just because it is difficult for most of us to

argue with, speaking as it does a different mental language from our own. These minds do not drive through a portion of experience; they wait for experience to make itself into shapes in their minds, they assimilate and correlate, find resemblances in different things, differences in similar things. At their best, in Faraday, Einstein, or, in my generation, Constantine, they are the great generalizers; at their worst they are infantilely fantastic and removed from all reality.[82]

Miles further characterized Constantine as "sympathetic, even interested," adding: "But irritably I was thinking how he and I saw people with different eyes, how individuals 'round him were shapes in an abstraction. A clever, wonderfully intricate, beautifully coloured abstraction of an ideal world—but that was his vision of things, and it was so alien to mine that he might have been speaking in a language I did not understand."[83]

Reflecting on his distrust of idealism and on his beliefs in the need for a realistic understanding of how social change is effected by people, Miles writes of his wife's parents: "They were ineffectual because their human beings were ideal; we may be ineffectual, but our human beings must at least be real. We want a liberal culture; but it has got to be based on human beings driven by their fears and desires; human beings who are cruel and cowardly and irrational, with just a streak of aspiration. . . ."[84]

One aspect of the changing social organization of science is portrayed in *The Search* through the focus on the establishment of a new research institute in crystallography. Miles wants the directorship. The senior Constantine was pushing hard for it. His was the new vision of science. Within this portrayal we can see the early crystallization of Snow's marriage between science and politics. It is all here: the personal ambition and politics, the vision, the public affairs. Here is a classic example of what Snow called committee politics. Snow's explorations in consciousness (*New Lives for Old*) are here revealed as mature, yet exuberant. The conversation at one of the meetings of the deciding board goes as follows:

> "For my part," said Austin, "I am in favour of Institutes of this nature. With safeguards. Such obvious safeguards as attaching them, both formally and in fact, to some University. We must see that an Institute doesn't become a research factory, doesn't altogether lose the atmosphere and contrast of a University."
>
> "That's exactly what we do want to lose," Constantine burst out. . . . "It's exactly that which will keep our scientific organi-

zation medieval, even when our individual science is years beyond its present level. Why should we pay all this lip service to
Universities? . . . [They are] cluttered up with superstitions and
religion and morals and social barriers, and [they add] on a little
science as patronizingly as they dared. We've got a problem here,
a definite problem, which is the job of the Institute to solve."

Fane spoke over his shoulder, smiling: "I'm afraid I've not Mr.
Constantine's faith in prior thought. If a thing's been done before
we may not get the best, but we know how to avoid the worst."

"That's what you mean by tradition?" said Constantine
quickly. Fane nodded.

"There might be more pretentious definitions. We ought to admit, though, that there is no end to tradition. Where you're dealing with something quite new, qualitatively new, different from
anything we've ever had before; I know we usually pretend it
isn't new, and smuggle it under the wing of our tradition. Like
science in the University. But it's an inept and frightened and
inefficient way of doing things." Constantine's head was flung
back, and his eyes were looking, not at Fane or any of us, but
into the distance.

"Somehow we rub along," said Desmond. "Patch up the system here and there. We put Institutes into Universities and call
them university labs. It seems to work."

"Our friend Desmond is right," Austin boomed. "That is the
way we introduce our changes, unobtrusively, discreetly—why,
anonymously, almost."[85]

For Snow, this would always ultimately be the essence of directed
social change. The individual, bringing his or her intelligence to bear
on public affairs, working with others, and pushing a result or outcome that—though perhaps revolutionary or incremental—appears
anonymous to the outsider.

In the end, similar to Snow in research, Miles commits an error in
judgment and loses the directorship. It becomes clear to him that he
had been placing his science second to his ambitions. In a painfully
honest passage of inner conflict and moral decision that one cannot
dissociate from Snow's own life, Miles says, after being told that he
was being offered the assistant directorship:

I ought to get out of science. There is nothing for me now. Not
for years. Macdonald was right (I resented him for being right).
With patience and penitence and effort [I might get an Insti-
tute]. . . . Why should I be patient and penitent? Why should

drab and jealous men . . . get me in the end? Make me have a respectable success—after working respectably enough, dully enough. I should be tamed as everyone else was tamed. Either I got out of science or else I had to be patient and conform. If I got out, what could I do? I cannot afford gestures. Money and leisure I must have. I want them for themselves—and for . . . the freedom of which they are a sign. . . . What can I do? . . . Industry? Scientific industry? . . . Scientific journalism? . . . It was a bad time to be unattached. Perhaps the world will never recover from this collapse (it was the August of 1931). Whatever I do, there will be some unpleasant years. In science the unpleasant years will be safe. . . . Yet to think of going back. Watching the dullards gloat. Working under Tremlin. Having everyday a reminder of the old dreams. It occurred to me that I'd forgotten my devotion to science. It occurred to me that I had no devotion to science.[86]

The Search stands today as one of the great novels of its kind, and certainly one of Snow's best. It brought the Nobel Prize–winning physicist I. I. Rabi to write that it is "a novel that describes the world of science as lived by scientists from the inside."[87] In *The Search* Snow succeeded in expressing his concerns and symbolically examining the modern dilemma of humanity's having pushed back the frontiers of knowledge, yet to little spiritual advantage. Snow claimed, however, that it was a "false start" in his literary career; his true start was to be *Strangers and Brothers*.

The subject of personal power and public affairs is strongly reflected throughout Snow's novel sequence. In discussing the theme of "possessive love," to which Snow sometimes referred instead of personal power and which he also identified in 1935 as being one of his key concerns, what he focuses on is ego domination or dependency between individuals. There are many examples of this kind of relationship throughout the series between pairings of individuals whom Snow has us watch closely. However, the most important relationships center on Lewis Eliot: his relationship with his manic-depressive (and ultimately suicidal) wife, Sheila Knight, is one in which the domination of wills, the exertion of power, and the willful denial of the self are paramount. There is no mutual trust. On the other hand, a more satisfactory relationship exists between Lewis and his second wife, Margaret, one that is symbiotic and that is based on mutual respect.

Lewis also has deep relationships with George Passant, Roy Calvert, and Charles March. George is a flawed idealist to whom Lewis

mian for me. But when my children refuse to bring any of their friends to see their aged parent if they have to make themselves un-comfortable, I'm compelled to stretch a point. I'd rather have you not looking like a penguin than not at all."[94]

In an excellent piece of drama, *The Conscience of the Rich* main-tains a level of tension rarely achieved in modern fiction. The split between Charles and his father, which is developed with subtlety and mastery by Snow, brilliantly represents not only the complex tension between social, political, and economic institutions in Brit-ain during the 1930s but also manages to be indicative of the splits between the rich and the poor, the conservative and the liberal, and between generations. But in the final analysis what Leonard March is fighting against is the loss of power and protection over those he loves. As Lewis Eliot humorously recounts after a March family cri-sis: "They left out what none of us would find it necessary to tell in a family story: the fact that there was deep feeling in the quarrel. . . . That Katherine, arguing with her father, felt more overawed and frightened than she could admit; that Mr. March felt a moment of anxiety, such as we all know as we see someone beginning to slip from the power of our possessive love."[95] What Snow demonstrates here is that, at least in this instance, his understanding of interper-sonal relations, private power, and ambition is thorough and truly compelling.

As has already been said, the themes of closed politics are best demonstrated through the novels *The New Men, The Masters, The Affair,* and *Corridors of Power. The New Men* has already been men-tioned. While the complete study that these books alone deserve is beyond my scope here, a sketch can certainly be provided of the committee, hierarchy, and court politics found. In each of these four novels Lewis Eliot is either part of, or party to, political activities in which both personal power and public affairs are at stake. In the case of *The Masters*—which has been called the "most popular" and the "most self-contained novel of the series"[96]—the personal power struggle is between Paul Jago and Thomas Crawford. The public affair is the eminent election of a new Master for the Cambridge college.

Working within the highly structured and organizationally lay-ered environment of the college, Snow provides a range of characters through which to animate the politics of social change. Chrystal, an established scientist, is an empire builder who is "still capable of losing himself in hero-worship." Arthur Brown is managerial and thrives on having a position of respect within the college. Winslow, the bursar, is wealthy, aloof, and singularly unpopular. Nightingale peaked too early intellectually and is, as a consequence, consumed with envy, bitterness, and insecurity in middle age. Jago, the senior Tutor, is mercurial, "a man of deep feeling and passionate pride." Despard-Smith, a cleric whose spirit has long dried up, lives out his days in bitterness and disappointment over the lack of recognition given him by his peers.[97] And finally, M. H. L. Gay, the elder Fellow, is among the most spirited of the group. Lewis Eliot is, of course, a junior Fellow along with Roy Calvert. The year is 1937.

The novel begins with its central drama. The Master of the college, Vernon Royce, is—without knowing it—dying. He believes he has only an ulcer and will be back in charge at the beginning of term. The Fellows are told by Royce's wife, Lady Muriel, that he in fact has inoperable cancer.[98] A replacement must be made ready to step in for the sake of the college. The choice very quickly comes down to two men of very different sensibilities and skills: Jago or Thomas Crawford, the humanist or the scientist. The remainder of the novel is essentially an observation of the Fellows agonizing over their choice, and the implications of what their decision will have for themselves and the college.[99]

Arthur Brown, the manipulator and tactician *par excellence* presents Jago's name as Royce's successor to his closed group composed of Lewis, Calvert, and Chrystal. Nightingale, a theoretical chemist, is later added, as is the nuclear physicist Walter Luke. Upon his return from Switzerland, Francis Getliffe is greatly disturbed both by the suggestion of Jago and by Lewis's support for him. Getliffe makes plans for another candidate, and a second faction immediately develops that submits the physiologist Crawford. In quiet support are Winslow, Despard-Smith, and Gay.

The characteristics, accomplishments, and aspirations of the thirteen Fellows, interspersed by reports of the Master's condition, influential visits by the industry tycoon Sir Horace Timberlake, and finally the death of the Master, give momentum to the book in much the same way that the maneuvering and shifting of allegiances lend suspense. All the while, Lewis communicates his fresh view of the politics within a closed society of men.

In so doing, Snow continues his development of themes: of acts of will and of being involved in affairs; of not being radical, but realistic; of having ambitions quietly fulfilled and of making a difference. Speaking of Brown and Chrystal, Lewis says:

These two were the solid core of the College, I thought. Year by year they added to their influence; it was greater now than when

I first came four years before. It had surprised me then that they should be so influential; now that I had lived with them, seen them at work, I understood it better.[100]

For, though they were the least conceited of men, they had complete confidence in their capacity to "run things." Between them, they knew all the craft of government. They knew how men in a College behaved, and the different places in which each man was weak, ignorant, indifferent, obstinate or strong. They never overplayed their hand; they knew just how to take the opinion of the college after they had settled a question in private. They knew how to give way. By this time, little of importance happened in the College which they did not support. . . . They accepted the world around them; they had no doubt they were being useful in the parts they played. As they piloted their candidate through a Fellowship election, or worked to secure [a sizable benefaction] from Sir Horace, they gained the thrill that men feel at a purpose outside themselves. . . . [In] College they formed the active, if sometimes invisible, part of a progressive government.[101]

Snow portrays the force of ambitions and the vision that some have of how to make changes in society. Of Jago he says:

[He] enjoyed the dramatic impact of power, like Chrystal; but he was seeking other things as well. He was an ambitious man, as neither Brown nor Chrystal were. In any society, he would have longed to be first. . . . He longed for all the trappings, titles, ornaments and show of power. . . . [But] there was something else. He had just said to Chrystal "we can make this a great College." He believed that there were things that only he could do. Money did not move him in the slightest; but there was a quality pure, almost naive, in his ambition. He had dreams of what he could do with his power.[102]

But Lewis cautions, saying, in a way that reflects Jago, "Envy and pique and vanity, all the passions of self-regard: you could not live long in a society of men and not see them often weigh down the rest."[103]

Both Crawford and Jago are cautiously considered by the other camp. Calvert considers Jago's appeal to be the fact that he's "a man who knows something about himself. And is appalled. And has to forgive himself to get along."[104] In reply to Francis Getliffe's statement that Jago was not a distinguished scholar and was not what a

Master should be,[105] Eliot countered that "it's not so much what he's done as what he is, and as a human being there's a great deal in him."[106] Chrystal simply states: "Jago would do."

Of Crawford, Brown says he would be a disaster.[107] As a scientist he "wouldn't lift a finger for any of us."[108] "He'd have no feeling. And no glow. And not a scrap of imagination."[109] Getliffe, "a radical, like many scientists of his generation," counters that Crawford is one of the best biologists alive.[110] The choice for Master is between the scientist described as "confident, impervious, conceited, self-assured" and a humanist who is said to be "sympathetic, emotional, anxious, and liberal." It is clear, however, that the pivotal question does not rely on the simple distinction between the fields of arts and sciences. As the authoritative M. H. L. Gay puts it: "I should never give a second's thought to such a question. . . . I have never attached any importance to boundary-lines between branches of learning. A man can do distinguished work in any, and we ought to have outgrown these arts and science controversies before we leave the school debating society."[111]

An influential factor leading to the ultimate choice of Crawford over Jago, however, is the increased income for the college that comes from Sir Horace Timberlake. His somewhat less than scholarly nephew is a student at the college, and the implication is that if the Tutors can get him through, then Sir Horace might be interested in making a substantial benefaction. He "relished the power of giving or withholding money,"[112] and he makes the conditions quite clear.

> "I'm only thinking aloud, you know what I mean. But it seems to an outsider that you haven't anything like your proper number of fellowships. Particularly on what I might call the side of the future. You haven't anything like enough fellowships for scientists and engineers. And this country is dead unless your kind of institution can bring out the first-rate men. I should like to see you have many more young scientific fellows. I don't much mind what happens to them, so long as they have their chance. They can stay at the university, or we shall be glad to take them in industry. But they are the people you want."
>
> "Even the possibility of a benefaction is exciting," said Jago. "But I do agree with my colleagues. If the fellowships were limited to one subject, it would change the character of our society."
>
> "You will have to change the character of your society in twenty years," said Sir Horace. . . . "History will make you. Life will make you. You won't be able to stop it. . . ."[113]

Echoing this point from another perspective, Lewis says: "We talked about personal politics, of which, not only in the college, we had now seen a good deal. One point struck us both: will, sheer stubborn will, was more effective than cunning or finesse or subtlety."[114]

The Affair, which takes place fifteen years after *The Masters*, portrays a similar struggle. Snow's setting is once again the college, and again he examines the inside workings of closed politics. But this time—instead of the election of a Master—the focus of Snow's novel is to show that justice (or rather, the decisions of a rational society) eventually triumphs despite the moral shakiness of the individuals who make the decisions.

The object of the story is Donald Howard, a young scientist who is accused of fraud and who had been dismissed from the college six months previously. He had been elected as a Fellow on the strength of research results presented in a dissertation under the supervision of the late C. J. B. Palairet. Howard—who is a Marxist, a wimpish character, and a rather unspectacular scholar[115]—never makes any claims in his defense. Howard's wife has pressed for the case to be reopened. Lewis Eliot is drawn in as an expert in law. The principal investigators are asked to reconsider the evidence of the case, which hinges on a diffraction photograph.

At the outset, there is a very high degree of agreement within the college. The majority are satisfied that justice has been done: that Howard had engaged in "a piece of simple unadulterated fraud." The discovery came when two American researchers published in *Nature* that they hadn't been able to replicate the results of Palairet and Howard. Closer investigation by Skeffington and Nightingale shows that the photo—one of a series—had been enlarged to show the desired effect. The first note of discord comes from Skeffington, who tells Lewis and his brother Martin after the college Christmas dinner that he believes the story of Laura Howard. Martin and Lewis are subsequently convinced enough to consider the case further. The dissenters are permitted to reexamine the late professor's papers, which had been willed to the college. The process from this point is almost identical with those described in *The Masters* and *The New Men*. By December 28, Lewis and Martin are convinced that an injustice has taken place. However, there is a great deal of reticence among the Fellows, and it takes until February for the trio to convince enough Fellows of the merits of their concern to have the Master issue a memo to the Court of Seniors authorizing the reopening of the case. Of Skeffington, Lewis says: "I was thinking, Skeffington was a brave and honourable man. He had not had an instant's hesitation, once he believed that Howard was innocent. He was set on rushing in. Personal relations did not matter, his own convenience did not matter, nor how people thought of him. Both by nature and by training he was single-minded: the man had his rights, one had to make sure that justice was done. Yet, inside that feeling, there was no kindness towards Howard."[116]

The proceedings drag on with arguments between factions trying, on the one hand, to ensure justice and, on the other hand, to ensure the stability of the conservative college (that is, keep it out of the papers, keep an unlikable sort out of the college, and so on). The exasperated Court of Seniors unhappily explode at one point, "Now we listen to the voice of Science, disinterested and pure, the voice of Intellect at its highest,"[117] while Tom Orbell (who started this appeal with his Lewis–Laura Howard dinner in London in September) also criticizes the proceedings by crying: "God knows I don't like Howard, but was one word said last night, was one word even thought, about the man himself? It was so de-humanized it made my blood boil. Have they forgotten what it's like to be human?"[118] Lewis simply observes that he had forgotten "how intense and open the emotions could show in a closed society."[119] The events parallel those in earlier novels: faction meetings, dinners, formal hearings, High Table discussions, and so on.

The real edge of mystery enters the story when the photo in question turns up missing. Lewis and Skeffington deduce who could have both wanted the picture removed and had access to the Palairet papers. At length Nightingale, who was pictured as the ageing and bitter bachelor in *The Masters*, now is portrayed as a happy individual—married and bursar of the college. He still retains his personal qualities (pride, meticulousness) and in his college position he is beyond reproach. It is only the retired Paul Jago who can convince Arthur Brown that the present Nightingale is just as capable of removing the photograph for his own purposes as the former Nightingale who had slandered Jago's wife, thus causing her attempted suicide. After all, as a successful bursar Nightingale would not wish anything to cloud the distinguished reputation of Dr. C. J. B. Palairet, FRS, who had just left the college £35,000 and in whose name Nightingale is planning to construct a college building. In the final analysis, Howard is proven innocent. Collective reason has delivered both practical and abstract justice over individual morals and prejudice.

Thus, throughout Snow's fiction, the themes of private power and closed politics in the intersecting guise of committee, hierarchy, and court politics are all consistently dealt with. What Snow examines is the relationship between personal power and public affairs. What he examines is the motivating consciousness of social change embodied in the individual who—unlike the contention of many modernist writers—does not simply possess "free will" but is dramatically responsible for each "act of will." These are meaningful decisions of which the mature, rational person is constantly aware and that are most often tied to the fulfillment of personal ambitions. These ambitions are associated both with the inner tension for self-realization and definition and with the selfless urge to contribute to the shaping of the human condition. Professionalization, of which so much concern has been expressed, is—for Snow—but a social and political adaptation to the realities of the world so that individuals may fruitfully continue to pursue their ambitions. Snow recognized the emerging character of the twentieth century as being associated with science and its products. He also recognized the tightening bureaucratization of the West, but unlike others, he did not see the government departments, universities and colleges, or professional offices that had come to dominate as being either impermeable to people or unalterable. Social change, for Snow, was simply a matter—albeit a complex matter—of sheer will. Snow's success and significance is in presenting, with realism and drama, the complexity, potential, and chance implied in life. Change for Snow, however, did not in any way imply a rejection of the capitalist system. Indeed, there is every indication that he was fundamentally sympathetic to it—attributing its apparent distress during this century initially to a natural reticence in coming to terms with the new character of the age and subsequently to the undisciplined growth of unbridled "liberal values which placed the individual above all else."[120]

Of course, many would argue that "unbridled" liberalism and "unbridled" capitalism are indeed coterminous, and they would thus use Snow's remarks to argue that he was, down deep, a representative of mid-twentieth-century conservative thinking. But this would be to miss his ultimate point. Like so many other liberal intellectuals in the earlier half of this century, Snow believed that the capitalist economic system and the democratic political system *could* be humanized in such a way as to encourage individuals to further develop their sense of personal individuality while not reneging on their social responsibilities. This, Snow believed, could be done in such a way as to mitigate against the fragmenting aesthetic, cognitive, and political tendencies that represent the struggle that is modernity.

Part Four

EPILOGUE

7

C. P. SNOW AND THE
STRUGGLE OF MODERNITY

Literature deteriorates only to
the extent that people deteriorate.
—GOETHE

THERE SHOULD BE no doubt as to the importance of C. P. Snow's work. At the very least his fiction deserves to be read by successive generations of readers, and his lectures ought to be required readings in university curricula. Together they are not only enjoyable and insightful, but they speak directly to the condition of modernity. In so saying, however, we must also recognize his limitations and the weight that modernity came to represent in his framework.

Snow was born in the burnout of Victorian liberalism. His early context thus imbued him with a lifelong dream of social stability, social progress, the primacy of the individual, and the power of rationality. His creative, cognitive, and political framework tried, through an articulate realism, to find a comforting (or comfortable) totality in an otherwise estranging modernity. But the sheer weight of modernity, with its will to chaos, ultimately reduced this framework to the simplicity, distortions, and dominance of the "two cultures" scenario's popular reception. Under this weight, and under the distance that modernity forces between any experience of self-identity and our quest for totality, Snow and his framework decayed. But insofar as this is so, his decay must be seen in context as a grand failure that was more his generation's than his own. If my thesis can be seen against the backdrop of a philosophy of civilization in which society needs a critical self-understanding before it can go on (i.e., progress), then Snow can be seen as an example par excellence of that trajectory that realizes the mythical lost generation of 1914 in the true lost generation of the Thatcher years.

Snow never permitted himself to be caught up in the rapture of causes. He did, however, start his career with a good measure of hopefulness, which is widely evident from the title of such works as

Time of Hope to the sheer optimism of his decision in 1935 to embark on a project that would consume thirty-five years of his life and energy. He refused, throughout his life, to admit to the power or utility of despair. However, as Saguna Ramanathan's critical introduction to Snow's novels has shown, his own "time of hope" carried within itself a sense of transition and ultimate decline. As Snow's life, like his novels, unfolded slowly, events and experiences eroded the hopefulness of his youth. Snow recognized this decay within himself. He recognized that he, like all human beings, was alone.

Of course, the personal reasons underlying Snow's "darkening vision" will never be fully understood. But some of their likely causes can be suggested. Snow's unique career was one that thrived on having proximity to power and action. Thus the time he spent in the labs at Cambridge imbued him with a blend of knowledge and experience that would never leave him and that would always be portrayed in light of the "heroic." The time he spent in government endowed him with an insider's view of policymaking and public affairs that few of us have been privileged to see. And the time he spent writing charged and recharged his sense of the urgency to link thought and experience. These together gave Snow a tone of authority that fed his writing but that did not advance his framework. As Snow aged, the proximity between his own "corridors of power" (e.g., Cambridge and Whitehall) and himself grew, reinforcing his sense that he would always be something of an outsider. The once constant stream of insights into the important forces of modernity began to dry up. As long as Snow could be privy to high-level political and creative decision processes, he was creatively empowered. But as he slowly ceased to walk those corridors, he also lost the insightful edge that made his fiction so believable. The bouts with melancholia and depression that his friends supported him through grew more frequent. The distance between Snow, the completion of the project that he began decades before, and the fast-moving world of modernity grew and Snow was brought face-to-face with the realization that his framework no longer seemed able to accommodate all that it was intended to embrace. By 1964, Snow was able to write in a letter to Prime Minister Harold Wilson that "I no longer believe that individual human people can have a decisive effect."[1]

This slow collapse of Snow's realist framework manifests itself in what is effectively two sides of the same flaw. First, the social and cultural contexts from which Snow emerged convinced him at an early age that—through the growing power of rationality and within the existing social system—he could improve himself, achieve a sense of totality and place, and achieve a balance between his private and public self. As a result, Snow placed a disproportionate value on social signifiers—such as getting a Cambridge doctorate, being appointed to the House of Lords, and "collecting" awards—with the false expectation that these would de facto result in a personal sense of value (totality) and erase his sense of marginality. With this strategy, however, modernity was predestined to win the struggle. Second, and by extension, Snow's realism ultimately could not appreciate that the sorts of organizations in which he had spent most of his life are only accessible to a very small number of people and that the number of people who have a decisive effect within these institutions is even smaller. Similarly, Snow never seemed to overcome his aversion to radical or extreme behavior—even though he was sometimes sympathetic to it in his youth. He never finally revised this conviction that radical individuals working outside of organizations could ever have any appreciable and positive effect on the direction of social change. Clearly Snow's conceptual framework underestimated the dominance and distortions of mass society. It was also largely blind to the systematic connections between "massification" and the avant-garde experience. Thus if the study of the struggle of modernity is also to be a study of modern culture—and not just of chosen sections of it—then Snow's framework needed to realize that the silences of modernity are as meaningful as its voices.

In closing, it must be said of Snow that he has taught us something meaningful about our private and public selves. And in the process—using his own words—"our idea of him has now changed enough for us to find a stable place for him to stand. Not so flattering, but much less prone to shock and supported by the firmest truths that we can discover. Truths, even bleak truths, are safer than false hopes."[2]

NOTES

1. Literature, Science, and the Modern Mind

1. See Martin Jay, *Marxism and Totality*; Daniel Bell, *The Cultural Contradictions of Capitalism*; and Christopher Lasch, *The Culture of Narcissism* (New York: Warner, 1979).

See also Jurgen Habermas, *The Philosophical Discourse of Modernity*; Lawrence E. Cahoone, *The Dilemma of Modernity*; William E. Connolly, *Political Theory and Modernity*; Timothy J. Reiss, *The Discourse of Modernism*; David Frisby, *Fragments of Modernity*; David Kolb, *The Critique of Pure Modernity: Hegel, Heidegger, and After*; Eugene Lunn, *Marxism and Modernity*; and Michael H. Levinson, *A Genealogy of Modernism*, and "The Fate of Modernity."

2. See Janet Wolff, "The Invisible Flaneuse."

3. Emile Durkheim, *The Elementary Forms of Religious Life*, trans. Joseph Ward Swain, pp. 489–490; Georg Lukacs, *History and Class Consciousness* (Cambridge: MIT Press, 1971), p. 198; Lucien Goldman, "Interdependencies between Industrial Society and New Forms of Literary Creation," in *Cultural Creation and Modern Society*, trans. Bart Grahl, p. 77.

4. Jurgen Habermas, *Philosophical Discourse*, pp. 6–7.

5. Irving Howe, "The Idea of the Modern," in *Literary Modernism* ed. Irving Howe (New York: Fawcett, 1965), p. 34.

6. Michael Walzer, *Obligations* (Cambridge: Harvard University Press, 1970), p. 21.

7. See Allan Bloom, *The Closing of the American Mind* (New York: Simon and Schuster, 1986); E. D. Hirsch, Jr., *Cultural Literacy: What Every American Needs to Know* (New York: Houghton Mifflin, 1987); William J. Bennett, *Our Children and Our Country* (New York: Simon and Schuster, 1988); and Lasch, *Culture of Narcissism*, p. 175.

"The new reconstitutive liberalism, however, is showing hopeful signs for re-energizing the conception of the individual" (Stuart Hall, *A Hard Road to Renewal: Thatcherism and the Crisis of the Left* [Oxford: Polity, 1988]).

8. It seems that Snow told Nolan of Macmillan Publishing's plan for a unified series of *Strangers and Brothers*. Nolan then offered to paint covers for some of the series. These resulted in the covers for *The Masters* and *Corridors of Power* as well as *The Affair* and *Homecomings* (which feature the same cover).

9. These are quoted from *The Redfern Gallery Presents Sidney Nolan*, London, May 1955, p. 12.

10. Hugh Kenner, *The Pound Era* (Berkeley: University of California Press, 1971); Harry Levin, "What Was Modernism?"; Irving Howe, "The Culture of Modernism."

11. On the level of aesthetics, our dominant image of modernity has become closely associated with a very small cadre of *avant-garde* artists. Indeed, many leading cultural critics have, for many decades now, actually *equated* modernity with the literary and visual *avant-garde*. Frank Kermode, Hugh Kenner, and Irving Howe, for example, have tended to use the terms interchangeably. As Howe as written, "the modernist writers and artists constitute . . . an *avant-garde*" (Irving Howe, *Decline of the New*, p. 15). However useful for analytical purposes, this demarcation is far too limiting for any understanding of modernity as a pervasive condition. It artificially separates the artistic impulse from the sociocultural totality that is its source and thus has become co-opted by modernity. If the artistic strategies of modernity and the *avant-garde* could be reduced to the level of pure linguistics, then one might be justified in attempting such a narrow and all-inclusive "theory of modernity." But one cannot. As Peter Bürger has argued in his *Theory of the Avant-Garde*, our aesthetic view of modernity has changed from being a view that promoted creative innovation to one that thrived on cultural negation. In so doing, aesthetic modernity— narrowly conceived—has lost its concern with the status of art in society. It has lost, in effect, its urge to totality. And in so doing, it has rejected an essential postulate of modernity that accepts interpretation and creation as essentially political—politics has become the absolute horizon of modernity. It is thus inauthentic for the strategists of narrow modernism to claim exclusive insight into our contemporary condition and to exclude other possible interpretive strategies. As we will discuss in some detail, realism— notably literary, scientific, and political realism—also has much to usefully say to us about the struggle of modernity and about our personal quests for totality in a period in which both the conceptions and the reality of "the individual" are being radically altered.

12. Lionel Trilling, *Freud and the Crisis of Our Culture* (Boston: Beacon, 1955), p. 102.

13. See Leo Marx, *The Pilot and the Passenger*; Lisa M. Steinman, *Made in America: Science, Technology, and American Modernist Poets* (New Haven: Yale University Press, 1987); and Cecilia Tichi, *Shifting Gears: Technology, Culture, and Literature in Modernist America*.

14. C. P. Snow, "The State of Siege." This address was first delivered as the John Findley Green Foundation Lecture at Westminster College, Fulton, Missouri, in 1968. It was subsequently published in a school magazine. This

quote is taken from *Public Affairs* (New York: Macmillan, 1971), p. 203.

15. Lionel Trilling, "A Sense of the Past," p. 23.

16. Hugh Kenner, *The Mechanic Muse*, p. 10.

17. Ibid.

18. See Paul Boytinck, *C. P. Snow: A Reference Guide;* William Cooper, *C. P. Snow* (London: Longman and Green, 1959); Robert Gorham Davis, *C. P. Snow;* Nora C. Graves, "The Two Cultures Theory in C. P. Snow's Novels"; Robert Graecen, *The World of C. P. Snow;* Frederick Karl, *C. P. Snow: The Politics of Conscience;* Saguna Ramanathan, *The Novels of C. P. Snow: A Critical Introduction;* Jerome Thale, *C. P. Snow;* Ruth M. Walsh, "C. P. Snow: Poet of Organizational Behaviour."

19. Robert Fulford, in a conversation with the author, Toronto, September 1989.

20. "Snow's role was to combat [traditional aristocratic ideologies] in the name of science and technology, in what I think Leavis rightly describes as a kind of neo-Wellsianism. His literary traditionalism (defense of realism and suspicion of modernism) go along, I think, paradoxically, with this since realist aesthetics are also part of the Wellsian package." Personal letter to the author from Terry Eagleton, March 1, 1984.

21. John Halperin, *C. P. Snow: An Oral Biography*, p. 60.

22. This is reported in William L. Shirer, *The Rise and Fall of the Third Reich* (New York: Norton, 1960). Snow's names appeared as "Charles Snow—scientist" and "C. P. Snow—novelist."

23. These were *Nights Ahead, The Fool of the Family* (1949, coauthored with William Gerhardi), *Family Party* (1951, coauthored with Pamela Hansford Johnson), *Her Best Foot Forward* (1951), *Spare the Rod* (1951), *The Pigeon with the Silver Foot* (1951), *To Murder Mrs. Mortimer* (1951), and *The Young and Ancient Men* (1952).

24. The *Strangers and Brothers* sequence of novels is made up of *Strangers and Brothers* (1940, later retitled *George Passant*), *The Light and the Dark* (1947), *Time of Hope* (1949), *The Masters* (1951), *The New Men* (1954), *Homecomings* (1956), *The Conscience of the Rich* (1958), *The Affair* (1960), *Corridors of Power* (1964), *The Sleep of Reason* (1968), and *Last Things* (1970).

Novels that stand outside the series are *Death under Sail* (1932), *New Lives for Old* (1933), *The Search* (1934), *The Malcontents* (1972), *In Their Wisdom* (1974), and *A Coat of Varnish* (1979).

25. Paul Ricoeur, *Hermeneutics and the Human Sciences;* John B. Thompson, *Critical Hermeneutics;* Paul de Man, "Literary History and Literary Modernity."

2. Strangers and Brothers against the Grain

1. John Snow, Snow's great-grandfather, in many ways represented the ideal of Jeremy Bentham and Samuel Smiles's Victorian "Self-Help" movement credo, in which the Mechanics' Institutes movement played an important role.

2. Philip Snow, *Stranger and Brother*, p. 11.

3. As a result of his bankrupt status, Snow's father could not own any real estate or property. This was confirmed in an interview with Philip Snow in Angmering on Sea, W. Sussex, in May 1989.

4. Jack Simmons, *Leicester: Past and Present*, vol. 1, *Ancient Borough to 1860* (London: Eyre Methuen, 1974), p. 184; and Jack Simmons, *Leicester: Past and Present*, vol. 2, *Modern City, 1860–1974* (London: Eyre Methuen, 1974), p. 151.

5. See George Dangerfield, *The Strange Death of Liberal England*; Richard Bentley, *The Liberal Mind: 1914–1929*.

6. This was a phrase Snow was to use often while lecturing in the United States between 1960 and 1979 regarding science and its relationship with government. In these talks "science" nearly always meant physics and biochemistry. Note the title of Snow's final book: *The Physicists: The Generation That Changed the World*. For a discussion of "radical science," see the work of Gary Werskey, "The Visible College"; and Marcus Gilbert, "The Social Relations of Science Movement," M.Sc. thesis, Sussex University, 1971.

For Snow's scientific research, see *Nature* and the *Proceedings of the Royal Society* during the period 1929–1935. These are discussed in depth in chapter 5.

7. Leon Edel, *Bloomsbury: A House of Lions* (New York: Avon Book, 1979); Richard Deacon, *The Cambridge Apostles* (New York: Farrar, Straus and Giroux, 1985).

8. G. H. Hardy was a member of both the Society of Apostles and the Heretics' Club, which at the time was under the leadership of P. M. S. Blackett, and among J. D. Bernal's favorite books was James Joyce's *Ulysses*. Aside from such minimal contacts, however, the "two cultures" actually existed at Cambridge. They were, in fact, cherished and nurtured for their elitist qualities.

9. Kenner, *The Pound Era*.

10. Ian Watt, *The Rise of the Novel*; Raymond Williams, *The English Novel*.

11. See, for example, Modris Ekstein's *Rites of Spring: The Great War and the Birth of the Modern Age* (Toronto: Lester and Orpen Dennis, 1989).

12. The phrase "cubist of letters" was a title given Stein by the *New York Times*. Stein's diary recollections of Fry and Bell are quoted in Humphrey Carpenter, *Geniuses Together: American Writers in Paris in the 1920s* (London: Unwin Hyman, 1987), p. 23.

13. Lesley Johnson, *The Culture Critics*.

14. Michael Holroyd, *Lytton Strachey and the Bloomsbury Group* (Harmondsworth: Penguin, 1971), p. 53.

15. Ibid.

16. T. E. Hulme, "Grafton," in *Further Speculations*, January 1914, pp. 114, 115, 117, 118.

17. Quoted in Julian Symons, *Makers of the New: The Revolution in Literature, 1912–1939*, p. 32.

18. Ibid., pp. 32, 45, 60.

19. Ezra Pound, *Sculpture*, quoted in ibid., p. 68.

20. Manifesto, in *Blast*, June 1914, pp. 1, 7, 148. Among those associated with vorticism were the Imagistes Richard Aldington and H. D. (Hilda Doolittle) Aldington.

21. F. T. Marinetti, "A Futurist Manifesto," in *New Age* 15 (May 7, 1914): 16.

22. F. T. Marinetti, in *Observer*, June 7, 1914, p. 7.

23. Ezra Pound, "Vorticism," in *Fortnightly Review* 96 (1914): 461; Wyndham Lewis, "The Melodrama of Modernity," in *Blast* 1 (June 1914).

24. D. H. Lawrence, *Kangaroo* (Harmondsworth: Penguin, 1980), p. 54.

25. Quoted in *The Modern Age*, ed. Boris Ford (Harmondsworth: Penguin, 1978), p. 14.

26. Quoted in ibid.

27. Ruth Benedict, *Patterns of Culture* (New York: Norton, 1934), p. 18.

28. Quoted in T. E. B. Howarth, *Cambridge between the Wars*, p. 27.

29. These statistics were provided in May 1987 by the Central Statistics Office (London) and by the University Statistical Record (Cheltenham).

30. Malcolm Cowley, *Exile's Return: A Literary Odyssey of the 1920s* (New York: Viking, 1951), p. 38.

31. Quoted in Andrew Sinclair, *The Red and the Blue: Intelligence, Treason, and the University* (London: Weidenfeld and Nicholson, 1986), p. 21.

32. Arthur Koestler, quoted in Clive Bell, *Civilization: An Essay* (London: Chatto and Windus, 1928), p. 41.

33. Wyndham Lewis, "Kill John Bull with Art," in *Outlook* 34 (July 18, 1914): 74. W. H. Auden, quoted in Robert Hewison, *Under Siege: Literary Life in London, 1939–45* (Newton Abbott: Reader's Union, 1978), p. 1. Cyril Connolly, *Enemies of Promise* (London: Routledge and Kegan Paul, 1938), p. 14.

34. Connolly, *Enemies of Promise*, p. 23.

35. Cyril Connolly, *Horizon*, December 1940, p. 6.

36. George Orwell, *Collected Essays* (Harmondsworth: Penguin, 1976), vol. 2, p. 137.

37. C. P. Snow, *Strangers and Brothers*, p. 206.

38. This was the phrase he used in a *New Statesman* article from October 1940.

39. *New Statesman*, December 14, 1940, p. 13.

40. Mrs. Robert Henley, "The Liquidation of the Free-Lances (by One of Them)," *New Statesman*, October 6, 1946.

41. C. P. Snow, "A New Means of Destruction," 1939.

42. Quoted in Hewison, *Under Siege*, p. 31.

43. George Orwell, *The Collected Essays, Journalism and Letters of George Orwell*, ed. Sonia Orwell and Ian Angus (London: Secker and Warburg, 1968), vol. 1, p. 73.

44. Quoted in Hewison, *Under Siege*, p. 23.

45. Werskey, "The Visible College," p. 20.

46. Interview with Sir Herman Bondi, Churchill College, Cambridge, May 1987.

47. Werskey, "Visible College," p. 21.

48. G. H. Hardy, *A Mathematician's Apology*, p. 34; C. P. Snow, *A Variety of Men*. Snow points to Rutherford's lack of sensitivity in questions regarding applied science by using as example his 1933 prediction that the world was not to expect a new source of energy to emerge from the splitting of the atom. Others, however, including Andrew Sinclair, have suggested that Rutherford was fully aware of the possible applications of atomic energy but made his statements in order to dampen press speculation. Indeed, Rutherford found the results so disturbing that he forbade any publication of the results until they had been proved. See Sinclair, *The Red and the Blue*, p. 51.

49. C. P. Snow, *Chemistry*, in *Cambridge University Studies, 1933*, ed. H. Wright (London, 1933), p. 103.

50. Government expenditures on science grew from roughly £0.5 million in 1912 to more than £4.0 million in 1938. Werskey, "Visible College"; Sinclair, *The Red and the Blue*. See Philip Gummett, *Scientists in Whitehall*.

51. See Gummett, *Scientists*; Norman Vig, *Science and Technology in British Politics*.

52. Hardy Papers, no. 137, p. 4, Archives of the NUScW and AScW, Warwick University, cited with permission.

53. Quoted in Deacon, *Cambridge Apostles*, p. 94.

54. Michael Polanyi, "The Republic of Science", in *Knowing and Being*, edited by Marjorie Greene (Chicago: University of Chicago Press, 1969).

55. From an interview with Gary Werskey, London, May 26, 1987.

56. Read Bain, "Scientist as Citizen," *Social Forces* 11 (March 1933): 413–414.

57. B. E. Schaar, "Scientific Method and Social Relations," *Science*, December 16, 1932, pp. 555–556. In 1937, Waldemar Kaempffert reflected similarly on scientists' behavior during the world war, recalling "the days of the war when even supposedly objective scientists lost their heads" (letter from Kaempffert to James McKeen Cattell, November 18, 1937, Cattell Papers, Library of Congress).

58. "Science—and Other Values," *New Republic*, September 16, 1931, p. 114.

59. Watson Davis expressed this commonplace attitude when he wrote, "The remakers of civilization, the true molders of history, whose names so seldom are found in the chronicles of history, are the investigators engaged in scientific research. They are the catalysts of civilization" (Watson Davis, "Science and Civilization," in *The Advance of Science*, ed. Watson Davis [New York: Garden City, 1934], p. 369).

60. P. M. D. Collins, "The British Association for the Advancement of Science [BAAS] and Public Attitudes to Science, 1919–1945," chapter 4.

61. J. B. S. Haldane, *Daedalus, or Science and the Future* (London: Kegan Paul Trench Trubner, 1924), p. 4.

62. Bertrand Russell, *Icarus, or the Future of Science* (New York: Dutton, 1924), pp. 62–63.

63. Julian Huxley, *Scientific Research and Social Needs* (London: Watts, 1934), p. ix, quoted in Collins, "BAAS and Public Attitudes," p. 71.

64. Julian Huxley, *Listener*, October 11, 1933, p. 527.

65. Huxley, *Scientific Research and Social Needs*, p. 149.

66. Julian Huxley, *Listener*, January 3, 1934, p. 25.

67. Ibid., p. 908.

68. Ibid., p. 25.

69. Ibid.

70. *Listener*, October 11, 1933, p. 526.

71. *Listener*, January 3, 1934, p. 24.

72. *Listener*, December 20, 1933, p. 942.

73. Richard Gregory, *Discovery, or the Spirit and Service of Science* (London, 1919), p. 50.

74. Werskey, "Visible College," pp. 38–39.

75. Werskey, "Visible College," chapter 6.

76. Gary Werskey, "Radical Cambridge."

77. C. P. Snow, "Rutherford and the Cavendish," 1960, p. 247.

78. Neal Wood, *Communism and British Intellectuals* (London: Gollancz, 1959), p. 79n.

79. Joseph Needham, foreword to *Science at the Cross Roads*, 2d ed. (London, 1971), p. ix.

80. J. D. Bernal, *The Social Function of Science*, pp. 406, 393.

81. Hyman Levy, *Modern Science: A Study of Physical Science in the World Today* (London, 1939), p. 97.

82. Sir Norman Lockyer, the first editor of *Nature*, was the first chairman of the British Science Guild. Sir Richard Gregory followed Lockyer into both positions. See W. H. G. Armytage, *Sir Richard Gregory: His Life and Work* (London: Macmillan, 1957). Snow was an acquaintance of Gregory and Hopkins and was a friend of Huxley's. See the Huxley-Snow correspondence in the Huxley Archives at Rice University, Houston, Texas.

83. Quoted in Wood, *Communism and British Intellectuals*, p. 142.

84. Rainald Brightman, "Progressive Science and Social Problems," *Nature* 134 (September 1, 1934): 301.

85. Rainald Brightman, "Industrial and Social Interactions," *Nature* 134 (October 13, 1934): 550.

86. Ibid.

87. Gilbert, "Social Relations," p. 53.

88. Ibid., p. 119.

89. Gary Werskey, '*Nature* and Politics Between the Wars,' *Nature* 224 (1969): 466, quoting from the *Nature* leader of January 1932.

3. Blindness, Insight, and the Two Cultures

1. The official name of the Cambridge Rede Lecture is the "Sir Robert Rede Lecture." The endowment was left to the university in 1524 by Sir Robert Rede, who was the Chief Justice of the Common Pleas between 1506

and 1519. He had been a member of Buckingham College, a precursor to Magdalene, and afterward a Fellow of King's Hall. The income of the trust in 1914 was £9 9s. 0d. The lecturer is appointed by the vice-chancellor before the end of Michaelmas term and is required during his term in office to deliver one free lecture in full term at a time and place to be established by the vice-chancellor. The lecture, even today, is open to all comers free of charge.

In 1959, the Rede Lecture was held on Thursday May 7 at 5 o'clock at the Senate House, which is the official meeting place of the university where degrees are conferred. The seating capacity of the Senate House is 360. However, local newspapers reported that the lecture was to a "crowded audience," so—with standing room accounted for—there may have been as many as 400 present at Snow's talk. Reports also note that an unusual interest in the lecture was shown by the university's literary coterie.

2. See Arthur Kroker, *Technology and the Canadian Mind.*

3. See, for example, Dean O'Brien, "Between Two Cultures"; special issue of *Journal of Higher Education* on "The Liberal Arts College: Adaptation to the 1980s," Allan O. Pfinster and Martin J. Finkelstein, Ohio State University Press, 1984; and Henry Petroski, "Technology Is an Essential Component of Today's Liberal Arts Education," p. 88.

4. C. P. Snow, "The Two Cultures," 1956, pp. 413–414; "Britain's Two Cultures: A Study of Education in a Scientific Age," 1957, p. 12; "Britain's Two Cultures: A Revolution in Education," 1957, p. 5; *The Two Cultures and the Scientific Revolution* (Cambridge: Cambridge University Press, 1960), reprinted in two parts in *Encounter* 12, no. 1, June 1959, and 13, no. 1, July 1959; and "Two Cultures," *Science,* 1959.

5. C. P. Snow, "The 'Two Cultures' Controversy: Afterthoughts," 1960; "The Two Cultures and the Scientific Revolution," 1960; "Education and Sacrifice," 1963; "The Two Cultures: A Second Look," 1963; and *The Two Cultures and a Second Look,* 1964.

6. See Boytinck, *C. P. Snow.*

7. References to "Snow's two cultures" that do not reference the germane ideas of his lecture can be regularly found in books as well as in such leading periodicals as the *Sciences, New Scientist, Science and Public Policy,* the *Chronicle of Higher Education,* the *Times Literary Supplement, Bulletin of Science, Technology, and Society,* and the *New York Review of Books.* Marginal periodicals also refer superficially to Snow's thesis. See, for example, *Border/Lines,* Spring 1988.

Recent books that have come across my desk and that cryptically refer to Snow in this way include Maurice Goldsmith, *The Science Critic: A Critical Analysis of the Popular Presentation of Science* (London: Routledge and Kegan Paul, 1986); *One Culture: Essays in Science and Literature,* ed. George Levine; *Languages of Nature: Critical Essays on Essays on Science and Literature,* ed. Ludmilla Jordanova (New Brunswick: Rutgers University Press, 1987); Krishnan Kumar, *Utopia and Anti-Utopia in Modern Times;* and Marx, *The Pilot and the Passenger.*

8. De Man, "Literary History and Literary Modernity," p. 110.

9. For some recent examples, see *Bulletin of Science, Technology, and*

Society 7, no. 4, 1987, special issue on "Technology and Literature"; "Science and Technology in Modern British Fiction: The Two Cultures," *Essays in Arts and Sciences* 8, September 1984; *Science and Public Policy* 11, June 1984; "Two Cultures Are One Too Many," *New York Review of Books*, December 14, 1986; "The Two Cultures and Scientific Books," *Chronicle of Higher Education*, 1987; "Radical Science," *Border/Lines*, Spring 1988; and "Physics and Fiction: Order from Chaos," *New York Times Book Review*, April 21, 1985, p. 1.

10. See, for example, Cahoone, *Dilemma*; Marx, *The Pilot and the Passenger*; and *One Culture*, ed. Levine.

11. Witness, for example, "The Two Cultures in Contemporary Education," held at Simon Fraser University, Canada, February 1982; "The Two Cultures and Science Studies," held at Queen's College, Oxford University, July 1984; and "Bridging the Gap: The Two Cultures Revisited," held at Douglass College, Rutgers University, January–March 1986.

12. See John R. de la Mothe, *Science, Technology, and Society: A Network Directory of Teaching and Research in Canada, the United States, and the United Kingdom* (Ottawa: Science Council of Canada, 1982).

13. Davis, *C. P. Snow*, p. 5; Graves, *Two Cultures*.

14. Aldous Huxley, *Science and Literature*, p. 5; Gertrude Himmelfarb, "In Defense of the Two Cultures" and *Marriage and Morals among the Victorians* (New York: Alfred Knopf, 1986); Lance Schachterle, "What Really Distinguishes the 'Two Cultures'?" p. 91; *One Culture*, ed. Levine, p. 3. Lord Sherfield, "The Adentures of an Innumerate in the World of Science and Technology," p. 14. Raymond Williams, foreword to *Languages of Nature*, ed. Ludmilla Jordanova, p. 11; H. L. Nieburg, in *Science* and quoted on the cover of *Science and Culture*, ed. Gerald Holton. This collection contains essays by such prominent scholars as Herbert Marcuse, Edmund Leach, Talcott Parsons, Harvey Brooks, Margaret Mead, Don K. Price, Daniel Bell, Rene Dubois, and Oscar Handlin. Snow's friend William Cooper argued the contrary view—that "the fact that Snow has such a wide experience and understanding of life in England naturally gives what he writes a peculiar authority: his style, simple, unaffected and moving is such as to make what he writes immediately recognizable as plain truth" (in Cooper, *C. P. Snow*, p. 37). F. R. Leavis, *The Two Cultures? or, the Significance of C. P. Snow*, p. 29; Edward J. Bloustien, "The 'Two Cultures' Debate."

15. November 20, 1936, p. 904.

16. These points were confirmed by Philip Snow in an interview in Angmerring on Sea, W. Sussex, May 1989, and in an interview with Maurice Goldsmith, London, June 1987.

17. C. P. Snow, "The First Excitement That Knowledge Gives," 1939.

18. J. Needham and D. Needham, "A Crystallographic *Arrowsmith*," *Nature*, supplement, p. 890.

19. Ibid.

20. C. P. Snow, *Two Cultures and the Scientific Revolution*, 1960, pp. 17–18.

21. This lecture was succinctly reviewed by Mary Simpson, "The Snow Affair," p. 32.

22. C. P. Snow, "The Two Cultures," 1956, p. 413. All references that follow unless specifically noted are to this page.

23. C. P. Snow, "The Leavis Case and the Serious Case," 1970, p. 739, column 3. It is interesting to note in this context that Stephen Hawking, the remarkable Cambridge cosmologist, has predicted the end of science within the first two decades of the next century, should the problems of the grand unified theory be resolved.

24. All quotations here are from C. P. Snow, "The Two Cultures," 1956, pp. 413–414.

25. Formal agreement to give and publish the 1959 Rede Lecture was reached on December 19, 1958, by Snow and H. S. Bennett (for the Syndics of the University Press, Cambridge).

For his efforts, Snow received the sum of nine guineas, which was the same fee as it was when the lecture was established in 1525. See note 1 above.

The exchange of letters regarding Snow's invitation to give and publish the Rede Lecture took place between September 1958 and August 1959. These reveal a small but interesting dispute between Snow and the Press regarding the unacknowledged appearance of excerpts in *Encounters* and the *Saturday Evening Post.* I am grateful to Philip Snow and the Humanities Research Center at the University of Texas at Austin for allowing me access to these letters. The correspondence between Snow and the secretary of the Press, R. J. L. Kingsford, is especially interesting.

26. C. P. Snow, *Two Cultures and the Scientific Revolution,* 1960, pp. 4–5.

27. Ibid., p. 5.

28. Ibid., p. 3.

29. Ibid., pp. 5–6.

30. Ibid., p. 9.

31. Ibid., p. 10.

32. F. R. Leavis, *Two Cultures? The Significance of C. P. Snow* (London: Chatto and Windus, 1963), p. 36.

33. C. P. Snow, *Two Cultures and the Scientific Revolution,* 1960, p. 11.

34. This constitutes section 3 of the Rede Lecture.

35. C. P. Snow, *Two Cultures and the Scientific Revolution,* 1960, p. 31.

36. Ibid.

37. Ibid., p. 33.

38. Ibid., p. 23.

39. Ibid., p. 12.

40. Ibid., p. 25.

41. Ibid., pp. 26–27.

42. Ibid., p. 8.

43. Ibid.

44. Ibid., p. 29.

45. Ibid., p. 6.

46. Ibid., pp. 6–7.

47. Ibid., p. 27.

48. Ibid., p. 23.

49. Ibid., p. 12.

50. Michael Yudkin, "Towards One Culture?" *Cambridge Review* 82, no. 2008, June 10, 1961, pp. 600–605; Jon Cohen, "The Too Cultured," pp. 57–58; Lloyd Fallers, "C. P. Snow and the Third Culture," pp. 306–310. For a complete bibliography of the debate, see Boytinck, *C. P. Snow.*

51. Norman Cousins, "The Third Culture." This criticism is somewhat difficult to maintain given that a standard examination technique in our education systems relies on the "compare and contrast" types of question. See also Fallers, "C. P. Snow and the Third Culture," p. 301.

52. Martin Green, "A Literary Defence of the Two Cultures," pp. 735–736.

53. C. P. Snow, *Two Cultures and the Scientific Revolution,* 1960, pp. 16, 17, and 45. However, Snow did argue (in the preface to his 1958 New York edition of *The Search*) that it made no sense to even suggest that everyone should be made into scientists or technologists. In *The Two Cultures and a Second Look,* Snow also mentioned molecular biology as another example (p. 13).

54. Richard Wollheim, "Grounds for Approval?" pp. 168–169.

55. This lecture was given on February 28, 1962, in the Hall of Downing College. Although no journalists were allowed into the lecture, Leavis had leaked copies of his text to the press. He sold a handwritten copy to the editors of the *Spectator,* who in turn secreted a copy to Snow, asking for his consent to print it. Snow considered taking legal action but instead agreed it should be printed. He wrote to Leavis on March 5 to ask for a copy of his final address, but evidence that a first-class row was about to take place appeared in the *Times* on March 1 and *Sunday Times* on March 4. The lecture appeared in full on March 9 in the *Spectator.*

56. F. R. Leavis, *Two Cultures?,* p. 6.

57. Ibid., p. 9.

58. Ibid., p. 10.

59. Ibid., p. 11.

60. Ibid., pp. 12–13.

61. Among those who championed Snow were J. D. Bernal, William Gerhardi, J. H. Plumb, Dame Edith Sitwell, Stephen Toulmin, Susan Hill, J. D. Scott, Lord Boothby, Denis Lant, Anthony Storr, Lovat Dickinson, J. D. Bodington, G. Reichardt, Peter Green, G. Fraser, Ronald Millar, Sir Oliver Scott, Arnold Haskell, Michael Ayrton, and Bernard Miles.

Among those who championed Leavis were Charles E. Raven, J. N. A. Guinness, Geoffrey Wagner, T. T. Roe, Remington Rose, Oswald Harland, Robert Kabak, and Neville Denny.

62. J. D. Bernal, letter, *Spectator,* p. 365.

63. C. P. Snow, *The Two Cultures and a Second Look,* pp. 54–55.

64. Ibid., p. 62.

65. C. P. Snow, *Two Cultures and the Scientific Revolution,* 1960, p. 9.

66. C. P. Snow, *Two Cultures and a Second Look*, 1964, p. 68.

67. F. R. Leavis, *Two Cultures? the Significance of C. P. Snow*, p. 38.

68. C. P. Snow, *Two Cultures and a Second Look*, 1964, p. 64.

69. A most insightful and useful assessment of Snow's hypothesis can be found in Leo Marx, "Introduction to the Two Cultures Debate," seminar delivered at Rutgers University, January 20, 1986.

70. Alfred North Whitehead, *Science and the Modern World* (New York: New American Library, 1964), pp. 175–176.

71. Quoted in Peter Stransky and William Abrahams, *Journey to the Frontier* (London: 1966), p. 46.

72. Matthew Arnold, "Literature and Science," pp. 486–501. T. H. Huxley, "Science and Culture," pp. 526–537.

73. Lynn White, Jr., "Science and the Sense of Self," *Daedalus*, spring 1978, p. 54; and Leo Marx, "The Two Cultures Revisited," Rutgers University seminar, 1986.

74. As we discussed in chapter 2, the reactions of the literary community to the modern world were in fact quite energetic and diverse. Moreover, had someone used a similar technique to stereotypically refer to the scientific community, Snow himself would have responded very strongly against its validity, both in terms of fact and in terms of technique.

75. The major Luddite attacks were carried out in the years 1811–1817 in three areas of England: the West Riding, South Lancashire, and Nottingham. Three trades were involved: the croppers (which was a skilled trade responsible for trimming, cleaning, pressing, and shearing woollen cloth), the cotton weavers, and the framework knitters. The croppers were a section of the working class that had a reputation among the owners for being the least manageable group within this industry. They were regularly reported in the scholarly and historical literature as being "independent." The croppers had sufficient control over their work to impose fines on any owners who attempted to avoid any of the cloth-finishing procedures, and in addition, a committee of workers themselves adjudicated all complaints by the owners about the quality of their work.

Luddite demands on management included the gradual introduction of worker-displacing machinery accompanied by alternative employment, taxes of 6*d.* per yard for machine-dressed cloth with the money going to an unemployment fund, a legal minimum wage, controls on sweated labor of women and children, prohibitions on shoddy work, and the right to legal trade unions (a right that had been removed by the Combinations Act of 1799).

The acts of the Luddites, while terrifying to the middle-class onlookers of the time, developed out of a previous background of a combination of parliamentary lobbying and controlled direct action in the workplace. In the years immediately preceding the insurrection, workers in the clothing trades maintained trade union integrity by a variety of methods: for example, they boycotted workers who undersold their labor. Over the period 1803–1806, the workers made repeated attempts to use existing legal statutes to control the introduction of new machines. The Yorkshire croppers, for example, spent between £10,000 and £12,000 on legal fees at a time when the average annual wage for a skilled cropper was £75. The destruction of machinery itself only began in 1811 after attempts at political action through the parliamentary route had failed. Even so, the machine breaking was reportedly carried out in a disciplined and almost military fashion. Destruction of machines was confined to wide frames that made inferior goods at lower prices; only cheaply made goods were slashed; Luddite bands were financed out of trade union funds; renegade bands were severely dealt with; and so on.

See David Albury and Joseph Schwartz, *Partial Progress: The Politics of Science and Technology;* Eric Hobsbawm, *The Age of Revolution* (London: Sphere, 1977); and E. P. Thompson, *The Making of the English Working Class* (London: Penguin, 1968).

76. E. P. Thompson, *English Working Class*, p. 594.

77. C. P. Snow, *Two Cultures and the Scientific Revolution*, 1960, pp. 60–61.

78. This is quoted from an English seminar at New York University in 1968 and communicated in a letter to the author from A. H. Nicholson dated January 14, 1985. See also Snow's oration "Recent Thoughts on the Two Cultures."

79. Philip Snow writes that Snow "was also too busy to accept an invitation from the Prime Minister Harold Macmillan, to serve on the Robbins Committee on Higher Education, although it was a matter close to his heart" (*Stranger and Brother*, p. 127).

4. Literature and the State of Siege

1. Recent authors have convincingly typified liberalism as being the deepest political voice of modernity. See, for example, Nancy Rosenblum, *Another Liberalism;* and John A. Hall, *Liberalism.*

2. See, for example, George Lukacs, *The Meaning of Contemporary Realism;* Georg Lukacs, *Theory of the Novel;* and especially Georg Lukacs, *Studies in European Realism* (London: Merlin, 1970).

3. See Edmund Husserl, *Crisis of the European Sciences;* Lukacs, *Studies in European Realism.*

4. *Oxford English Dictionary*, Compact (micrograph) ed. (New York: Oxford University Press, 1971), vol. 1, p. 1296, definition 4.

5. Quoted in "Conversations with Milan Kundera on the Art of the Novel," *Salmagundi*, Winter 1987, p. 1.

6. Milan Kundera, *New York Review of Books*, March 6, 1988.

7. In the preface to *Strangers and Brothers*, Snow wrote, "I had the idea out of the blue—in what seemed like a single moment—in Marseilles on 1 January 1935. . . . I was staying in Marseilles for the night, having flown down from London, and was off on a boat to Italy the next day. I was extremely miserable. Everything, personal and creative, seemed to be going wrong. Suddenly I saw, or felt, or experienced, . . . both the outline of the entire *Strangers and Brothers* sequence and its inner organization, that is, the response or dialectic between Lewis Eliot as observer and as the focus of

direct experience. As soon as this happened, I felt extraordinarily happy. I got the whole conception . . . in a few minutes" (Omnibus ed., 1971).

8. Cooper, *C. P. Snow.*

9. In an often told story, related to me by Maurice Goldsmith, one evening in 1948 Snow encountered Leonard Russell, the book editor of the London *Sunday Times,* in a corner of the Saville Club. Snow brooded unfavorably on the new fiction of sensitivity and "plotted its overthrow." Russell was sympathetic. Soon after, Snow handed Russell an article entitled "Credo" that further articulated his views. A short time later, after reading the paper, Russell sent Snow a telegram offering him a regular column reviewing fiction for the *Sunday Times.* Snow accepted.

Snow began as book reviewer for the London *Sunday Times* on January 9, 1949, and held the post until December 18, 1952. In his public statement of resignation, Snow observed that he found it impossible to maintain indefinitely his "interest in any kind of new fiction." It is thus somewhat interesting that when Snow took up the post of book reviewer for the *Financial Times* nearly two decades later, he reviewed primarily nonfiction.

C. P. Snow, "Science, Politics, and the Novelist: Or, the Fish and the Net," 1961, pp. 1–17.

10. Snow's attack on the modern novel began as early as 1932 when, in his early novel *Death under Sail,* Snow's principal character reflected on "the extraordinary prudery of the Irish Catholic" and who went on to find it "responsible equally for . . . censorship in Boston, gang warfare in America [and] Mr. James Joyce. . . ."

11. C. P. Snow, "The English Realist Novel," *Moderna Sprak* 51 (1957): 269.

12. Despite Snow's literary perspective, it is absurd to suggest (as some prominent American critics have) that he named his main, autobiographical character, Lewis Eliot, as a gibe to Wyndham Lewis and T. S. Eliot. Both of these writers almost entirely escaped Snow's direct invective.

13. C. P. Snow, *Richard Aldington,* 1938.

14. Richard Aldington, "Science and Conscience: A Letter from Mr. Aldington," *Discovery* 1, no. 9, December 1938, pp. 421–424. Snow reciprocated with a 26-page pamphlet entitled *Richard Aldington: An Appreciation.* Snow planned to include Aldington in a second volume of *A Variety of Men* that was never written.

15. C. P. Snow, "Science, Politics, and the Novelist," 1961, p. 5. This is consistent with what we now refer to as the modernist period. See Symons, *Makers of the New.*

16. C. P. Snow, "Science, Politics, and the Novelist," 1961, p. 5. However, as we discussed in chapter 2, the origins of the modern novel can be placed more helpfully in the late nineteenth century and pre-1914 years.

17. C. P. Snow, "Storytellers for the Atomic Age," 1955, p. 1.

18. C. P. Snow, "Books and Writers," *Spectator,* 1950, p. 320; "Storytellers for the Atomic Age," p. 5.

19. C. P. Snow, "Storytellers for the Atomic Age," p. 1.

20. C. P. Snow, *The Realists,* 1978, p. 8.

21. C. P. Snow, "Science, Politics, and the Novelist," 1961, p. 5.

22. C. P. Snow, "Storytellers for the Atomic Age," 1955, p. 1. This was confirmed and expanded upon in an interview with H. S. Hoff in London, May 1987.

23. C. P. Snow, "New Trends in First Novels," 1953, p. 3.

24. C. P. Snow, "Science, Politics, and the Novelist," 1961, p. 9.

25. Ibid., p. 3.

26. Ibid., p. 6.

27. Ibid., p. 10.

28. Ibid., pp. 9–10.

29. See C. P. Snow, Trollope, 1975; and C. P. Snow, The Realists, 1978.

30. C. P. Snow, "Books and Writers," 1950, p. 82.

31. Snow's favorite example of this was Joyce's Finnegans Wake.

32. See, for example, Maurice Merleau-Ponty, Phenomenology of Perception (New York: Basic, 1962).

33. See Karl Popper, "Scientific Reduction and the Essential Incompleteness of All Science," in Studies in the Philosophy of Biology, ed. Francisco Jose Ayala and Theodosius Dobzhansky (Berkeley: University of California Press, 1974).

34. Rubin Rabinovitz makes just such a claim; see his "C. P. Snow vs the Experimental Novel."

35. William Cooper, "Reflections on Some Aspects of the Experimental Novel," International Literary Annual 2 (1959).

36. C. P. Snow, "The English Realistic Novel," 1957, p. 269. Snow was especially fond of William Cooper, in whose novels—namely Scenes from a Provincial Life (1950), The Struggles of Albert Woods (1952), Young People (1958), Scenes from a Married Life (1961), Scenes from a Metropolitan Life (1982), and Scenes from a Later Life (1983)—Snow appears as a principal character. Cooper was a lifelong friend of Snow's who wrote C. P. Snow for the British Council Writers Series (no. 113) in 1959. For his part, Snow dedicated Homecomings (1956) to Cooper.

37. This was confirmed to me in dozens of letters from scholars who met Snow in America during this period.

38. C. P. Snow, "Storytellers for the Atomic Age," 1955, p. 1.

39. C. P. Snow, "Science, Politics, and the Novelist," 1961, p. 1.

40. C. P. Snow, "Challenge to the Intellect," 1958, p. iii.

41. C. P. Snow, "Science, Politics, and the Novelist," 1961, p. 1.

42. Ibid., p. 12.

43. C. P. Snow, "The Scientific Profession and Degrees of Freedom," 1969, p. 2.

44. Raymond Williams, Marxism and Literature, p. 49.

45. C. P. Snow, "Science, Politics, and the Novelist," 1961, p. 1.

46. Ibid., p. 2.

47. Useful outlines of the sequence can be seen in the work of William Cooper, Frederick Karl, Saguna Ramanathan, and Jerome Thale.

48. See Malcolm Bradbury, No, Not Bradbury (London: Andre Deutsch, 1987), pp. 176–181.

49. Ibid., p. 178.

50. This is true despite the thesis by Susan Turnquist Meixner ("Partisan Politics and the Sequence Novels of Evelyn Waugh, C. P. Snow and Anthony Powell") which argues that Snow was consistently a spokesman of the British Labour party.

51. C. P. Snow, preface to *The Realists*, 1978, p. 7.

52. See, for example, Rabinovitz, "C. P. Snow vs the Experimental Novel."

53. Georg Lukacs has made a considerable contribution to our understanding of this process. For a useful discussion, see Frederic Jameson, "Reflections on the Brecht-Lukacs Debate," in *The Ideologies of Theory*, vol. 1.

54. C. P. Snow, "Storytellers for the Atomic Age," 1955, p. 28.

55. See Theodore Adorno and Max Horkheimer, *The Dialectic of Enlightenment;* and Walter Benjamin, "The Work of Art in an Age of Mechanical Reproduction."

56. C. P. Snow, "Storytellers for the Atomic Age," 1955, p. 1.

57. "The Many Sided Life of Sir Charles Snow," *Life*, April 6, 1961, p. 136.

58. C. P. Snow, "Storytellers for the Atomic Age," 1955, p. 1.

59. J. Robert Moskin, "A Conversation with C. P. Snow," p. 21; C. P. Snow, "Science, Politics, and the Novelist," 1961, p. 6.

60. Pamela Hansford Johnson, "Three Novelists and the Drawing of Character: C. P. Snow, Joyce Cary, and Ivy Compton-Burnett," p. 83.

61. C. P. Snow, *The Realists*, 1978, p. 7.

62. Johnson, "Three Novelists," p. 82.

63. C. P. Snow, "Science, Politics, and the Novelist," 1961, p. 13.

64. Frederick Karl, *C. P. Snow: The Politics of Conscience*, pp. 20–21.

65. C. P. Snow, "Science, Politics, and the Novelist," 1961, p. 15.

66. Ibid., pp. 16–17.

67. C. P. Snow, "The English Realistic Novel," 1957, pp. 267–268.

68. Ibid., p. 84.

69. C. P. Snow, *The Search*, 1958, p. iv.

70. Jerome Thale, "C. P. Snow and the Art of Worldliness," p. 89.

71. Bernard Bergonzi, "The World of Lewis Eliot," *Twentieth Century* 167 (March 1960): 216.

72. Helen Gardner, "The World of C. P. Snow," p. 409.

73. C. P. Snow, author's note to *The Conscience of the Rich*, 1958, p. vii.

5. The Unneutrality of Science

1. This is Goya's title for one of his Caprichos, inscribed on the etching itself. It also provided the title of C. P. Snow's *The Sleep of Reason*, 1968.

2. At the heart of the rhetoric surrounding the principle of complete neutrality and its denial of the role played by constitutive and contextual values in guiding factual research is adherence to the famous tenet of positivism. This is the fact-value dichotomy or the belief that facts and values are completely separable, and that there are facts that are not value-laden. Despite the fact that scholars including John Stuart Mill, Lionel Rob-

bins, Milton Friedman, and others have affirmed the fact-value dichotomy, there are a number of serious reasons for doubting both it and the pure science ideal associated with it. For example, to ascribe to such a belief is to subscribe to the belief that there can be "pure facts" as well as presuppositionless research.

See Norwood Russell Hanson, *Patterns of Discovery* (London: Cambridge University Press, 1958); Thomas Kuhn, *The Structure of Scientific Revolutions*; Michael Polanyi, *Personal Knowledge*; Stephen Toulmin, *Foresight and Understanding* (New York: Harper and Row, 1961); and Karl Popper, *The Open Society and Its Enemies* (Cambridge: Cambridge University Press, 1979).

3. As did Aldous Huxley, *Literature and Science*, p. 1.

4. See, for example, John Forge, "A Realistic Theory of Science?" *Social Studies of Science* 19 (1989); Roy Bhaskar, *Scientific Realism and Human Emancipation*; and *Scientific Realism*, ed. Jarrett Leplin.

5. "In order to ensure that theoretical terms were meaningful in their lights, positivists required that these terms be explicitly defined with respect to observational terms. So 'electron' would not be interpreted literally, but would be defined with respect to such things as clicks in Geiger tubes, flashes on fluorescent screens and other phenomenon normally regarded (that is, by non-positivists) as observable manifestations of electrons. Moreover the theoretical statements are not, in the positivist view, supposed to describe the world. Rather, their role is to provide an economical basis for generating predictions about observable matters. While the positivist criteria for meaningfulness and the demand for the explicit definition of theoretical terms has been largely abandoned as a basis for reconstructing science, empiricists and others have nevertheless tended to retain the positivists' conception of the role of theoretical statements" (Forge, "A Realistic Theory of Science?" p. 182).

6. Forge, "A Realistic Theory of Science?" p. 183.

7. See Bhaskar, *Scientific Realism and Human Emancipation*; Joseph Rouse, *Knowledge and Power: Toward a Political Philosophy of Science* (Ithaca: Cornell University Press, 1987); *Scientific Realism*, ed. Leplin; and Ernan McMullin, "The Case for Scientific Realism," in *Scientific Realism*, ed. Leplin. As Ian Hacking has pointed out, it is not surprising that Snow was a scientific realist, as both physics and physical chemistry provide the strongest evidence for this form of realism. See Ian Hacking, "Experimentation and Scientific Realism," in *Scientific Realism and Human Emancipation*, ed. Leplin, p. 154.

8. Bhaskar, *Scientific Realism and Human Emancipation*, p. 5.

9. Ibid.

10. Interview with Thomas Kuhn, February 17, 1989.

11. These are *New Lives for Old* (1933), *The Search* (1934), *The Light and the Dark* (1947), *Time of Hope* (1949), *The Masters* (1951), *The New Men* (1954), *Homecomings* (1956), *The Conscience of the Rich* (1958), *The Affair* (1960), and *Corridors of Power* (1964).

12. Snow himself makes this claim in Halperin, *C. P. Snow*, p. 59. This is

also verified by the Kapitza Club membership lists of 1931–32, which include the names of J. D. Bernal, Patrick Blackett, John Cockcroft, Philip Dee, Paul Dirac, Neville Mott, Mark Oliphant, W. A. Wooster, and C. P. Snow. My thanks are due to the Cavendish Laboratory Archives for information on this point.

13. The exception here is provided in W. H. Brock, "C. P. Snow: Novelist or Scientist?" pp. 345–347.

14. Ibid. See Ron Freedman, "The Science Policy Foundation, 1964–1984," *Science and Public Policy* 11, no. 3, June 1984, pp. 161–172. In an interview with Gary Werskey in London, May 10, 1987, it was asserted that Snow was a member of the club. See Werskey, *The Visible College*, pp. 263–264. However, Sir Solly Zuckerman, in a description of the dining club that he began, makes no mention of Snow's involvement. See Solly Zuckerman, *From Apes to Warlords* (London, 1980), appendix 1.

15. Michael Polanyi, "The Republic of Science," *Minerva* 1 (1962): pp. 54–73.

16. C. P. Snow, "The First Excitement That Knowledge Gives," 1939.

17. Ibid.

18. Ibid.

19. The Snow household library included the following: Neumann's *History of Music*, Arthur Mee's 8-volume *Children's Encyclopedia, Discoveries and Inventions of the Nineteenth Century, Ports of Britain*, Anita Loos's *Gentlemen Prefer Blondes, Heroes of the Great War*, bound volumes of the *Penny Magazine*, and P. F. Warner's *My Cricketing Life*. Among the periodicals to appear regularly in the Snow home were the *Tatler*, the *Graphic*, the *Illustrated London News, John o' London's, Wide World Bystander, Strand, Punch*, the *Times*, the *Daily Herald, Morning Post, Daily Telegraph, News Chronicle*, the *Leicester Mercury*, the *Leicester Evening Mail*, and the *Leicester Chronicle*. According to Philip Snow, Charles was a voracious reader of them all. Interview with the author, Angmerring on Sea, W. Sussex, May 29, 1985.

20. *The Search*, 1958, pp. 3–4. These events are also based on fact, as was attested by Philip Snow in an interview at Angmerring on Sea, W. Sussex, May 29, 1984. See also Philip Snow, *Stranger and Brother*; and C. P. Snow, preface to *Strangers and Brothers*, Omnibus ed., 1971.

21. When Snow attended, the school was divided into two schools—one for boys, the other for girls. In 1959, the two schools were joined, and the "new" unified school was formally opened by Charles Snow.

22. C. P. Snow, *The Search*, 1958, p. 9.

23. Ibid., p. 13.

24. This is the equivalent of today's GCE O levels.

25. Philip Snow, *Stranger and Brother*, p. 17.

26. Ibid., p. 10.

27. Ibid.

28. Ibid., p. 11.

29. Telephone interview with W. H. Brock, director of the Victorian Studies Center, Leicester University, June 1988.

30. Bert Howard (1900–1963) was to become the character of George Passant in Snow's novels. Snow acknowledged his influence on the period between 1922 and 1927 in particular but remained in touch with him until his death. Howard attended Snow's wedding in 1950.

31. C. P. Snow, in an interview with John Halperin, quoted in Halperin, *C. P. Snow*, p. 21.

32. Ibid., p. 85. This is contrary to the views put forward by J. C. W. Brand.

33. See H. G. Orme and W. H. Brock, *Leicestershire's Lunatics: Institutional Care of Leicestershire's Lunatics during the Nineteenth Century* (Leicester, 1987). This was done until 1957, when Leicester University gained full university status.

34. Louis Hunter (1899–1986), took his D.Sc. from London University in 1928 for his investigations into the role of hydrogen bonding in organic chemistry. After many years of both teaching the full range of subjects in chemistry and managing to initiate a successful reseach focus with only limited resources, Hunter was appointed to Leicester University's first chair in chemistry and was made vice-principal for the period 1952–1957. Following this he was made pro-vice-chancellor (1957–1960), after which, in 1965, he retired from the university. Throughout his career, he played an active role in the Royal Institution of Chemistry, the Chemical Society, and the British Association for the Advancement of Science. See *Chemistry in Britain*, September 1987, p. 878.

A. C. Menzies (1897–1974), was educated at Christ's Hospital. After World War I, he took up the Open Scholarship at Christ's College, Cambridge, and subsequently obtained a first in the Natural Science Tripos in 1921. After four years as a lecturer in physics at the University of Leeds, he then went to the University College at Leicester and later, in 1932, to the University of Southampton where he was professor of physics. During this early period, he made significant original contributions to atomic and Raman spectroscopy. In 1945 he became director of research at the scientific instrument maker Adam Hilger Ltd. He continued in this post until his retirement in 1964. C. P. Snow was his first research student. See the *Times* (London), June 7, 1974, p. 21.

35. Snow's lack of experimental acumen became apparent to me during interviews with Philip Snow, Maurice Goldsmith, J. C. D. Brand, and Sir Herman Bondi.

36. Philip Snow, *Stranger and Brother*, p. 25.

37. Interview with W. H. Brock, the Victorian Studies Center, University of Leicester, June 1988; see his brief article "C. P. Snow: Novelist or Scientist?" p. 345.

38. Raman spectroscopy is named after the Indian physicist Sir Chandrasekhara Venkata Raman (1888–1970). It is that form of spectroscopy that is based upon the Raman effect, which may be described as the scattering of light of several frequencies from a transparent gas, liquid, or solid that is illuminated by light of a single frequency. This scattered "Raman light" is of low intensity and results from an exchange of energy between the photons of light from the source and the molecules of the sub-

stance. Those photons that absorb energy from the molecules emerge with a higher energy, whereas those that yield energy to the molecules emerge with a lower frequency. The study of such energy exchange gives important information about the structure of the molecules and is used in chemical analysis. C. V. Raman began his work on the scattering of light in 1921. The Raman effect was discovered in 1928, and he received the Nobel Prize for his work in 1930.

39. *Reports and Accounts,* Leicester, University College, December 1, 1927, p. 11.

40. These can be found in the *Philosophical Magazine,* London, 1928, and *La Réunion Internationale de Chimie Physique,* Paris, 1929, respectively. The second of these was delivered at the invitation of Menzies, who was the convenor of both the Spectroscopy Group of the Physical Society and the Colloquium Spectroscopium Internationale.

41. C. P. Snow, "The Relation between Raman Lines and Infrared Bands," 1929, p. 379.

42. This is recalled in a letter written from Christ's College by Sydney Grose in 1964, which is cited in Philip Snow, *Stranger and Brother,* p. 160.

43. C. P. Snow, in Halperin, *C. P. Snow,* p. 85.

44. C. P. Snow, in an interview with John Halperin, in Halperin, *C. P. Snow,* p. 21.

45. See *The Search,* 1958, p. 171.

46. Interviews with Harry Hoff and Maurice Goldsmith, London, May and June 1987.

47. As Snow wrote in *The Search,* "there was Rutherford himself; Neils Bohr, the Socrates of automatic science, who talked to us amiably one night in his Danish-English for something like two and a half hours; Dirac, of whom I heard it prophesied very early that he would be another Newton; Kapitza, with a bizarre accent and an unreproducible genius; Eddington, who made some of his Carroll-like jokes; and all the rest, English, Americans, Germans, Russians, who were in atomic physics at the time when the search was hottest." pp. 88–89.

48. C. P. Snow, *The Search,* 1958, p. 86. Snow echoed this sentiment repeatedly throughout his life. As an example, see his unpublished lecture at the University of Texas at Austin on the history of physics (March 29, 1978), C. P. Snow Archives, Harry Ransom Humanities Research Center of the University of Texas at Austin (hereafter HRHRC).

49. C. P. Snow, *The Search,* 1958, p. 107.

50. C. P. Snow, quoted in Halperin, *C. P. Snow,* p. 17.

51. C. P. Snow, *The Search,* 1958, p. 26. The character of Austin was actually a caricature of F. W. Aston (1877–1945), D.Sc., FRS, FIC, Nobel laureate, Fellow of Trinity College, Cambridge, and author of *Mass Spectra and Isotopes* (London: Edward Arnold, 1933), of which Snow wrote chapters 14 and 15—"Isotope Effect in Molecular Spectra" and "The Isotope Effect in Atomic Spectra," respectively—in the 1933 and 1942 editions.

52. These sections represent pages 25–47 and 167–176 of *The Search* (1958), respectively.

53. Ibid., pp. 26–27.

54. C. P. Snow, *The Search*, 1958, p. 35.

55. Jacob Bronowski, *Science and Human Values*, p. 63.

56. C. P. Snow, *The Search*, 1958, p. 39.

57. Following Kuhn, "normal science" can be defined as science that uses past achievement as a model and as a guide for formulating and solving new problems about the world. Since the paradigm cannot be reduced to any set of explicit rules, neither can normal science work on new problems. Clearly not all science can be "normal." At times of both major and minor paradigmatic challenge, as was potentially the case with the Ponds-Fleischman cold-fusion experiments of 1989, normal science is forced into a period of reevaluation.

58. An important development in the replacement of the Bohr theory was the formulation of the uncertainty principle in 1926 by Werner Heisenberg. This principle set the limits of accuracy that may be attained in simultaneous measurement of the position and velocity of such particles as electrons and atoms, or in the simultaneous measurement of energy and time in such systems.

59. pp. 170–171.

60. A. S. Eddington, *The Nature of the Physical World* (Cambridge: Cambridge University Press, 1930), p. 352.

61. C. P. Snow, *The Search*, 1958, pp. 170–172.

62. Ibid., p. 168.

63. Ibid., p. 30.

64. Ibid., pp. 168–169. The scientist to whom Snow referred was Paul Dirac.

65. C. P. Snow, *The Search*, 1958, p. 47.

66. Snow himself makes this point in Halperin, *C. P. Snow*, p. 21.

67. Personal correspondence between the author and Sir Hans Kornberg, master of Christ's College, Cambridge, October 21, 1985. Snow claimed to have worked at the Cavendish (Halperin, *C. P. Snow*, p. 17). This was not true, however, as the labs only became a subdepartment of the Cavendish in 1930. See *Biographical Memoirs of Fellows of the Royal Society* (E. K. Rideal), vol. 22, 1975.

68. C. P. Snow in *Biographical Memoirs of Fellows of the Royal Society* 15 (1969): 4.

69. Eric Keightley Rideal (1890–1974), elected FRS 1930, pursued a wide range of research from pure physics to biology and published research articles and books from 1912 to 1974. He authored papers with, among others, Snow, Blackett, and Philip Bowden. See *Biographical Memoirs* 22: 381–413.

70. Quoted in ibid., p. 385.

71. Philip Bowden, quoted in *Biographical Memoirs* 15: 3.

72. Rideal's research interests extended to insoluble monolayers on the Langmuir trough, colloids and surface chemistry, and homogenous kinetics; his articles occasionally included biological problems as well.

73. Quoted from an unpublished MS dated March 14, 1968, C. P. Snow Archives, HRHRC.

74. R. W. G. Norish, Royal Society Letters, A, 1976, p. 54.

75. C. P. Snow, *The Search*, 1958, p. 312.

76. C. P. Snow, "Chemistry," *University Studies Cambridge 1933*, ed. Harold Wright, p. 97. As W. H. Brock also notes in "C. P. Snow: Novelist or Scientist?" this essay also represented Snow's first, and very successful, attempt to explain the nature of scientific activity in lay terms. This was an accomplishment that was to become important to him in his role as editor of *Discovery* (1937–1940).

77. These were: "Band Spectra of Molecules without Unused Valency Electrons," *Réunion Internationale de Chimie Physique*, Paris, 1928; "The Relation between Raman Lines and Infrared Bands," 1929; "Infrared Investigations 1," pp. 442–452 (with A. M. Taylor); "Infrared Investigations 2," pp. 453–464 (with Rawlins and Rideal); "Infrared Investigations 3," pp. 462–483 (with Rideal); "Infrared Investigations 4," pp. 355–359, (with Rideal); "Infrared Investigations 5," pp. 294–316; "Optical Rotatory Power of Quartz," *Proceedings of the Royal Society* 127A (1930): 271–278 (with Lowry); "Excited Radicals," *Physical Review* 35 (1930): 563–564; "Vibration-Rotation Spectra," *Transactions of the Faraday Society*, 1929, pp. 930–936; "Colours of Inorganic Salts," *Nature* 125 (1930): 349–350 (with Rawlins); "Fine Structure of Absorption Bands," *Proceedings of the Cambridge Philosophical Society*, November 23, 1931; "Photochemistry of Vitamins," *Nature* 129 (May 14, 1932): 720 (with Bowden); "Photochemistry of Vitamins," *Nature* 129 (June 25, 1932): p. 943 (with Bowden); "Photochemistry of Vitamins," *Nature* 130 (November 19, 1932): 774 (with Bowden); "Absorption Spectra of Vitamin A," *Nature* 131 (1933): 582–583 (with Bowden and Morris); "Modified Ionic States," *Proceedings of the Cambridge Philosophical Society* 28 (1931–1932): 522–530 (with Rawlins).

78. For example, see Snow's 1966 American Association for the Advancement of Science lecture entitled "Government, Science, and Public Policy," 1966, p. 650.

79. See, for example, Halperin, *C. P. Snow*; Graves, "The Two Cultures Theory in C. P. Snow's Novels"; personal communication with Saguna Ramanathan, July 14, 1987; personal communication with W. H. Brock, June 29, 1988; and personal communication with R. Norman Jones, July 7, 1988.

80. As Snow said: "I made an infrared [spectroscope]. I changed that: I don't know why" (Halperin, *C. P. Snow*, p. 82).

81. Snow briefly describes his 1939 meeting with Bragg on the Cambridge train platform in *The Two Cultures and the Scientific Revolution*. As a result, Snow became technical director of the Ministry of Labour from 1940 to 1944, during which time he interviewed the thousands of scientists and engineers that he described in the Rede Lecture with his friend the scientist and author Harry S. Hoff (aka William Cooper). This detail was discussed in an interview with Harry Hoff at the Athenaeum, London, May 1987.

82. Halperin, *C. P. Snow*, p. 61.

83. The insert regarding Bernal is my own. C. P. Snow, *The Physicists*, 1981, p. 153.

84. Ibid., pp. 153–154.

85. See, for example, ibid.; C. P. Snow, in Halperin, *C. P. Snow*; C. P. Snow, in *University Studies Cambridge 1933*, ed. Wright.

86. Not the eleven attributed to Snow by Boytinck, *C. P. Snow*; nor the twenty-two attributed to Snow by Brock, "C. P. Snow, Novelist or Scientist?" p. 346.

87. Bowden appears as Francis Getliffe in *The Conscience of the Rich, The Light and the Dark, The Masters, The New Men, The Affair, Corridors of Power, The Sleep of Reason*, and *Last Things*. See Snow's note on Bowden in *Biographical Memoirs* 15 (1969).

88. According to Aston's preface, Snow wrote chapters 14 and 15 entitled "Isotope Effect in Molecular Spectra" and "The Isotope Effect in Atomic Spectra," respectively. See F. W. Aston, *Mass Spectra and Isotopes*, 1933, reprinted in 1942, 1944, 1946, 1948, and 1960.

89. Originally thought of as a form of peer review, authors wishing to have papers submitted to reputable journals had senior scientists communicate their work on their behalf. By the 1960s, this practice had practically stopped, and authors submitted their own papers.

90. For my discussion on Snow's research, I am deeply indebted to a small number of people. First, I am especially grateful to Dr. Michael Hogben, associate professor of chemistry at Concordia University, Montreal, and Dr. J. C. D. Brand, Professor Emeritus, Department of Chemistry, University of Western Ontario. Brand's article entitled "The Scientific Papers of C. P. Snow" (*History of Science* 2, part 2, no. 72, June 1988, pp. 111–127) represents the only substantive assessment of Snow's research to date. I would like to thank Dr. Brand for discussions and permission to quote from his article and from a prepublication draft. I would also like to note my thanks in this regard to Dr. W. H. Brock (Leicester University) and Dr. Gerhard Herzberg (National Research Council, Canada).

91. As J. C. D. Brand has pointed out, examples of this include Hund and Mulliken who had both begun to develop a theory of states of individual electrons, which are now called molecular orbitals, and Hill and Van Vleck who had explained the fine details of the energy levels for pi and sigma states in terms of the coupling of molecular rotation and electron spin. See F. Hund, "Molecular Spectra," pp. 759–795; R. S. Mulliken, "Assignment of Quantum Numbers for Electrons in Molecules," *Physical Review* 32 (1928): 761–772; and E. Hill and J. H. Van Vleck, "Rotational Distortion in Multiplets in Molecular Structure," *Physical Review* 32 (1928): 250–272.

92. C. V. Raman and K. S. Krishnan, "A New Class of Spectra Due to Secondary Radiation," pp. 399–419.

93. C. P. Snow and Taylor, "Infrared Investigations 1," pp. 442–452; C. P. Snow, Rawlins, and Rideal, "Infrared Investigations 2," pp. 453–464; C. P. Snow and Rideal, "Infrared Investigations 3," pp. 462–483; Snow and Rideal, "Infrared Investigations 4," pp. 355–359.

94. A spectrometer is an instrument used to measure spectra or to determine wavelengths of the various radiations or separations of the particles according to their energies.

95. See J. C. D. Brand, "Scientific Papers of C. P. Snow."

96. Ibid.

97. R. H. Gilette and E. H. Eyster, "The Fundamental Rotation-Vibration Band of Nitric Oxide," pp. 1113–1119, quoted in Brand, ibid., p. 7.

98. E. K. Plyler and E. F. Barker, "The Infrared Spectrum and Molecular Configuration of N_2O," *Physical Review* 38 (1931): 1827–1836.

99. This can be summarized in a table:

Mode of Vibration of CO_2		Raman	Infrared	CM^{-1}
nu_1: symmetric stretch	$\overset{\leftarrow}{O} - C - \vec{O}$	active	inactive	1330
nu_2: bend	$\overset{\uparrow}{O} - \underset{\downarrow}{C} - \overset{\uparrow}{O}$	inactive	active	667
nu_3: asymmetric stretch	$\vec{O} - \overset{\leftarrow}{C} - \vec{O}$	inactive	active	2349

100. See Dickenson, Dillon, and Rasetti, "The Rotational Raman Spectrum of Nitrogen and Oxygen," *Zeitschrift fur Physik* 61 (1930): 600.

101. The modern assignment for N_2O is:

Mode of Vibration of NNO		Raman	Infrared	CM^{-1}
nu_2: bend	$\overset{\uparrow}{N} - N - \overset{\uparrow}{O}$	inactive	active PQR	589
nu_1: symmetric stretch	$N - \overset{\leftarrow}{N} - \vec{O}$	active	active PR	1285
nu_3: asymmetric stretch	$\vec{N} - \overset{\leftarrow}{O} - \vec{N}$	active	active PR	2224

102. Dennison's swift analytical mind had evidently seen through Snow's N_2O problem, and he relayed this to Barker upon his return to Michigan.

103. J. C. D. Brand, "Scientific Papers of C. P. Snow," p. 117.

104. Ibid., p. 118.

105. J. D. Bernal, "Properties and Structures of Crystalline Vitamins," p. 721.

106. C. P. Snow, *The Search*, 1958, p. 172.

107. F. P. Bowden and C. P. Snow, "Photochemistry of Vitamins A, B, C, D," p. 943.

108. I. M. Heilbron and R. A. Morton, "Photochemistry of Vitamins A, B, C, D," *Nature* 129 (1932): 866–867.

109. All above quotes are from Heilbron and Morton, pp. 866–867.

110. For invaluable comments on IR spectra, I am indebted to Prof. S. Daunt and Prof. M. G. Hogben (Department of Chemistry, Concordia University).

111. J. C. D. Brand, p. 118.

112. C. P. Snow in Halperin, *C. P. Snow*. Although the episode was certainly a setback, its impact need not necessarily have been terminal for

Snow's research career. After all, Bowden went on to have a most successful career, albeit he never dabbled in photochemistry again.

113. C. P. Snow, *The Search*, 1958, p. 271.

114. See J. D. Bernal, *Science in History*, (Cambridge: MIT Press, 1968), vol. 3, p. 864.

115. H. Bethe, "Term Splittings in Crystals," *Annalen der Physik* 3 (1929): 133–208.

116. H. Sauer, "The Line Absorption of Chrome Alum Crystals," *Annalen der Physik* 87 (1928): 197–237.

117. J. C. D. Brand, "Scientific Papers of C. P. Snow," p. 119.

118. See James R. During, *Chemical, Biological, and Industrial Applications of Infrared Spectroscopy* (New York: Wiley, 1985).

119. This proposed research dealt with the isoelectronic molecule glyoxal (CH)-(CHO). Snow and Eastwood commented on the exceptionally sharp lines and close spectral resemblance to acrolein. Through such research, Snow and Eastwood were at the point of doing significant work, notably because they would have had access to the high-performance instruments at Manchester University through W. L. Bragg.

120. C. P. Snow, *The Search*, 1958, p. 150.

121. J. D. Bernal, letter, *Spectator*, p. 365.

122. C. P. Snow in Halperin, *C. P. Snow*, p. 21.

123. Ibid., pp. 67, 87.

124. C. P. Snow, *The Physicists*, 1981, p. 68.

125. See C. P. Snow, "J. D. Bernal," in *The Science of Science*, ed. Maurice Goldsmith and Alan Mackay, (London: Souvenir Press, 1964), p. 22; C. P. Snow, introduction to Hardy, *A Mathematician's Apology*. Dates were also confirmed in interviews with Maurice Goldsmith (London, June 1987), Erik Millstone and Brian Easlea (Brighton, February 1984), Gary Werskey (London, June 1986), Joe Palca (Washington, D.C., April 1987), and Collin Divall (Manchester, June 1987), whom I would like to thank for bringing the Snow-Huxley correspondence held in the Huxley Archives at Rice University to my attention.

Snow distinguished the intellectual left from the trade union left calling it a typically *New Statesman* sort of thing. See his comments in Halperin, *C. P. Snow*, p. 67.

126. C. P. Snow in ibid., p. 67.

127. Ibid., p. 67.

128. C. P. Snow, *The Search*, 1958, pp. 218–219.

129. Ibid., pp. 35–36.

130. C. P. Snow, MSS, notes for a talk at Northwestern University, 1975, C. P. Snow Archives, HRHRC.

131. Quoted in Nail Bezel, *Annals of Science* 32 (1975): 555.

132. Ibid., p. 21.

133. Including J. C. D. Brand.

134. It is important to note that *Youth Searching* and *The Devoted* were *not* the same book as W. H. Brock has claimed ("C. P. Snow: Novelist or Scientist?" p. 346). Indeed, *Youth Searching* was written and destroyed before

Snow ever went to Cambridge. *The Devoted* was partially written in 1939, never appeared in book form, but was cannibalized in the writing of *Strangers and Brothers* (1940). The name of Snow's girlfriend at that time is now forgotten.

135. For example, Snow would certainly have disapproved of J. B. S. Haldane's attempt at stirring up "United Front" meetings in Trafalgar Square. An example of Snow's reaction to such matters can be seen in his portrayal of relations between Martin and Lewis Eliot regarding the atomic bomb in his novel *The New Men*.

136. C. P. Snow, MSS, undated C. P. Snow Archives, HRHRC.

137. C. P. Snow, MSS entitled "Man's Idea of Himself: Is It Changing?" undated (but most likely written in 1977), C. P. Snow Archives, HRHRC, p. 3.

138. See, for example, his notes and handwritten corrections to speeches he gave in the United States and India between 1966 and 1977 entitled, or earmarked, "Science and Technology: Our Common Problem," "Science and the Advanced Society," and "Man's Idea of Himself: Is It Changing?" MSS, C. P. Snow Archives, HRHRC.

139. These are what Snow called "our modest criteria" for defining an advanced society ("Science and the Advanced Society," p. 2). Of course, anyone aware of the enormous problems currently being faced by our countries' very large populations of "street people" and increasing rates of illiteracy would have very substantial grounds for bickering with Snow.

140. C. P. Snow, "Science in a Modern World," 1938, p. 317.

141. Notes for an address given at the British Embassy in Washington, D.C., by C. P. Snow on January 26, 1966, entitled "Science and the Advanced Society," p. 7.

142. "Science and Technology: Our Common Problem," p. 1.

143. C. P. Snow, MSS, notes for "Science and Technology: Our Common Problem," delivered in India, pp. 1–2.

144. Ibid., p. 2.

145. See *The Frascati Manual*, published by the Organization for Economic Cooperation and Development (Paris, 1980).

146. C. P. Snow, "Scientific Prophecies," 1939, p. 1.

147. Ibid., p. 2.

148. C. P. Snow, "Science and Technology: Our Common Problem," p. 4.

149. C. P. Snow, "Science and the Advanced Society," p. 2.

150. Ibid., p. 2.

151. Ibid., p. 3.

152. "Man's Idea of Himself: Is It Changing?" pp. 4, 12, 13.

153. See Marie Jahoda, *The Social Psychology of Unemployment* (London: Macmillan, 1978).

154. C. P. Snow, "Science and the Advanced Society," unedited record, Washington, D.C., January 26, 1966, pp. 4–5.

155. C. P. Snow, "Science and Technology: Our Common Problem," pp. 5–6.

156. C. P. Snow, quoting his friend Alexander Dvardovsky, in ibid., p. 7.

157. Ibid., p. 5.

158. C. P. Snow, "The Moral Un-Neutrality of Science," delivered to the American Association for the Advancement of Science (AAAS) in 1960, published in *Science* in 1961 and reprinted in *Public Affairs,* 1971, p. 187.

159. C. P. Snow, "Science in a Modern World," 1938, p. 318.

160. C. P. Snow, notes for an address at MIT entitled "Scientists and Decision-Making," HRHRC, pp. 2–3.

161. Ibid., p.4.

162. C. P. Snow, "Science in a Modern World," 1938, p. 318. Two salient points need to be made here. First, Snow exactly echoed the views of G. H. Hardy regarding scientists and war when he wrote at the same time that "incidentally, military inventions do not require Rutherfords or Bohrs; second-rate technicians are quite adequate" (p. 318); and second, despite the questions that arise out of scientific research, Snow vehemently disagreed that there are "things that men should not even try to know." "I do take, however, that there is a responsibility to understand [what we are trying to know and] to persuade . . . people that this [search] is part of life—an interesting, valuable part of life that may in fact affect us deeply" ("Science in an Advanced Society," p. 5).

163. C. P. Snow, "Science in a Modern World," 1938, p. 319.

164. Ibid.

165. See Halperin, *C. P. Snow,* p. 96.

166. Ibid., p. 87.

6. Personal Power and Public Affairs

1. Snow is incorrectly portrayed as a highly partisan supporter of the British Labour party by Susan Turnquist Meixner in *Partisan Politics and the Sequence Novels of Evelyn Waugh, C. P. Snow, and Anthony Powell.* It should be noted, however, that in a regular series of meetings that were held from 1956 to 1962 at the expense of Marcus Brumwell—who was a devoted Labour supporter and a successful advertising agent—Snow did meet with Harold Wilson, Hugh Gaitskell, Frank Cousins, P. M. S. Blackett, Solly Zuckerman, and Jacob Bronowski to advise the Labour party on science policy. Bernal sent his advice through Blackett and Snow but was not present himself, as Wilson would have nothing to do with "the Red scientist." These details were confirmed by Maurice Goldsmith in interviews held at the London Athenaeum in May 1987. They are also briefly discussed in Maurice Goldsmith's biography of Bernal *Sage: A Life of J. D. Bernal* (London: Hutchinson, 1980), pp. 140–141.

Suggestions that Snow was an ideologue were made by Frederick Karl in *C. P. Snow: The Politics of Conscience.*

2. However, Snow's interest in public affairs is discernible from as early as July 1924 when Snow wrote an editorial in the *Newtonian* (the Alderman Newton school newspaper), continuing through his years as editor of *Dis-*

covery (1937–1940); in his fiction (1932–1979); in his lectures and public talks at colleges and universities in the U.S., Canada, and the Soviet Union; and ending in 1981 with the posthumous publication of *The Physicists: A Generation That Changed the World.*

3. Morris Speare, *The Political Novel: Its Development in England and in America* (1924; reprint, New York: Russell and Russell, 1966), p. ix. For Snow, the phrase "social form" was interchangeable with "political system." See "Grounds for Hope?" in the *New York University Education Quarterly* 7, no. 4, 1977, p. 1.

4. Snow's novels deal with the reforming and liberating spirit of the 1920s, the Iberian conflict of the 1930s, nazism, the bomb, the narrowing of loyalties in the cold war, and generally (but consistently) with the problems of power and conscience in a managerial, highly technological society.

5. C. P. Snow, *The Realists*, 1978, p. 1.

6. Quoted in Philip Snow, *Stranger and Brother*, p. 171.

7. An extensive examination of unpublished manuscripts and notes for lectures in the U.K., the U.S., India, and Canada reveals no direct references to party politics or policies. Even in invited talks to Labour party meetings, Snow's presentations were extremely general. I am indebted in this search to the C. P. Snow Archives (HRHRC), the Julian Huxley Archives (Woodson Research Center, Rice University), and to Gary Werskey.

8. C. P. Snow, *Public Affairs*, 1971, p. 7.

9. The English Dreamers spoke out against the ills of industrialized society. Eliot's stance on modern culture articulated a preservation of the traditions of society (at the cost of democracy if necessary), while Leavis defined modern culture as a moral ideal similar to the ideals of the Romantic poets. See Lesley Johnson, *The Culture Critics.*

10. C. P. Snow, "Science, Politics, and the Novelist: Or, the Fish and the Net," 1961, p. 15.

11. C. P. Snow, *Public Affairs*, 1971, pp. 9–10. "The growing moral discontent of the West" is a phrase that Snow used repeatedly after 1968—a date that can be loosely used to identify his emerging "darkening vision." This aspect of Snow's perspective is examined in some detail toward the end of this chapter.

12. Ramanathan, *The Novels of C. P. Snow.* I am grateful to Prof. Ramanathan for her correspondence regarding delicate points central to this study.

13. C. P. Snow, "Scientists and Decision-Making," talk given at MIT in 1966, quoted from an unpublished transcript provided by the HRHRC.

14. C. P. Snow, "Science in a Modern World," 1938, p. 320.

15. The Godkin Lectures on the Essentials of Free Government and the Duties of the Citizen were established at Harvard University in memory of Edwin Lawrence Godkin (1831–1902). The theme of the lectures by Snow was one that he revisited frequently during the next five-year period. See, for example, the text of his presentation to the U.S. House of Representatives (delivered on January 25, 1966), reprinted as "Government, Science, and Public Policy," pp. 650–653. For a report of the lectures themselves, see

the *Harvard Crimson* for Wednesday November 30, 1960 (pp. 1, 2), and Friday December 2, 1960 (pp. 1, 3).

16. C. P. Snow, *Science and Government*, 1961, p. 10. For Lord Cherwell's reaction to Snow's rendering of events, see the earl of Birkenhead, *The Prof in Two Worlds: The Official Life of Professor F. A. Lindemann, Viscount Cherwell* (London: Collins, 1961). See also David Shusterman, *C. P. Snow* (Boston: G. K. Hall, 1975).

17. C. P. Snow, *Science and Government*, 1961, pp. 48–49.

18. Ibid., p. 51.

19. Ibid., p. 63.

20. Ibid.

21. Ibid., p. 64.

22. Ibid., p. 27.

23. Ibid., pp. 82–83.

24. C. P. Snow, *Appendix to Science and Government*, 1962, pp. 3, 13, 36.

25. C. P. Snow, *Public Affairs*, 1971, pp. 9–10.

26. Jacques Ellul, *The Technological Society* (New York: Vintage, 1964), p. 85. The position of the technological utopians is outlined by Bernard Gendron in *Technology and the Human Condition*. Snow is included, by Gendron, in this group (p. 13).

27. See Snow's prewar editorials in *Discovery*, which in many ways reflect the views of the "Science of Science" radicals regarding the social function of science.

28. See Hardy, *A Mathematician's Apology*, p. 81.

29. See Kenneth Prewitt, "Scientific Illiteracy and Democratic Theory," *Daedalus*, Spring 1983, pp. 49–64; Jon D. Miller, "Scientific Illiteracy: A Conceptual and Empirical Review," *Daedalus*, Spring 1983, pp. 29–48; Jon D. Miller, *The American People and Science Policy* (New York: Pergamon, 1983).

30. A third theme was "possessive love." This will be discussed later in the chapter as, although it represents a weak link, or even a failure, in Snow's work, it *does* become animated as yet another nuance of power relationships—those dealing with private power. C. P. Snow, preface to *Strangers and Brothers*, Omnibus ed. (1971), vol. 1, p. xii.

31. C. P. Snow in Halperin, *C. P. Snow*.

32. C. P. Snow, "Science and the Advanced Society," talk given at the British Embassy, Washington, D.C., January 26, 1966, HRHRC, p. 8.

33. C. P. Snow. "The Scientific Profession and Degrees of Freedom," 1970; quoted with permission.

34. Ibid.

35. Throughout Snow's career he only initiated, or threatened to initiate, legal actions against two individuals as a result of "literary exchanges." This includes the period of the sometimes notorious "two cultures" debate. One of these threats was carried out and settled out of court. The other remained only a threat.

36. Talks given at the Education Faculty of New York University and published in the *New York University Education Quarterly*, dated Summer

1976 (pp. 2–5); and the New York City campus of Pace University on April 27, 1977. The quote is from pp. 64–65 of the Pace University archive transcripts; quoted with permission.

37. This phrase, which Snow was very fond of quoting, comes from Blaise Pascal and means "we die alone."

38. C. P. Snow, *The New Men*, 1960, p. 301.

39. Ibid.

40. See Kenneth Hamilton, "C. P. Snow and Political Man," p. 425.

41. It should not be construed from this that Snow is a crude environmentalist. The role of rationality allows Snow and his heroes to understand, and act upon, the environment.

In addition, Snow puts very little faith in modern psychology and psychoanalysis and states that "this was the trouble with psychoanalysis from the beginning. The concepts were such that they could neither be verified nor falsified. They were circular systems. Very pleasant for the operators, not very pleasant for the person with any sort of critical mind. They were more like certain kinds of art. Art, as it happens, of a sort that I'm not especially fond of" (talk given by C. P. Snow, April 26, 1977, on the Pleasantville campus of Pace University, New York City; quoted with permission of Pace University).

42. John Dewey, *School and Society* (Chicago: University of Chicago Press, 1979), p. 123.

43. Lord Annan, *The Curious Strength of Positivism in English Political Thought* (London: Free Association, 1959), p. 187.

44. C. P. Snow, "Science, Politics, and the Novelist," 1961, p. 3. Although this definition sounds characteristically Snovian in its simplicity, it is not very far from the definition used by others who have pursued the problem at great length. See, for example, John Kenneth Galbraith, *The Anatomy of Power* (London: Hamish Hamilton, 1984).

45. C. P. Snow, "The Scientific Profession and Degrees of Freedom," 1970, p. 2.

46. C. P. Snow, untitled address given on April 27, 1977, at the New York City campus of Pace University, quoted, with permission, from the unpublished transcript, HRHRC, p. 51.

47. C. P. Snow, "Grounds for Hope?" 1976, p. 3.

48. Ibid., p. 3.

49. "Interview with C. P. Snow," *Review of English Literature*, July 3, 1962, p. 105.

50. C. P. Snow, *Public Affairs*, 1971, pp. 9–10.

51. Snow quoted this phrase often. See, for example, his address at Westminster College in Fulton, Missouri, entitled "The State of Siege" (reprinted in *Public Affairs*). This phrase is in fact inscribed on the base of Snow's memorial urn, which is in the Fellows' Garden of Christ's College, Cambridge.

52. Confirmed in an interview with Harry S. Hoff in London, May 21, 1987.

53. C. P. Snow, *Strangers and Brothers*, Hudson River ed., 1977, p. 29.

54. Ibid., p. 48.

55. Karl, *C. P. Snow*, pp. 20–21.

56. Thale, "The Art of Worldliness," p. 33.

57. C. P. Snow, *New York University Education Quarterly*, summer 1976, p. 3.

58. C. P. Snow, Pace University, September 17, 1977, p. 47.

59. Ibid., pp. 35–36.

60. C. P. Snow, "The Scientific Profession and Degrees of Freedom," 1970, p. 6.

61. Ibid., p. 4.

62. Don K. Price, *The Scientific Estate*, p. 270.

63. C. P. Snow, notes for a presentation made at MIT in 1966 on "Scientists and Decision-Making," HRHRC.

64. C. P. Snow, *Science and Government*, 1964, p. 132.

65. Ibid., p. 132.

66. Ibid., p. 133.

67. Ibid., pp. 133–134. Snow's reference to General Electric is interesting given that Snow was in fact invited in 1945 to join the English Electric Company (later General Electric) as the director of technical personnel by Sir (later Lord) George Nelson, who was then chairman. Snow had met Sir George while at the Ministry of Labour and accepted the postwar position on March 3, 1947. He stayed with the firm until October 22, 1964, when he left to become Parliamentary Secretary in the House of Lords to the Ministry of Technology. During this period Snow continued to write his novels while in a basement office of the International Science Policy Foundation on Craven Street, London.

68. Ibid., p. 135.

69. Ibid.

70. Ibid.

71. Ibid., pp. 135–136.

72. C. P. Snow, *The Masters*, 1951, p. 36.

73. These individuals, many of whom are based loosely on real characters, are found in the fiction of C. P. Snow. Arthur Miles is the main character in *The Search* (1934). Jack Cotery is found in *Time of Hope* (1949) and *Strangers and Brothers* (1940). George Passant is in these as well as in *The Masters* (1951) and *Homecomings* (1956). Martin Eliot is in *Time of Hope*, *The New Men* (1954), *Homecomings* (1956), and *The Affair* (1960). Charles March is in *The Conscience of the Rich* (1958).

74. Snow had been a reader of Wells since he was a child in Leicester, but he only met Wells in October 1934; although they got along well, they did not become friends. Despite the arguments made by J. C. D. Brand, Snow did not get his "two cultures" thesis from Wells. See C. P. Snow, "H. G. Wells," 1966.

75. Interview with Harry S. Hoff in London, May 21, 1987. Hoff (aka William Cooper) also makes this point in his 1962 pamphlet *C. P. Snow* (London: Longman, Green and Co.), p. 13.

76. The idea of a rejuvenating agent was something of a preoccupation during this period. H. G. Wells wrote of a rejuvenating process, while Somer-

set Maugham was to take the topic seriously enough to endure the injections that are believed to have extended his physical, if not his mental, life.

77. C. P. Snow, *New Lives for Old,* 1935, p. 239.

78. Ibid., p. 358.

79. C. P. Snow, "First Excitement," 1939.

80. C. P. Snow, *The Search,* 1958, p. 38.

81. C. P. Snow, talk given at London School of Economics Student Union, February 1967.

82. C. P. Snow, *The Search,* 1958, p. 259.

83. Ibid., p. 197.

84. Ibid., pp. 309–310.

85. Ibid., pp. 214–215.

86. Ibid., pp. 276–278.

87. I. I. Rabi, in *Nature,* 1935, and the cover of 1958 Scribner's edition.

88. C. P. Snow, *Strangers and Brothers,* Omnibus ed., 1971, p. 22. This relationship parallels Snow's own relationship with H. E. Howard on whom Passant is based.

89. The character of Roy Calvert is based on Charles Allbury, a close friend of Snow's, who was killed in 1941.

90. C. P. Snow, *The Light and the Dark,* 1979, p. 195.

91. Ibid.

92. Ibid., pp. 318–319.

93. See Snow's preface to the English ed. of *The Conscience of the Rich.*

94. C. P. Snow, *The Conscience of the Rich,* p. 19.

95. Ibid., p. 34.

96. See Davis, *C. P. Snow,* p. 31; Karl, *C. P. Snow,* p. 67; Hortense Calisher, "Can There Be an American C. P. Snow?" p. 41.

97. C. P. Snow, *The Masters,* 1951, pp. 16, 22, 18, 47, 4, 313.

98. The machinations described by Royce's family in dealing with his illness are also clear examples of "private power" of the sort portrayed in *The Conscience of the Rich.*

99. While it has been said—whether it matters or not, by an American— that the events described by Snow seem overdone, I am assured by a current Cambridge Master that a recent election at Snow's old college *very much* replicated those described in *The Masters.* "The Loser" now holds a prominent diplomatic position.

100. C. P. Snow, *The Masters,* 1951, p. 27.

101. Ibid., pp. 27–28.

102. Ibid., pp. 51–52.

103. Ibid., pp. 232–233.

104. Ibid., p. 49.

105. Ibid., p. 69.

106. Ibid., p. 34.

107. Ibid., p. 33.

108. Ibid., p. 71.

109. Ibid., p. 71.

110. Ibid., p. 70.
111. Ibid., p. 266.
112. Ibid., p. 100.
113. Ibid., pp. 99–100.
114. Ibid., p. 191.
115. As Howard claims during the hearings: "I'm not interested in any damned discoveries. All I'm interested in is cooking up a thesis. Then I can publish a paper or two by hook or by crook. That's the way everyone's playing the game. And I'm going to play the same game too" (p. 324).
116. C. P. Snow, *The Affair*, p. 824.
117. Ibid., p. 871.
118. Ibid.
119. Ibid.
120. See C. P. Snow, "Grounds for Hope?" 1977.

7. C. P. Snow and the Struggle of Modernity

1. C. P. Snow, unpublished letter to the prime minister, dated October 24, 1964.
2. C. P. Snow, MSS, 1974, HRHRC.

SELECT BIBLIOGRAPHY

Adams, Robert. "Pomp and Circumstance: C. P. Snow." *Atlantic Monthly,* November 1964, pp. 95–98.

Adorno, Theodore, and Max Horkheimer. *The Dialectic of Enlightenment.* New York: Prism Books, 1984.

Albury, David, and Joseph Schwartz. *Partial Progress: The Politics of Science and Technology.* London: Pluto Press, 1982.

Allen, Walter. "Shorter Review: The Two Cultures." [Designated simply as "WA."] *New Statesman,* June 6, 1959, p. 806.

Arnold, Matthew. "Literature and Science." In *Prose of the Victorian Period,* edited by William E. Buckler. Boston: Houghton Mifflin, 1958.

Aston, F. W. *Mass Spectra and Isotopes.* London: Edward Arnold, 1933.

Ayrton, Michael. A letter in *Spectator,* March 23, 1962, pp. 365–366.

Bahktin, M. M. *The Dialogic Imagination.* Edited by Michael Holquist, Jr. Austin: University of Texas Press, 1981.

Bantock, G. H. "A Scream of Horror." *Listener,* September 17, 1959, pp. 427–428.

Barber, Benjamin. *Strong Democracy.* Berkeley and Los Angeles: University of California Press, 1984.

Barzun, Jacques. "One Culture, Now Two." In *Science: The Glorious Entertainment.* New York: Harper and Row, 1964.

Bell, Daniel. *The Cultural Contradictions of Capitalism.* New York: Basic Books, 1976.

Benjamin, Walter. "The Work of Art in an Age of Mechanical Reproduction." In *Illuminations.* New York: Schocken, 1969.

Bentley, Richard. *The Liberal Mind: 1914–1929.* Cambridge: Cambridge University Press, 1977.

Bergonzi, Bernard. "The World of Lewis Eliot." *Twentieth Century* 167 (March 1960).

Berman, Marshal. *All That Is Solid Melts into Air.* New York: Simon and Schuster, 1986.

Bernal, J. D. "Properties and Structures of Crystalline Vitamins." *Nature* 129 (1932).

———. A letter in *Spectator*, March 23, 1962.

———. *The Social Function of Science*, Cambridge: MIT Press, 1979.

Bernard, Kenneth. "C. P. Snow and Modern Literature." *University Review* (Kansas City), Spring 1965, pp. 231–233.

Bhaskar, Roy. *Scientific Realism and Human Emancipation*. London: Verso, 1986.

Bloustien, Edward J. "The 'Two Cultures' Debate: Implications for Education and Public Policy." *Bridging the Gap: The Two Cultures Revisited* Seminar Series. Rutgers University, March 3, 1986.

Bodington, J. D. A letter in *Spectator*, March 23, 1962, p. 369.

Boothby, Lord. Letters in *Spectator*, March 16, 1962, p. 331; March 30, 1962, p. 359.

Boulding, Kenneth. "The Two Cultures." In *Technology and Western Civilization*, edited by M. Kranzberg and C. W. Pursell. Vol. 2. London: Oxford University Press, 1967.

———. Personal communication, February 16, 1982.

Bowden, F. P., and Snow, C. P. "Photochemistry of Vitamins A, B, C, D." *Nature* 129 (1932).

Boytinck, Paul. *C. P. Snow: A Reference Guide*. Boston: G. K. Hall and Co., 1980.

Brock, W. H. "C. P. Snow: Novelist or Scientist?" *Chemistry in Britain*, April 1988.

Bronowski, Jacob. *Science and Human Values*. New York: Harper and Row, 1965.

Brooks, Harvey. *The Government of Science*. Cambridge: MIT Press, 1968.

Buckley, Vincent. "C. P. Snow: *How Many Cultures?*" *New York Times Magazine*, July 15, 1962.

Buckley, William F., Jr. "The Voice of Sir Charles." *National Review*, May 22, 1962, p. 358.

Cahoone, Lawrence E. *The Dilemma of Modernity*. Albany: State University of New York Press, 1988.

Calisher, Hortense. "Can There Be an American C. P. Snow?" *Reporter* 15 (November 1, 1956).

Casey, John. "Literature and Society." *Caribbean Quarterly* 8, no. 2 (June 1962), pp. 73–93.

Clarke, George A. "Review of the *Two Cultures*." *Ethics*, October 1960, pp. 72–73.

Cohen, Jon. "The Too Cultured." *First Person* 1, no. 3 (Spring–Summer 1961).

Collins, Frederick, W. "Where There Is No Understanding." *New Republic*, April 11, 1960, pp. 17–18.

Collins, P. M. D. "The British Association for the Advancement of Science and Public Attitudes to Science, 1919–1945." Ph.D. diss., Leeds University, 1978.

Connolly, William E. *Political Theory and Modernity.* New York: Basil Blackwell, 1988.

Cooper, William. *C. P. Snow.* London: Longman and Green, 1959.

———. "Reflections on Some Aspects of the Experimental Novel." *International Literacy Annual* 2 (1959).

Cornelius, D. K. *Cultures in Conflict: Perspectives on the Snow-Leavis Controversy,* edited by Edwin St. Vincent. Chicago: Scott, Foresman and Company, 1964.

Cousins, Norman. "The Third Culture." *Saturday Review,* May 7, 1966, p. 42.

Cyril, Ray. A letter to the editor in *Times Literary Supplement,* April 30, 1970, p. 478.

Dangerfield, George. *The Strange Death of Liberal England.* London: Paladin, 1972.

Davis, Robert Gorham. *C. P. Snow.* Columbia Essays on Modern Writers, no. 8. New York: Columbia University Press, 1965.

Davenport, Basil. "Review of the Two Cultures." *Book-of-the-Month-Club News,* June 1960, pp. 10–11.

de Man, Paul. "Literary History and Literary Modernity." In *Blindness and Insight: Essays in the Rhetoric of Contemporary Criticism.* Minneapolis: University of Minnesota Press, 1983.

Denny, Neville. A letter in *Spectator,* April 6, 1962, p. 442.

Desl, M. S. A letter in *Spectator,* April 6, 1962, p. 442.

Dixon, John R. "Two Semantic Cultures." *ETC: A Review of General Semantics,* 23, no. 1 (March 1966), pp. 77–83.

Dolbier, Maurice. "Building Bridges between Two Cultures." *New York Herald Tribune Book Review,* March 2, 1958, p. 2.

Downs, Hugh. "Let's All Be Eggheads." *Science Digest,* May, 1966, p. 90–93.

Dunn, John. "Science and C. P. Snow." *Listener,* November 11, 1971, pp. 656–657.

Eagleton, Terry. "Capitalism, Modernism, and Postmodernism." In *Against the Grain: Selected Essays.* London: Verso, 1986.

Easlea, Brian. *Liberation and the Aims of Science.* Brighton: Sussex University Press, 1980.

Eisely, Loren. "The Illusion of the 'Two Cultures.'" *American Scholar* 33, no. 3 (Summer 1964), pp. 387–399.

Estall, H. M. "The Snows of Yesteryear." *Humanities Association Review* 26 (1975), 1–9.

Fairlie, Henry. "Cults, Not Cultures." *Spectator,* November 1, 1963, p. 554.

Fallers, Lloyd. "C. P. Snow and the Third Culture." *Bulletin of the Atomic Scientists* 17, no. 8 (October 1961).

Faulkner, Peter. "William Morris and the Two Cultures." *Journal of the William Morris Society,* Spring 1966, pp. 9–12.

Finkelstein, Sidney. "The Art and Science of C. P. Snow." *Mainstream,* September 1961, pp. 31–57.

Foster, Kenelm. "Snow against the Poets." *Blackfriars: A Monthly Review Edited by the English Dominicans*, May 1964, pp. 220–226.

Fowler, Albert. "The Negative Entropy of C. P. Snow." *Approach*, Winter 1966, pp. 7–13.

Fraser, G. S. A letter in *Spectator*, March 23, 1962, p. 366.

Fried, Albert. "The Scientific Culture of C. P. Snow." *New Politics* 1, no. 4 (1962), pp. 105–110.

Frisby, David. *Fragments of Modernity*. Cambridge: MIT Press, 1986.

Fuller, Edmund. "Lord Snow's Humane Advices." *Wall Street Journal*, January 3, 1972, p. 6.

———. "Snow-Leavis Affair." *New York Times Book Review*, April 22, 1962, pp. 24–25.

Gainham, Sarah. A letter in *Spectator*, March 23, 1962, p. 366.

Gardner, Helen. "The World of C. P. Snow." *New Statesman*, March 1958.

Geertz, Clifford. "Thick Description: Towards an Interpretive Theory of Culture." In *The Interpretation of Cultures*. New York: Basic Books, 1973.

Gerhardi, William F. A letter in *Spectator*, March 16, 1962, pp. 329–332.

Gilette, R. H., and E. H. Eyster. "The Fundamental Rotation-Vibration Band of Nitric Oxide." *Physical Review* 56 (1939).

Graecen, Robert. *The World of C. P. Snow*. Suffolk: Scorpion Press, 1962.

Graham, Loren R. *Between Science and Values*. New York: Columbia University Press, 1981.

Gray, John. *Liberalism*. Milton Keynes: Open University Press, 1986.

Graves, Nora. "The Two Cultures Theory in C. P. Snow's Novels." Ph.D. diss., University of Southern Mississippi, 1967.

———. "The Two Cultures Theory in C. P. Snow's Novels." *Swansea Review*, October 1969.

Green, Martin. "A Literary Defence of the Two Cultures." *Kenyon Review*, Autumn 1962.

———. "Lionel Trilling and the Two Cultures." *Essays in Criticism* 13, no. 4 (October 1963), pp. 375–385.

———. *Science and the Shabby Curate of Poetry: Essays about the Two Cultures*. London: Longman, Green and Company Ltd., 1964.

Green, Peter. A letter in *Spectator*, March 23, 1962, p. 366.

Gummett, Philip. *Scientists in Whitehall*, Manchester: Manchester University Press, 1980.

Habermas, Jurgen. "Modernity: An Incomplete Project." In *The Anti-Aesthetic*, edited by Hal Foster. Port Townsend: Bay Press, 1983.

———. *The Philosophical Discourse of Modernity*. Cambridge: MIT Press, 1987.

Hall, John A. *Liberalism*. London: Paladin, 1988.

Halperin, John. *C. P. Snow: An Oral Biography*. Brighton: Harvester, 1984.

Hamilton, Kenneth. "C. P. Snow and Political Man." *Queen's Quarterly* 69, no. 3 (Autumn 1963).

Hand, Harry E. "The Paper Curtain: The Divided World of Snow and Leavis

Revisited." *Journal of Human Relations* 14, no. 3 (Third quarter, 1966), pp. 351–363.

Hardy, G. H. *A Mathematician's Apology.* Cambridge: Cambridge University Press, 1980.

Harland, Oswald. A letter in *Spectator,* March 23, 1962, p. 367.

Haskell, Arnold L. A letter in *Spectator,* March 16, 1962, p. 333.

Heinemann, Margot C. A letter in *Spectator,* March 23, 1962, pp. 366–367.

Hill, Susan. A letter in *Spectator,* March 16, 1962, p. 332.

Himmelfarb, Gertrude. "In Defense of the Two Cultures." *American Scholar* 50 (1981).

Hodgson, P. E. "Culture and Subculture." *Month,* March 1964, pp. 177–181.

Holton, Gerald, ed. *Science and Culture.* Boston: Beacon, 1965.

———. *The Scientific Imagination: Case Studies.* Cambridge: Harvard University Press, 1978.

Howarth, T. E. B. *Cambridge between the Wars.* Hogarth Press: London, 1978.

Howe, Irving. "The Culture of Modernism." In *Decline of the New.* New York: Horizon, 1970.

———. *The Political Novel.* New York: Random House, 1978.

Hudson, Liam. "A Differential Test of Arts/Science Aptitude." *Nature,* April 30, 1960.

Hund, F. "Molecular Spectra." *Zeitschrift Fur Physik,* 1928.

Husserl, Edmund. *Crisis of the European Sciences.* New York: Beacon, 1978.

Huxley, Aldous. *Science and Literature.* London: Chatto and Windus, 1963.

Huxley, T. H. "Science and Culture." In *Prose of the Victorian Period,* edited by William E. Buckler. Boston: Houghton Mifflin, 1958.

Jaki, Stanley L. "A Hundred Years of Two Cultures." *University of Windsor Review,* Fall–Winter 1975, pp. 55–75.

Jameson, Frederic. *The Ideologies of Theory: Essays, 1971–1986.* 2 vols. Minneapolis: University of Minnesota Press, 1988.

Jay, Martin. *Marxism and Totality.* Berkeley: University of California Press, 1986.

Jay, Peter. A letter in *Spectator,* March 16, 1962, p. 333.

Jenson, Jay. "Review of the Two Cultures." *Journalism Quarterly* 37, no. 4 (Autumn 1960), p. 608.

Johnson, Gerald W. "Footnote to a Current Dialogue." *American Scholar* 32 (Winter 1962–63), pp. 66–72.

Johnson, Lesley. *The Culture Critics.* London: Routledge and Kegan Paul, 1979.

Johnson, Pamela Hansford. "Three Novelists and the Drawing of Character: C. P. Snow, Joyce Cary, and Ivy Compton-Burnett." In *Essays and Studies* (London) vol. 3 (1950).

Jones, C. R. O. A letter in *Spectator,* March 16, 1962, p. 333.

Jurczak, Chester A. "Humanities or Science?" *Duquesne Review* 8, no. 1 (Fall 1962), pp. 3–11.

Kabak, Robert. A letter in *Spectator*, April 6, 1962, p. 442.

Karl, Frederick. *C. P. Snow: The Politics of Conscience*. Carbondale: Southern Illinois University Press, 1965.

Kazin, Alfred. "A Gifted Boy from the Midlands." *Reporter*, February 5, 1959, pp. 37–39.

———. *The Open Forum*. New York: Harcourt, Brace, and World Inc., 1965 (This ̇edition only).

Kenner, Hugh. *The Mechanic Muse*. London: Oxford University Press, 1987.

Kirk, Russel. "Can We Apprehend Science." *Teacher's College Record* (New York), April 1963, pp. 536–544.

Kolb, David. *The Critique of Pure Modernity: Hegel, Heidegger, and After*. Chicago: University of Chicago Press, 1986.

Kroker, Arthur. *Technology and the Canadian Mind*. Montreal: New World Perspectives, 1986.

Kuhn, Thomas. *The Structure of Scientific Revolutions*. Chicago: University of Chicago Press, 1968.

Kumar, Krishnan. *Utopia and Anti-Utopia in Modern Times*. London: Basil Blackwell, 1987.

Lant, Dennis. A letter in *Spectator*, March 16, 1962, p. 332.

Leavis, F. R. *The Common Pursuit*. London: Chatto and Windus, 1952.

———. "The Significance of C. P. Snow." *Spectator*, March 9, 1962, pp. 297–303.

———. "Two Cultures? The Significance of C. P. Snow." *Melbourne Critical Review* 5 (1962): 90–101.

———. *Two Cultures? The Significance of C. P. Snow*. London: Chatto and Windus, 1962.

———, and Denys Thompson. *Culture and Environment: The Training of Critical Awareness*. London: Chatto and Windus, 1962.

———. *The Two Cultures? Or, the Significance of C. P. Snow*. New York: Pantheon, 1963.

———. *Nor Shall My Sword: Discourses on Pluralism, Compassion, and Social Hope*. London: Chatto and Windus, 1972.

———. *Education and the University: A Sketch for an "English School."* Cambridge: Cambridge University Press, 1979.

Lepkowski, Wil. "Science and the Humanities: Bridging the Gap." *Chemical and Engineering News*, December 1, 1980.

Leplin, Jarrett, ed. *Scientific Realism*. Berkeley and Los Angeles: University of California Press, 1984.

Levin, Harry. "What Was Modernism?" In *Refractions*. New York: Oxford University Press, 1960.

Levine, George, and Owen Thomas, eds. *The Scientific vs the Humanist*. New York: W. W. Norton and Co., Inc., 1963.

———, ed. *One Culture: Essays in Science and Literature*. Madison: University of Wisconsin Press, 1987.

Levinson, Michael H. *A Genealogy of Modernism: A Study of English Literary Doctrine, 1908–1922*. Cambridge: Cambridge University Press, 1984.

———. "The Fate of Modernity." Special issue of *Theory, Culture, and Society* 2, no. 3 (1985).

Lindemann, F. A., earl of Birkenhead. *The Prof in Two Worlds: The Official Life of Professor F. A. Lindemann, Viscount Cherwell.* London: Collins, 1961.

Lowrance, William W. *Modern Science and Human Values.* New York: Oxford University Press, 1985.

Lukacs, Georg. *The Theory of the Novel.* Cambridge: MIT Press, 1971.

———. *The Meaning of Contemporary Realism.* London: Merlin, 1979.

Lunn, Eugene. *Marxism and Modernity.* Berkeley and Los Angeles: University of California Press, 1982.

Marx, Leo. *The Pilot and the Passenger: Essays on Literature, Technology, and Culture in the United States.* New York: Oxford University Press, 1988.

———. "What Kind of Knowledge Do We Need?" In "Science and Technology Policy Under Free Trade," edited by John de la Mothe. *Technology in Society.* New York: Pergamon, *II*, 2, 1989.

Meixner, Susan Turnquist. "Partisan Politics and the Sequence Novels of Evelyn Waugh, C. P. Snow, and Anthony Powell." Ph.D. diss., University of Kansas, 1979.

Merton, Robert. *The Society of Science.* Chicago: University of Chicago, 1977.

Miles, Bernard. A letter in *Spectator*, March 23, 1962, p. 367.

Millar, Ronald. A letter in *Spectator*, March 16, 1962, p. 333.

Morris, Max. "A Review of the Two Cultures." *Marxism Today* 3, no. 12 (December 1959), pp. 374–380.

Moskin, J. Robert. "A Conversation with C. P. Snow." *Saturday Review,* April 6, 1974.

Needham, J., and D. Needham. "A Crystallographic *Arrowsmith*." *Nature* 134 (December 8, 1934).

New Statesman and Nation. Two cultures correspondence, October 13, 1956, p. 453; October 20, 1956, p. 486; October 27, 1956, p. 519.

"Operation Snow Removal." National Review, March 27, 1972, p. 194.

O'Brien, Dean. "Between Two Cultures." In *Theory of Knowledge and Problems of Education*, edited by Donald Vandenberg. Urbana: University of Illinois Press, 1969.

Panter-Downes, Mollie. "A Letter from London." *New Yorker*, March 24, 1962, pp. 167–174.

Parsons, Ian. A letter in *Spectator*, March 23, 1962, p. 365.

Peterson, A. D. C. "How to Break the Barrier between Science and the Arts." *New Scientist*, November 22, 1956.

Petroski, Henry. "Technology Is an Essential Component of Today's Liberal Arts Education." *Chronicle of Higher Education*, November 14, 1984.

Plumb, J. H. A letter in *Spectator*, March 30, 1962, p. 296.

Polanyi, Michael. "The Two Cultures." *Encounter* 13, 1959, p. 61–64 (reprinted in *Knowing and Being* [Chicago: University of Chicago Press, 1969]).

———. *Personal Knowledge.* Chicago: University of Chicago Press, 1960.

———. "The Republic of Science." *Minerva* 1 (1962).

Price, Don K. *The Scientific Estate.* Cambridge: Harvard University Press, 1967.

Quoodle [pseud.]. "The Two Cultures." *Spectator,* February 19, 1963, p. 225.

Rabi, I. I. *Nature,* 1935, and cover of 1958 Scribner's edition of *The Search.*

———. "Scientists and Humanists: Can the Minds Meet?" *Atlantic Monthly* 197 (1956), pp. 64–67.

Rabinovitz, Rubin. "C. P. Snow vs the Experimental Novel." *Columbia University Forum,* Fall 1967, p. 39.

Raman, C. V., and K. S. Krishnan. "A New Class of Spectra Due to Secondary Radiation." *Indian Journal of Physics* 2 (1928).

Ramanathan, Saguna. *The Novels of C. P. Snow: A Critical Introduction.* London: Macmillan, 1978.

Raven, Charles E. A letter in *Spectator,* April 6, 1962, p. 396.

Read, Robert. "Mood of the Month"—X." *London Magazine,* August 1959, pp. 39–43.

Rees, [Sir] Richard. A letter in *Spectator,* April 6, 1962, p. 442.

Reichardt, G. A letter in *Spectator,* March 16, 1962, p. 332.

Reiss, Timothy J. *The Discourse of Modernism.* Ithaca: Cornell University Press, 1982.

Ricoeur, Paul. *Interpretation Theory: Discourse and the Surplus of Meaning.* Fort Worth: Texas Christian University Press, 1976.

———. *Hermeneutics and the Human Sciences.* Cambridge: Cambridge University Press, 1981.

Roberts, Catherine. "Nightingales, Hawks, and the Two Cultures." *Antioch Review,* Summer 1965, pp. 221–228.

Roe, T. T. A letter in *Spectator,* March 23, 1962, p. 365.

Rose, Remington. A letter in *Spectator,* March 23, 1962, p. 366.

Rosenblum, Nancy L. *Another Liberalism: Romanticism and the Reconstitution of Liberal Thought.* Cambridge: Harvard University Press, 1987.

Roskill, S. W. A letter in *Spectator,* April 6, 1962, p. 442.

Rousseau, G. S. "Are There Really Men of Both Cultures?" *Dalhousie Review* 52 (1972), pp. 351–372.

Russell, Bertrand. "Science as an Element of Culture." *New Statesman,* May 31, 1913.

Schachterle, Lance. "What Really Distinguishes the 'Two Cultures'?" In *Annals of Scholarship.* New York, 1986.

Schenck, Hilbert. "Revisiting the Two Cultures." *The Centennial Review of Arts and Science—Michigan State,* Summer 1964.

Schlesinger, Arthur M. "The One against the Many." *Saturday Review,* July 14, 1962.

Scott, [Sir] Oliver. A letter in *Spectator,* March 16, 1962, p. 333.

Shapiro, Charles. "The Civil War of Sir Charles." *Saturday Review,* May 18, 1963.

Sherfield, Lord. "The Adventures of an Innumerate in the World of Science and Technology." *Science and Public Affairs* (London), no. 1 (1986).

Simpson, Mary. "The Snow Affair." *Bulletin of the Atomic Scientists* 19 (April 1963).

————. "The Two Cultures Revisited." *Bulletin of the Atomic Scientists,* September 1965.

Sisk, John P. "Writers and Scientists: The Two Cultures." *Ramparts* 1, no. 2 (September 1962), pp. 17–22.

Sitwell, [Dame] Edith. A letter in *Spectator,* March 16, 1962, p. 331.

Snow, C. P. "The Relation between Raman Lines and Infrared Bands." *Philosophical Magazine* 8 (1929).

————, and A. M. Taylor, "Infrared Investigations of Molecular Structure, Part I, Apparatus and Technique." In *Proceedings of the Royal Society,* A, 124 (1929).

————, and F. I. G. Rawlins, and E. K. Rideal. "Infrared Investigations of Molecular Structure, Part 2, The Molecule of Nitric Oxide." In *Proceedings of the Royal Society,* A, 124 (1929).

————, and E. K. Rideal. "Infrared Investigations of Molecular Structure, Part 3. The Molecule of Carbon Monoxide." In *Proceedings of the Royal Society,* A, 125 (1929).

————, and E. K. Rideal. "Infrared Investigations of Molecular Structure, Part 4. The Overtone of Nitric Oxide." In *Proceedings of the Royal Society,* A, 126 (1930).

————. "Infrared Investigations of Molecular Structure, Part 5." In *Proceedings of the Royal Society,* A, 128 (1930).

————. "Chemistry." In *University Studies Cambridge 1933,* edited by Harold Wright.

————. *New Lives for Old.* London: Victor Gallancz Ltd., 1933 (published anonymously).

————. *The Search.* New York: Scribner's Sons, 1934.

————. "Humanity of Science." *Spectator,* 158, 1936.

————. "The Enjoyment of Science." *Spectator,* June 12, 1936.

————. "What We Need from Applied Science." *Spectator,* November 20, 1936.

————. "The Humanity of Science." *Spectator,* April 16, 1937.

————. "Science and Conscience: A Letter from Mr. Aldington." *Discovery* (Cambridge) n.s., vol. 1, no. 9, December 1938.

————. *Richard Aldington: An Appreciation.* London: Heinemann, 1938.

————. "A New Means of Destruction." *Discovery* (Cambridge) 8, no. 14 (September 1939).

————. "Science in a Modern World." *Discovery,* October 1938.

————. "Scientific Prophecies." *Discovery,* January 1939.

————. "Blueprint for Future Science." *Discovery,* March 1939.

————. "The First Excitement That Knowledge Gives." *Discovery* (Cambridge) 2, no. 13 (April 1939).

————. "Science and Air Warfare." *Discovery,* May 1939.

————. "Against Destructiveness." *Discovery,* September 1939.

————. "The Fate of Homo Sapiens." *Discovery,* October 1939.

————. "Scientists and War Discoveries." *Discovery,* February 1940.

———. Letters in *New Statesman,* October 6, December 14, 1940.

———. "Careers." *Political Quarterly* 15, no. 310 (1944).

———, and William Gerhardi. *The Fool of the Family.* 1949.

———. *Time of Hope.* London: Macmillan, 1949.

———. "Books and Writers." *Spectator,* September 22, 1950.

———. *To Murder Mrs. Mortimer.* 1951.

———, and Pamela Hansford Johnson, *Her Best Foot Forward.* 1951.

———. *The Masters.* London: Macmillan, 1951.

———. *Spare the Rod.* 1951.

———. *The Pigeon with the Silver Foot.* 1951.

———. *The Young and Ancient Men.* 1952.

———. "New Trends in First Novels." *Sunday Times,* December 27, 1953.

———. *The New Men.* London: Macmillan, 1954.

———. "The Well Endowed." *New Statesman and Nation,* December 25, 1954.

———. "Using Science." *New Statesman and Nation,* March 20, 1954.

———. "Storytellers for the Atomic Age." *New York Times Book Review,* January 30, 1955.

———. *Homecomings.* London: Macmillan, 1956.

———. "The Two Cultures." *New Statesman and Nation,* October 6, 1956.

———. "Irregular Right." *Nation* 182, no. 238 (1956).

———. "New Minds for the New World." *New Statesman and Nation* 52, no. 279, 1956 (published anonymously).

———. Letters in *New Statesman and Nation,* October 20, 27, 1956.

———. "The English Realist Novel." *Moderna Sprak* 51 (1957).

———. "Britain's Two Cultures: A Study of Education in a Scientific Age." *London Sunday Times,* March 10, 1957.

———. Letters in *London Sunday Times,* March 10, 17, 1957.

———. "Britain's Two Cultures: A Revolution in Education." *London Sunday Times,* March 17, 1957.

———. "The Corridors of Power." *Listener* 57 (1957).

———. *The Conscience of the Rich.* London: Macmillan, 1958.

———. *The Search.* New York: Charles Scribner's Sons, 1958 ed.

———. "Changing Nature of Love." *Mademoiselle* 46, no. 105 (1958).

———. "Men of Fission." *Holiday,* April 1958.

———. "Man in Society." *Observer,* July 13, 1958.

———. "Challenge to the Intellect." *Times Literary Supplement,* August 15, 1958, p. iii.

———. A letter in *New Republic,* August 18, 1958.

———. "New Men for a New Era." *London Sunday Times,* August 24, 1958.

———. "Future of Man." *Nation,* September 13, 1958.

———. "Books of the Year." *London Sunday Times Magazine* 11 (December 28, 1958).

———. Letters in *London Times,* January 22, May 8, 1959.

———. "The Missing Scientist." *Reporter,* February 19, 1959.

———. "The Two Cultures and the Scientific Revolution." *Encounter,* June–July 1959.

———. "The Two Cultures." *Science*, August 21, 1959.

———. "Conflict of Cultures." *Saturday Evening Post*, September 12, 1959.

———. *The Affair*. London: Macmillan, 1960.

———. *The New Men*. London: Macmillan, 1960.

———. "Rutherford and the Cavendish." In *The Baldwin Age*, edited by John Raymond. Souvenir Press: London, 1960.

———. "The 'Two Cultures' Controversy: Afterthoughts by C. P. Snow." *Encounter*, February, 1960.

———. "The Two Cultures and the Scientific Revolution." *Library Journal* 85, no. 13 (July 1960).

———. A letter in *New Statesman and Nation*, October 13, 1960.

———. A letter in *New York Times*, December 4, 1960.

———. "News Notes." *Science*, December 23, 1960.

———. A letter in *London Times*, December 28, 1960.

———. *The Two Cultures and the Scientific Revolution*. Cambridge: Cambridge University Press, 1960.

———. "Which Side of the Atlantic: The Writer's Choice." In *Writing in America*, edited by John Fischer and Rob B. Silvers. New Brunswick: Rutgers University Press, 1960.

———. A letter in *New York Times*, January 3, 1961.

———. "The Moral Un-Neutrality of Science." *Science*, January 27, 1961.

———. "Whether We Live or Die." *Life*, February 3, 1961.

———. "The Moral Un-Neutrality of Science." *Science Digest*, March 1961.

———. "A Secret War of Whitehall." *London Sunday Times Magazine* 25 (March 12, 1961).

———. A letter in *London Sunday Times Magazine* 25 (March 12, 1961).

———. "Both Cultures." *New Statesman*, April 1961.

———. A letter in *Bulletin of the Atomic Scientists*, October 1961.

———. "Western Values and Total War." *Commentary*, October 1961.

———. A letter in *Science*, November 1961.

———. "Science, Politics, and the Novelist: Or, the Fish and the Net." *Kenyon Review* 23, no. 1 (Winter 1961).

———. A letter in *Current Biography Yearbook 1961*, edited by Chas. Maritz.

———. "The Literati and the Scientists." In *The Fate of Man*, edited by Crame Brinton. New York: George Braziller, 1961.

———. *Science and Government*. Cambridge: Harvard University Press, 1961.

———. with Malcolm Muggeridge. *Encounter*, February 1962.

———. Letters in *New York Times*, March 10, 16; April 14, 22; June 14, 1962.

———. Letters in *Spectator*, March 16, 23, 1962.

———. "On Magnanimity." *Harper's* 37 (July 1962).

———. "Interview with C. P. Snow." *Review of English Literature*, July 3, 1962.

———. A letter in *New York Times*, September 16, 1962.

———. "Recent Thoughts on the Two Cultures." 1961 oration delivered at

Birkbeck College, London, published December 12, 1962.

———. *Appendix to Science and Government.* Cambridge: Harvard University Press, 1962.

———. *Science and Government.* New York: Mentor Books, 1962.

———. "Education and Sacrifice." *New Statesman,* May 17, 1963.

———. Letters in *New York Times,* October 25, November 16, 1963.

———. "The Two Cultures: A Second Look." *London Times Literary Supplement,* October 25, 1963.

———. "The Two Cultures Re-Affirmed." *Scientific American,* December 1963.

———. *The Two Cultures and a Second Look.* London: Cambridge University Press, 1964.

———. Letters in *London Times,* February 20, November 19, December 15, 1964.

———. "Short Reviews." *Scientific American,* June 1964.

———. Transcripts of programs. BBC Educational Channel, February 5, 11; March 23, 27; November 3; December 2; 1965.

———. A letter in *New York Times,* January 13, 1965.

———. "Can Science Save Britain's Industry?" *Business Week,* May 8, 1965.

———. "Government, Science, and Public Policy." *Science,* February 11, 1966.

———. Notes for a presentation made at MIT in 1966 on "Scientists and Decision-Making." Harry Ransom Humanities Research Center, University of Texas, Austin.

———. "H. G. Wells." In *A Variety of Men.* New York: Scribner's, 1966.

———. Letters in *New York Times,* January 26, 1966; June 12, 1967.

———. "State of Siege." 1968 John Findley Green Foundation Lecture, reprinted in *Public Affairs.*

———. "The Scientific Profession and Degrees of Freedom." MSS, notes for an address to Loyola University of Chicago in 1969. Harry Ransom Humanities Research Center, University of Texas, Austin.

———. *The Two Cultures and a Second Look.* Cambridge: Cambridge University Press, 1969.

———. "The Scientific Profession and Degrees of Freedom." Symposium on "Freedom and the Human Sciences." Loyola University of Chicago, MSS, dated January 20, 1970. Harry Ransom Humanities Research Center, University of Texas, Austin.

———. "The Leavis Case and the Serious Case." *London Times Literary Supplement,* July 9, 1970.

———. "Never Before." *London Financial Times* 26, October 8, 1970.

———. A letter in *London Sunday Times,* October 25, 1970.

———. "The Two Cultures: A Contemporary English Intellectual Discusses Science and the State of Man." Phonotape cassette, Learning Plans, 1970.

———. *Strangers and Brothers.* New York: Scribner's Sons, 1971.

———. *Public Affairs.* New York: Macmillan, 1971.

———. "The State of Siege." *Public Affairs.* New York: Scribner's, 1971.

————. "High Fliers and Others." *London Financial Times* 37 (November 23, 1972).

————. *Trollope.* London: Macmillan, 1975.

————. "Mind and Body." *London Financial Times,* October 30, 1975.

————. "Grounds for Hope?" *New York University Education Quarterly* 7, no. 4, 1977.

————. *Strangers and Brothers.* Hudson River ed. New York: Scribner's Sons, 1977.

————. MSS, Untitled address on April 27, 1977, Pace University, New York City Campus.

————. "Boys into Men." *London Financial Times,* November 17, 1977.

————. *In Their Wisdom.* Harmondsworth: Penguin, 1977.

————. *The Realists.* London: Macmillan, 1978.

————. *George Passant* (formerly *Strangers and Brothers*). Harmondsworth: Penguin, 1978.

————. *Time of Hope.* London: Penguin, 1978.

————. *Corridors of Power.* Harmondsworth: Penguin, 1979.

————. *Homecomings.* Harmondsworth: Penguin, 1979.

————. *Last Things.* Harmondsworth: Penguin, 1979.

————. *The Conscience of the Rich.* London: Penguin, 1979.

————. *The Affair.* London: Penguin, 1979.

————. *The Light and the Dark.* Harmondsworth: Penguin, 1979.

————. *The Search.* London: Penguin, 1979.

————. *The Sleep of Reason.* Harmondsworth: Penguin, 1979.

————. *A Variety of Men.* Harmondsworth: Penguin, 1979.

————. *The Physicists.* Boston: Little, Brown, 1981.

————. *A Coat of Varnish.* Harmondsworth: Penguin, 1981.

————. *Death under Sail.* Hudson River ed. New York: Scribner's, 1982.

————. "Science and the Advanced Society." MSS, Harry Ransom Humanities Research Center, University of Texas, Austin.

Snow, Philip. *Stranger and Brother.* London: Macmillan, 1982.

Stern, J. P. *On Realism.* London: Routledge and Kegan Paul, 1973.

Strickland, Geoffrey. "The Question of Tone: Reflections on the Snow-Leavis Controversy." *Delta: The Cambridge Literary Magazine,* Summer 1962.

Sumner, W. L. "Review of the Two Cultures." *Nature,* August 8, 1959.

Symons, Julian. "The Two Cultures, One Missing." *Encounter,* September 1959.

————. *Makers of the New: The Revolution in Literature, 1912–1939.* London: Andre Deutsch, 1988.

Thale, Jerome. "C. P. Snow and the Art of Worldliness." *Kenyon Review* 23 (1960).

————. *C. P. Snow.* London: Oliver and Boyd, 1964.

Thompson, John B. *Critical Hermeneutics.* Cambridge: Cambridge University Press, 1984.

Tichi, Cecelia. *Shifting Gears: Technology, Culture, and Literature in Modernist America.* Chapel Hill: University of North Carolina Press, 1987.

Toulmin, Stephen. A Letter in *Spectator*, March 16, 1962, p. 8.

Trilling, Lionel. "Reality in America." In *The Liberal Imagination: Essays in Literature and Society*. New York: Anchor Books, 1950.

———. "A Sense of the Past." In *Influx: Essays on Literacy Influence*, edited by Ed Primeau. New York: Kennikat Press, 1977.

Vig, Norman. *Science and Technology in British Politics*. London: Pergamon, 1968.

Virginia Quarterly Review 128, Autumn 1960, (review of *The Two Cultures*).

Wagner, Geoffrey. "In Search of the Snow of Yesteryear." *Commonweal*, May 31, 1962.

Wain, John. "A Certain Judo Demonstration." *Hudson Review*, Summer 1962.

Walsh, Ruth M. "C. P. Snow: Poet of Organizational Behaviour." Ph.D. diss., University of South Florida, 1976.

Watt, Ian. *The Rise of the Novel*. London: Chatto and Windus, 1957.

Werskey, Gary. "*Nature* and Politics between the Wars." *Nature* 224 (November 1, 1969).

———. "Radical Cambridge: Left-wing Scientists in the 1930s." Harvard University, February 1971. Mimeo.

———. "British Scientists and Outsider Politics, 1931–1945." *Science Studies* 1 (1971).

———. "The Visible College: A Collective Biography of British Scientists and Socialists of the 1930s." Ph.D. diss., Harvard University, 1977.

———. *The Visible College*. London: Allen Lane, 1978.

West, Anthony. "From the Top Drawer and the Bottom." *Show*, December 1962.

Willets, Ron. "A World without a Hero." *Marxism Today*, March 1961.

Williams, Raymond. *Marxism and Literature*. Oxford: Oxford University Press, 1978.

———. *The English Novel*. London: Hogarth Press, 1984.

Wilson, J. T. "An Interview with Edmund Wilson." *New Yorker*, June 2, 1962.

Wolff, Janet. "The Invisible Flaneuse: Women and the Literature of Modernity." *Theory, Culture, and Society* 2, no. 3, 1985.

Wollheim, Richard. "Grounds for Approval?" *Spectator*, August 7, 1959.

———. "Two Cultures and the Scientific Revolution: A Review." *Spectator*, August 7, 1959.

INDEX

Lightning Source UK Ltd.
Milton Keynes UK
UKOW04f0325281114

242265UK00003B/18/P